BELITTLED CITIZENS

NIAS – Nordic Institute of Asian Studies
New and Recent Monographs

NIAS Press is the autonomous publishing arm of the Nordic Institute of Asian Studies (NIAS), a research institute located at the University of Copenhagen. NIAS is partially funded by the governments of Denmark, Finland, Iceland, Norway and Sweden via the Nordic Council of Ministers, and works to encourage and support Asian studies in the Nordic countries. In so doing, NIAS has been publishing books since 1969, with more than two hundred titles produced in the past few years.

UNIVERSITY OF COPENHAGEN

Nordic Council of Ministers

BELITTLED CITIZENS

THE CULTURAL POLITICS OF CHILDHOOD ON BANGKOK'S MARGINS

GIUSEPPE BOLOTTA

Belittled Citizens
The Cultural Politics of Childhood on Bangkok's Margins
by Giuseppe Bolotta

Nordic Institute of Asian Studies
Monograph series, no. 154

First published in 2021 by NIAS Press
NIAS – Nordic Institute of Asian Studies
Øster Farimagsgade 5, 1353 Copenhagen K, Denmark
Tel: +45 3532 9503 • Fax: +45 3532 9549
E-mail: books@nias.ku.dk • Online: www. niaspress. dk

A CIP catalogue record for this book is available from the British Library

ISBN 978-87-7694-301-1 (Pbk)
ISBN 978-87-7694-718-7 (Ebk)

Typeset in 11 pt Arno Pro by Don Wagner
Printed and bound in Thailand
for Silkworm Books, Chiang Mai

Cover design: NIAS Press
Cover illustration: สักวันหนึ่ง.. เราจะโต๊.. เราจะโต [one day we will grow up],
courtesy: Headache_stencil.

CONTENTS

MAPS

FIGURES

Bold = colour image

Acknowledgments

This book is the result of years of research, relationships, reflections and human encounters, and I am indebted to the many people who have shared this long journey with me. First of all, to the hundreds of children I met in the slums of Bangkok and outside them, now young women and men, for sharing with me their knowledge, struggles, hopes and adventures. It was a tremendous privilege to witness their lives unfolding over the years. My gratitude also extends to their families, the given and the chosen, for their generous hospitality, advice and friendship. A special thanks to *mae* Pan, who welcomed me as a son into her house, providing shelter and protection.

I am most grateful to the many helpful monks, missionaries, humanitarian workers and activists for their dedication to the poor of Bangkok, and for making my research possible. My sincere thanks to Father Nicola, *phra* Payom, Sister Serafina, *phra* Manid, Father Niphot, *khru* Prateep, and to all the members of staff at the Saint Jacob's Centre, at the Suan Kaeo Foundation, at *wat* Saphansung, at the Duang Prateep Foundation and at the Four Regions Slum Network.

My research and this book have been possible thanks to the generous support of the University of Milano-Bicocca's Doctorate School in Cultural and Social Anthropology, the Faculty of Political Science at Chulalongkorn University, the École Française d'Extreme-Orient, and the Asia Research Institute at the National University of Singapore. My utmost gratitude goes to the many Thai and foreign scholars and friends who have contributed to shaping my analysis, shared their ideas and observations, and/or commented upon earlier drafts of this manuscript. In particular, I owe special thanks to Ugo Fabietti, Silvia Vignato, Pitch Pongsawat, Michael Herzfeld, Heather Montgomery, Eli Elinoff, Amalia Rossi, Rungsiri Nuchsuwan, Jirapa Pruikpadee, Boonlert Visetpricha, R. Michael Feener, Michelle Miller, Catherine Scheer, Catherine Smith, Philip Fountain, David Lancy, Spyros Spyrou, Thomas Stodulka, Mary Beth Mills, Barbara Watson Andaya, Edoardo Siani, and Simon Baker.

Part of my field research in Thailand was conducted in the framework of the EU project SEATIDE, Southeast Asia: Trajectories of Inclusion and Dynamics of Exclusion (2012-2016), funded by the Seventh Framework Programme of the European Commission (FP7). I would like to thank all the colleagues who undertook the scientific direction and coordination of SEATIDE: Franciscus Verellen, Yves Goudineau, Andrew Hardy, and Chayan Vaddhanaphuti.

This book is an expanded, revised, and significantly restructured version of my PhD dissertation, and the result of several rounds of proofreading and editing by Monica Janowski, Caitriona McBride and Silvia Sias. I am deeply grateful for their help and scrupulous attention to detail. A special thanks to the staff of NIAS Press, especially Gerald Jackson, Editor-in-chief, for his responsiveness, critical comments, and truly thorough editorial support during the writing, revision and production of this manuscript.

My deepest gratitude goes to Enrichetta Buchli, an irreplaceable mentor, and to my Thai language teachers, particularly to Andrea Macario, who initiated me into the poetics of Thai, making the learning of the language into an enchanting journey. Finally, I would like to thank my friends, who are often insufficiently acknowledged in most academic publications despite the crucial role that they play, providing constant emotional and moral support no matter what happens. I am alone responsible for any inaccuracies, errors or omissions in this book.

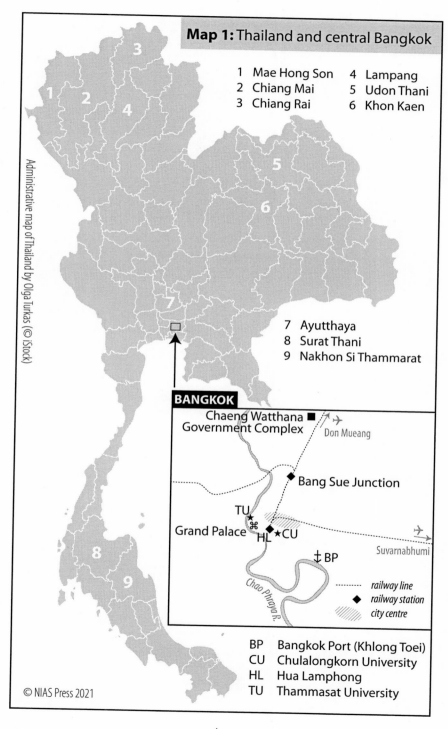

Map 1: Thailand and central Bangkok

1 Mae Hong Son
2 Chiang Mai
3 Chiang Rai
4 Lampang
5 Udon Thani
6 Khon Kaen

7 Ayutthaya
8 Surat Thani
9 Nakhon Si Thammarat

BANGKOK

Chaeng Watthana Government Complex

Don Mueang

Bang Sue Junction

TU
Grand Palace
⌘
HL
★CU

‡ BP

Suvarnabhumi

Chao Phraya R.

········· railway line
◆ railway station
▨ city centre

BP Bangkok Port (Khlong Toei)
CU Chulalongkorn University
HL Hua Lamphong
TU Thammasat University

Administrative map of Thailand by Olga Turkas (© iStock)

© NIAS Press 2021

ix

Introduction

One Sunday afternoon in August 2008, after a 14-hour flight and an epic 2-hour drive through the infamous traffic jams and gridlocked highways of Bangkok, my pink taxi finally dropped me off at the Saint Jacob's Centre,[1] a Catholic NGO providing residential care to underprivileged children and young people aged five to 18. It was my first volunteering experience abroad – and was not the usual context in which first-time travellers encounter the 'Land of Smiles'. With its towering skyscrapers, Buddhist shrines, tasty street food, futuristic shopping malls and vibrant nightlife, the capital city of Thailand is one of the world's top tourist destinations. As well as amenities like these, however, the megalopolis of 15 million inhabitants also hosts some of the largest slums in Southeast Asia, a city within a city, a city of the poor – mostly internal migrants from the rural and ethnic minority regions of the country. The charitable work of Saint Jacob's takes place in this alter-city, targeting its youngest members, who are publicly labelled *dek salam* ('slum children').[2] These children are the protagonists of this book.

Along the pathway leading to the huge playground of the NGO, a hundred children were chasing one another around, seemingly unaffected by the stifling tropical heat. I suddenly found myself surrounded and pulled in all directions. The guests of Saint Jacob's, out of breath and sweating all over, were playfully fighting for my attention. While I was trying to navigate my way through the children's myriad grasping hands, I noticed that Chiu, five years old, no more than a toothpick covered with skin, had moved away from the group. Sitting on the pavement with both hands covering his face, he seemed to be crying. When I got closer, I realised that the little boy, who was hiding a wry, toothless smile behind his hands, was actually just pretending. A moment later he was clinging

---

1   The names of all organisations and individuals, as well as those of some geographical locations, have been changed throughout the book in order to protect the anonymity of my informants.

2   The Thai terms for 'slum children' (*dek salam*) and 'slum' (*salam*), and even the politically-correct version of the latter, 'crowded community' (*chumchon aeat*), are all problematic as they carry unacceptably derogatory overtones. The use of these social labels is, however, fairly common (if contested) in Thai everyday speech and therefore they cannot be avoided. As I shall show, the genealogy, meanings, and situational connotations of these expressions vary significantly according to both speaker and social context. These important distinctions will be critically scrutinised throughout the book.

to my back, writhing and screaming so that his friends could clearly see that he was on the shoulders of the *farang* ('white person'). I was his living trophy. The *dek salam* were clearly accustomed to visiting European volunteers, and did not appear at all like the 'innocent victims' whom I was eager to help.

The chaos unleashed by my presence was suddenly interrupted by the arrival of the Thai staff at Saint Jacob's. The behaviour and attitude of the *dek salam* changed abruptly. Quiet, and in perfect order, they quickly settled into parallel rows, with older children at the head of each one. One by one, they assumed their usual positions in the courtyard and reverentially greeted the NGO staff with the *wai*: the Thai traditional salute, consisting of a slight bow, with the palms pressed together in a prayer-like fashion.[3] They were acting as proper *phu noi* ('small people') performing quiet deference to *phu yai* ('big people'). In doing this, they were recreating a hierarchically-organised cultural pattern of interaction that lies at the heart of Thailand's socio-political, ethnic, and even cosmic order, as I would later understand (e.g. Akin Rabibhadana 1963; Tambiah 1977; Bechstedt 1991; Aulino 2014).

I thought initially that this was the way in which Thai children were expected to behave in the presence of adults, but it slowly became clear that the terms *phu noi* and *phu yai*, unlike those of 'children' and 'adults' in a Western context, are not locally construed as fixed age groups but are what may be described as 'social shifters' (Durham 2000: 116) – relational categories that vary according to the interlocutor's social status, linking different class, ethnic, religious and gendered ways of being. For instance, while the Thai staff at Saint Jacob's were *phu yai* in relation to the children, they themselves played the role of childlike *phu noi* in the presence of the Catholic missionaries leading the NGO, or while interacting with state officials and Buddhist monks outside of Saint Jacob's.

Exhausted, jet-lagged, and quite confused by the (supposedly suffering) children's exuberant vitality, suddenly transformed into order and obedience, I stood there gawking, searching for clues. Prasit, the head of staff at Saint Jacob's, explained to me that the children (who all declare themselves to be Buddhists) were gathering for the daily collective prayer before dinner. The Thai version of Our Father, one of the most venerated Christian prayers, was recited in the canteen of the NGO, where a giant portrait of King Bhumibol Adulyadej (Rama IX) – worshipped in Thailand as the (Buddhist) nation's 'father' – was displayed, next to a crucifix. I noticed that Nung, a 10-year-old orphan, had his head and

---

3   The *wai* has its origin in the Indic Anjali Mudra, and similar salutations are used in a number of Asian countries (Phya Anuman Rajhadon 1963). Similar gestures can be observed, for example, in Cambodia and Laos. There are also similarities between the Thai *wai* and the Indian, Sri Lankan and Nepalese *namasté*.

eyebrows shaved: 'He spent a few weeks in a Buddhist foundation for poor children, where he was ordained as a novice and trained in meditation', Prasit patiently explained, as I plied him with questions. Half-annoyed and half-amused by my inquisitiveness, he added that many children were absent: some had spent the weekend in the slums with their 'families', however defined; others had yet to return from schools where they were attending a drug-prevention programme that was specifically designed for *dek salam* – the 'bad children of Bangkok', as they are often described.

During my 2-month stint of volunteering at Saint Jacob's, I was repeatedly confronted by my inability to grasp its little guests' multiple childhoods, and more broadly to capture the different cultural, material, and religious frameworks informing poor children's everyday lives in Bangkok. Although most schoolteachers saw *dek salam* as a threat to national stability, as citizens who are 'not-Thai-enough' and who therefore need discipline administered through an awkward combination of Buddhist morality and military zeal, to Father Nicola – the Italian missionary who headed Saint Jacob's – they were God's favourite children. Thai adults approached them as *phu noi*; Buddhist monks interpreted their socio-economic marginalisation in terms of karmic deficiencies. The humanitarian portrait of the Global South's 'child victim', the image that had brought me to Saint Jacob's and that Western aid agencies circulate to justify their work, further complicated the kaleidoscopic nature of the identities projected by these children.

What does childhood mean in Thailand? What constitutes childhood in a slum? How are the apparently secular debates around the rights of children interpreted in the context of a Catholic NGO within a primarily Buddhist country? What is the role of state education; and what is the role of families? These were the first, most obvious questions. Many others would arise as I spent more time in Thailand, grew fond of the guests at Saint Jacob's, and realised that the Catholic NGO for which I was volunteering was just one of many organisations addressing the vast population of slum children in Bangkok.[4]

With a growing global emphasis on child-focused humanitarian work in the 1970s, the Thai state was no longer the only institution involved in these children's lives. Aid agencies – Christian, Buddhist, and secular, local and international – have transformed the landscape of urban poverty in Bangkok into a cosmopolitan, child-centred field of power. These new actors have pluralised the educational and institutional environments that shape children's experiences

---

4   A 2007 survey by Bangkok Metropolitan Administration (BMA) estimated that there were about 2,000 slums in the city, with a total population of more than two million individuals – making up approximately 20% of the entire population of the inner core of the city (BMA2007).

and development, providing *dek salam* with unprecedented opportunities for socialisation and a hugely diverse range of cultural reference points to draw on in the construction of their selves and their worlds.

THAI POLITICS AND THE POLITICS OF CHILDHOOD

In 2010, I took off my humanitarian vestments and returned to Thailand to begin the long-term ethnographic study that became my PhD dissertation and is the basis of this book. I devoted the following six years to ethnographic investigation of the multiple social contexts within which, and in relation to which, *dek salam* spend their lives (slums, schools, Buddhist temples, Catholic NGOs, state and international aid organisations, social media). My research focused on two interlocking points of study. The first involved pinpointing the multiple agendas, positions and policies that are relevant to childhood on the margins of society – what one might describe as 'marginal childhood' – and investigating how these policies seek to define the institutional geographies in which *dek salam* move and live, as well as the parenting styles, pedagogical objectives, and relational attitudes of adults vis-à-vis Bangkok's poor children. The second focus of study was to bring out the children's own voices, embodied experiences and cultural practices in each of the different social settings in which they grow up. I was both fascinated by, and struggled with, the apparent ability of *dek salam* to take on a number of roles, in different contexts: from 'victim' to Buddhist novice, from Catholic to citizen, from student to daughter – an impressive interplay of 'subject positions' (Laclau and Mouffe 1985: 111; Foucault 1994) that provided the framework for a dynamic picture of the children's hybrid selves in formation.

This book is arranged in two parts that reflect these entangled axes of historically-informed ethnographic investigation. Part One (The Cultural Politics of Childhood) interrogates the multifaceted nature of 'slum childhood' in Bangkok, looking at each of the environments in which the children live, and using *dek salam* as a prism through which to trace broader socio-political, religious, and economic transformations in Thai society. Part Two (Children's Cultures and Selves) examines the active roles played by *dek salam* in processes of socio-political change, bearing in mind that marginal children's efforts to make sense of their selves in an era of authoritarian rule reflect the broader tensions facing the poor during a complex period of Thai history (2010–2016).

By focusing on an unusual link – between culture, politics and children – this book locates the historically- and socially-constructed character of childhood in a variety of political arenas (James and James 2005: 4). In doing this, I aim to problematise Western notions of childhood 'innocence' and of children as 'pre-political subjects' (Ticktin 2017), and to deliberately foreground 'political-ly unmarked' (Brekhus 1998) features of social life.

In a country now run by soldiers, blessed by a divinised, paternal king, royal fatherhood acts as a national ethos that seeks to infantilise the citizenry in ways that reflect the relationship between Thai conceptions of childhood and the wider construction of the Thai polity. An analytical emphasis on the political dimension of 'childhood' thus offers critical insights into contemporary Thai politics, and this is one of the central contributions of this study. Furthermore, by looking at 'marginal childhoods' as a window into Thailand's societal transformations, I invert the more conventional focus within Thai studies on monarchic, Buddhist, and state 'parenthood' as the overarching features of Thai political culture (e.g. Keyes 1971; Tambiah 1976, 1984; Thak Chaloemtiarana 2007; Ivarsson and Isager [eds] 2010).

This book presents two main arguments. Firstly, I argue that 'marginal child-hoods' and what may be described as the 'cultural technologies of childhood' – schools, religious aid agencies, NGOs – are reflective of endemic inequalities in Thailand's wider socio-political structure, as well as of transformations in the transnational governance of childhood that are related to globalisation. The spaces in which childhood is constructed are therefore deeply charged political spaces that both mirror the ways in which authoritarian power is being produced in Thailand and suggest its limits. These limits result from the shifting boundaries between national and international law. In an era of children's rights, the control exercised by the Thai state over (supposedly deviant) childhoods faces significant challenges from multiple child-focused agencies (international NGOs, missionary organisations, Buddhist foundations, etc.) that may well have different ideas of what is in the child's best interests. Secondly, I argue that poor children's access to these increasingly plural ideas of childhood opens up a space for both existential fragmentation and creative self-reformulations, which have the potential to pro-vide socially disadvantaged citizens, as they grow up, with unexpected religious, economic, and political resources with which to challenge generational structures of power in Thai society. In the following two sections, I trace the theoretical foun-dations of these arguments and describe the course of the book in greater detail.

PART ONE – THE CULTURAL POLITICS OF CHILDHOOD

Children's Day (*wan dek*), the Thai version of the International Day for the Protection of Children, is celebrated in Thailand in the second week of January. For the occasion, various government offices, including major military installa-tions, are open to children and their families. On *wan dek* in 2014, I went to the

Bangkok headquarters of the Royal Thai Armed Forces on Chaengwattana road, where celebrations for children were taking place, with the aim of examining the way in which the public characterisation of 'Thai childhood' was being staged (Bolotta 2016). During the day soldiers proudly showed excited children the best of the Thai Army's military arsenal: helicopters, tanks and war weapons of various kinds. The celebrations emphasised the fact that a 'good child' (*dek di*) is an authentically Thai child – something the children were also being taught every day at school. It means honouring the monarchy, Buddhism and the nation. Even during a day formally dedicated to their rights, children were instructed to always be grateful and to obey *phu yai*. To be a 'good child' is to emulate the example of Thai soldiers, who were portayed as the nation's brave and generous defenders, ready to sacrifice themselves for the good of 'Thainess' (*khwam pen thai* – literally 'the Thai mode of being') and the national family (Figure 1).

Universal Children's Day, the establishment of which was recommended worldwide by the United Nations in 1954, is officially aimed at promoting the rights of children. The UN convention on the Rights of the Child, signed by Thailand on 27 March 1992, sets out a number of children's rights, including the right for children to have their views heard in the context of a horizontal relationship with adults, and to be protected from violence. Given this, it was curious to see how Children's Day had been transformed in Bangkok into an ultra-nationalist military parade. Particularly striking was the fact that the event used weapons of war, the quintessential technological materialisation of violence, as instruments of pedagogy and as a form of entertainment, with the aim of solidifying rather than undoing hierarchy.

What came through at the Children's Day celebration was a tension that animates much of this book: that there is a clear contradiction at play between two different cultural and political conceptualisations of 'childhood'. On the one hand, we have the juridical definition of the child promoted by UN agencies in Geneva and acknowledged – often only formally – across the world. This definition underlines the status of children as full human beings who have the right to freely express their views on all matters affecting them. On the other hand, there is the local, militarised image of the 'good Thai child' (*dek thai di*), who is an obedient and loyal subject subordinate to both adults and to the will of the nation itself. As I will demonstrate, *dek salam* – publicly conceived of as the ethno-linguistic, class and moral nemesis of the 'good Thai child' – were not only aware of this tension but used it to good effect to challenge Thai hierarchies in shaping their own lives.

Since Margaret Mead's (1928) pioneering study of adolescence in Samoa, anthropological, sociological, and historical scholarship has amply demonstrated

Photo: Takeway, Wikimedia Commons.

Figure 1. Children's Day 2012. Chiang Mai Royal Thai Air Force base. Colour version, p. 229.

that the nature and experience of childhood vary enormously across time and space (e.g. Ariès 1962; Malinowski 1929; Whiting [ed.]1963; Benthall 1992; Levine 2003; Levine and Norman 2001; Lancy 2008). As a distinct concept, 'childhood' is a social construct, a set of historically and culturally specific ideas, practices and interpretations of the early years of human life, which interact in complex ways to define what childhood is and what it should be (James and Prout [eds] 1997). Hence, definitions of childhood cannot be based only on biology and chronological age. Variables such as gender, religion, class, and ethnicity play important parts in defining who is regarded as being a 'child' or considers himself or herself to be a 'child'. Children may be defined as 'persons who have not reached social maturity in their society and whose access to resources, experiences, practices and objectives relate to their specific positioning and self-ascertainment within (different and sometimes overlapping) social orders' (Martin et al 2016: 3; Montgomery 2009: 53; Pache Huber & Ossipow 2012: 27).

Importantly, in the context of modern nation-states 'the birth of a child is a political event' (Handwerker 1990: 1). Children, tomorrow's citizens, are often considered not-yet-complete subjects, to be socialised, educated and taught morality, with the aim of ensuring the continuity and reproduction of a normative socio-economic and political order (Coles 1986; Stephens 1995). Their minds and bodies are at the centre of public debates about ethnic purity, national identity and the transmission of fundamental cultural values in schools – the primary institutional device used by the state in the creation of 'normal' childhood. Public interventions and policies addressing 'abnormal' childhood reflect likewise specific projects of governance, visions of the world, and arrangements of citizenship (Scheper-Hughes and Sargent 1998; Goddard et al [eds] 2005; Wells 2009; Peacock 2014). As Nancy Scheper-Hughes and Carolyn Sargent put it:

> The cultural politics of *childhood* speaks on the one hand to the public nature of childhood and to the inability of isolated families or households to shelter infants and small children within the privacy of the home or to protect them from the outrageous slings and arrows of the world's political and economic fortunes. On the other hand, the *cultural politics* of childhood speaks to the political, ideological, and social uses of childhood [...]. Outside the home, childhood is the primary site of pedagogy and cultural learning. It is a primary nexus of mediation between public norms and private life [...]. Childhood also involves cultural notions of personhood, morality, social order and disorder. (Scheper-Hughes and Sargent 1998: 1–2)

In this book, I scrutinise slum children's multiple childhoods along these theoretical and scholarly lines of anthropological enquiry. The personal experiences of *dek salam* in Bangkok – the social settings and pedagogies they are confronted with and the different ways in which they are, as children, conceived of and constructed by adults – are embedded in daily affective interactions, institutional arrangements and cultural encounters, which are the micro-level outcomes of broader socio-political, religious, and economic processes, both national and global.

The lives of the children I met at Saint Jacob's unfolded in multiple social scenarios, institutional sites, public and private realms. In each of these contexts, children were interpreted differently by adults, and were confronted with conflicting sets of quite specific historical, religious and political notions of 'childhood', 'parenthood', 'morality', 'ethnicity', 'society', and, ultimately, 'citizenship'. Happy to immerse myself in the children's worlds, I decided to carry out fieldwork in each of the environments in which they lived. While I thought initially that I would mainly live in the slums, assuming that these (mostly matrifocal) homes were the children's primary living spaces, I eventually realised that *dek salam* were, in fact, hardly ever at home.

Wealthier children in Bangkok are increasingly busy with extra-domestic and extra-scholastic activities, including private tuition, sport and other leisure activities – some provided by their parents and some by the market – but they normally live with their (nuclear) families until they reach full legal adulthood. Compared to these upper-middle class children (whose lives, in this respect, are not unlike those of children in Europe), the lives of *dek salam* were definitely on the move. The highly unusual plurality of the social and institutional geographies in which slum children lived and moved was partly linked to what was regarded as their 'deviant' state, as *dek salam*: an anti-normative category of childhood that implied a wide range of measures intended to be socially corrective, to varying degrees both compassionate and repressive. Partly, though, these children's remarkable trans-local mobility is made possible by a whole new set of socio-political, economic, and technological possibilities that were not available to former generations of slum dwellers in Bangkok.

Following them around like a bulky shadow – 'a strange *farang* who speaks Thai like the missionaries but is not a priest', as one of the children, five-year-old Chiu, once ironically observed – I spent six months with them in the slums, eight months in their schools, and about one year in religious (Buddhist and Catholic) and secular child-focused NGO contexts. In each of these places, particular constructions of childhood moulded patterns of adult–child interactions in surprisingly different (though overlapping) ways. The ways in which schoolteachers, state officials, monks, missionaries, NGO workers and parents talked about *dek salam*, and their views on how the children should be taught and should grow up, thus became a fundamental locus of my ethnographic and historic investigation.

In exploring these diverse institutional and ideological endeavours to support–govern–save–convert *dek salam*, Part One of this book reveals the extent to which the 'futurity' inherent in childhood becomes a site of political contention (James and James 2005: 4). This sheds light on the competition between organisations (the Thai militarised state, engaged Buddhism, Catholic missionaries, Western NGOs) that have attempted, over the years, to define Thai society and the future of its urban poor through modelling marginalised children's minds and bodies. The structure of this section reflects the ethnographic approach adopted, with each chapter focusing on a specific living space – and on the cultural politics of childhood expressed there.

Chapter 1 takes a historical and ethnographic look at the hegemonic state ideology of the 'good Thai child' (*dek thai di*) as this is expressed in schools – the main institutional device for the promotion of 'Thainess' (*khwam pen thai*). By focusing on the schools attended by *dek salam*, it provides a detailed analysis of the contemporary Thai school environment. This includes its spatial and symbolic culture, nationalistic rituals, teaching methodologies, curriculum, textbooks, class activities and the daily routines of its students. Through school pedagogy, rituals and aesthetics, the state attempts to construct a childhood that is pure Thai, and to adjust *dek salam*, who are viewed as being 'not-Thai-enough', to this ethnno-nationalistic standard of childhood.[5] This analysis brings out the way in which the cultural politics of 'Thainess' at work in schools entrenches a public representation of the nation as family, of the royal family as the Buddhist paradigm of parenthood, and of citizens as grateful, subordinate, and obedient children. As a whole, this chapter demonstrates conclusively the way in which the governance of children at school and the political significance of 'childhood' in the public sphere articulate with the resurgent power of monarchical paternalism, and its military grammar, in wider Thai society.

Chapter 2 focuses on two Buddhist aid organisations that address child poverty in Bangkok: the Suan Kaeo Foundation, headed by *phra* ('monk') Payom Kanlayano, a popular disciple of influential Thai monk Buddhadasa Bikku; and *wat* ('temple') Saphansung, where *phra* Manid coordinates meditation trainings aimed at *dek salam*. By analysing *phra* Payom's and *phra* Manid's religious explanations of poor children's marginal condition on the one hand and the daily activities in which *dek salam* are involved while guests of these Buddhist charities on the other, this chapter brings out the ideological, religious and political tensions embedded in contemporary dialectics between the Buddhism of state 'Thainess' (which is displayed very clearly in schools) and the socially-engaged Buddhism of 'development monks' (*phra nak phatthana*). In this context, classic Buddhist notions of *karma* (*kam* in Thai), *dharma* (*thamma* in Thai), and *nirvana* (*nipphan* in Thai) can be seen framed in different ways in relation to politically-inflected concepts of childhood, children's obligations, and poverty, generating conflicting doctrinal formulations of morality and of the socio-political order.

Chapter 3 focuses on the Catholic NGO where I first met the children, the Saint Jacob's Centre, and discusses the particular construction of childhood that has shaped its educational project and its approach to *dek salam*. The missionaries leading the organisation, Father Nicola and Sister Serafina, articulate long-standing Christian evangelisation efforts in the region in new ways, engaging creatively with the secular global framework of children's rights. They provide slum children with subversive theological-political interpretations of childhood and poverty, interpretations that overturn their status, transforming them from not-yet-Thai *phu noi* into God's most beloved sons and daughters. The chapter situates the

---

5   Although the term 'Thai' is commonly used to refer to all the citizens of the modern nation-state of Thailand, in this book I also use it with its dominant ethno-political connotation, which refers primarily to the Central Thai or Siamese Tai – the Bangkok-based hegemonic group whose ethno-linguistic characterisation was used as the main reference for 'Thainess', the modern national identity. Accordingly, I use the term 'non-Thai' to refer to both *chao khao* ('hill tribes') and other minority Tai groups such as the northeastern Thai-Lao or the southern Thai-Malay, who are historically regarded and projected by the state as 'insufficiently Thai'.

work of Saint Jacob's in the historical context of royalist Thai Catholicism and the Buddhist cultural politics of the Thai state, and demonstrates the increasingly relevant (although usually invisible) political and economic roles of missionary aid organisations in Thailand's ethnic minority regions and city slums.

Focusing on the children's native environment, Chapter 4 presents a detailed analysis of urban slums as the Thai capital's ethno-linguistic and political 'other within' (Thongchai Winichakul 2000a). No longer closed communities of rural migrants, slums are analysed here as child-centred humanitarian landscapes, political arenas within which local, national and global social forces and interests converge and clash. This chapter underscores the symbolic value of children's 'victimhood' and its strategic deployment as part of slum dwellers' anti-eviction movements and broader political initiatives. In their position as the mothers of children classed as 'victims', women – especially single mothers – emerge here as key actors in negotiating between slum networks, child-focused NGOs, land-owners and the Thai state. The chapter reveals how women's emerging leadership as the new spokespersons of the urban poor is linked to the humanitarian polit-icisation of their children in the slums. It also provides a much-needed updated account of Bangkok's poorest areas and their evolving political significance in contemporary militarised Thai society.

PART TWO – CHILDREN'S CULTURES AND SELVES

In addition to investigating the multifaceted political significance of Bangkok's marginal childhoods, in (and beyond) mainstream Thai society, this book also details how children form their own sense of self[6] through these multiple cul-tural contexts and political processes. Part Two scrutinises children's embodied views and everyday practices; their negotiations of relationships; and their ways of interpreting the adults around them and the environments in which they live, both in the presence of adults and without adult supervision. The ways in which children understand their experiences and negotiate their multiple positionali-ties vary dynamically depending on whether they are interacting with parents,

---

6   Unlike other scholars addressing conceptions of the person in Thailand (see e.g. Cassaniti 2012), I do not use the term 'self' only to refer to specific theories of the individual or to doctrinal debates – such as, for example, debates about Hindu teachings of the self (*atta*) and Buddhist teachings of non-self (*anatta*). I refer to something more fundamental: the ability of human beings to be self-reflexive and self-conscious, and the processes through which a subject is able to objectify, think, and understand herself/himself (Holland et al 1998: 291-292; see also G.H. Mead 1934; Butler 1993; Cohen 1994; Philipps, 2006; and Bolotta 2017a: 97–99). This processual definition of the self recognises variations in conceptions of the person, both across cultures and between individuals (Spiro 1993).

missionaries, peers, or NGO workers, and on whether they are at school, surfing the net, or performing rituals in a temple.

In recent years, scholars have examined children's and young people's crucial roles in mediating socio-cultural transformations in rapidly changing societies, and in relation to planetary processes of development and humanitarianism, neoliberal capitalism and rampant consumerism, war and terrorism, environmental change and increasing socio-economic inequalities. An expanding body of literature in the field of childhood studies addresses anti-normative categories of childhood, from 'child witches' in the Democratic Republic of Congo (de Boeck, 2005) to 'street children' in Indonesia (Stodulka 2016; Beazley 2003), 'child soldiers' in Sierra Leone (Schepler 2014; Rosen 2007) and addicted children in Mexico (Pochetti 2017). As far as Thailand is concerned, the only available studies of this kind are, to the best of my knowledge, Heather Montgomery's (2001) thought-provoking ethnography of child prostitutes in Baan Nua and, more recently, Sorcha Mahony's (2018) study of children's growth, urban poverty, precariousness, and the search for a better life in the slums of Bangkok. These studies complicate Western, ethnocentric conceptualisations of 'children's happiness', 'children's innocence' and 'children's vulnerability', and persuasively demonstrate the active roles that children and young people play in the (un)making of society.

This strand of research prioritises children's cultural productions over those of adults, looking at children as competent social actors equipped with agency (as opposed to a view of children as passive, dependent or uncomplete) (James and Prout [eds] 1997; Morrow 1995). Proponents of this school of thought urge an ethnographic shift in anthropological and sociological research on childhood, from adult-centric studies of social structures to a child-focused approach primarily centred on children's own peer-cultures (e.g. Hirshfeld 2002; Delalande [ed.] 2009; Corsaro 2011). As Hirshfeld (2002) has argued:

> Mainstream anthropology has marginalised children because it has marginalised the two things that children do especially well: children are strikingly adept at acquiring adult culture and, less obviously, adept at creating their own cultures. [...] Children also create and inhabit cultures of their own making, cultures that in significant measure are independent of and distinct from those of the adults with whom they live. In making their own cultural traditions, children deploy singular conceptual skills that significantly constrain and mold not only their own cultural productions but also those of adults. (Hirshfeld 2002: 611–612)

As my fieldwork in Thailand progressed, I learnt to appreciate slum children's astonishing ability to deal competently with a variety of social situations, even

12

when such situations were remarkably unfriendly. At the same time, however, as my description above of the Thai National Children's Day suggests, *dek salam* are seriously constrained by adult social, political, economic, educational and religious structures. I felt that I should not underestimate the impact of these structures on children's lives. Relatedly, I should not overestimate children's ability to challenge adult norms and authority, however impressive.[7] It is important to recognise that Thai children themselves – unlike their peers in a number of Western contexts – tend to regard adults as *phu yai* or 'big people' rather than as equals. I thus decided to adopt a perspective that was both two-fold and holistic, one that would focus on the circular, non-linear relationship between the adult cultural politics of childhood (as discussed in Part One) and children's evolving subjectivities.[8] In fact, as Mahony (2018) has poignantly observed, the constrained agency of marginalised children is exercised in multiple, often conflicting, social spheres and aspirational fields, in such a way that 'action in one sphere of life can have "spill-over" effects in other spheres, and without acknowledging the existence of these multiple spheres [...], we cannot properly understand the ways in which agency operates when severely constrained, often bumping up against itself in different realms of practice [...] to produce counter-productive outcomes' (Mahony 2018: 4).

In order to capture children's social worlds from the bottom-up (and not only through lenses, practices, debates and perspectives current among adults), I accessed each field site as *dek salam* normally did (Fine and Sandstrom 1988; Christensen and Prout 2002). Although I did not manage this without contradictions, paradoxes and ambiguity – in the best anthropological tradition (e.g. see M. Jackson 1998) – I tried my best to take part in the routines in which *dek*

---

7   A number of scholars have observed that the notion of 'children's agency', if decontextualised, might subtend a Western-centric cultural and political bias, assuming that children would be always as self-sufficient, independent, and competent as adults (see e.g. Komulainen 2007; Lancy 2009; Lewis 2011). As Spyros Spyrou (2018) has convincingly pointed out, the normative 'fixation with the unitary child-agent' of scholars working within the discipline of childhood studies can, in fact, obscure rather than disclose the complex relational fabric of childhoods. In this book, therefore, I look at children's agency critically and reflexively, mindful of its historical, cultural and situational specificities.

8   I moulded my ethnographic participation into children's lives, conforming to their usual daily experience, requests and comfort, without trying to confine or artificially organise their self-expression within alien-to-the-context, standardised research settings. While the emergence of these settings responds to an increasing scholarly awareness of children's social competence, using age-based research techniques that are independent of the cultural context have the potential to reproduce the very 'children's difference' that scholars in the discipline of childhood studies aim to deconstruct (see e.g. Spyrou 2018; Punch 2002). For a more detailed analysis of interdisciplinary research on/with children, see also Bolotta et al 2017.

salam were involved, as one of them – an attempt that often failed miserably. During my time at Saint Jacob's and at other Buddhist and secular NGOs, for instance, I slept in the same dormitory as the children, whereas adult guests were normally accommodated in separate, and more comfortable, venues. During school lessons, I usually sat in the middle of the classroom, rather than standing next to teachers. I was a big, white, student-researcher – awkward, but aligned with the children. In the slum, I asked the children to show me their everyday itineraries, and they led the clumsy *farang* into the labyrinthine settlement, through its material and social locations. Obviously, for both research and practical reasons I also built positive relationships with the adults in charge, and the children were smart enough to understand that I – as a European researcher, supposedly wealthy – had considerable influence over the local *phu yai*, something they could use to their advantage. Initially, I felt spatially and emotionally disoriented by these continual shifts in the research setting. Over time, however, both my own multi-situated positionality and that of the children became a cross-contextual, recognisable feature of our atypical relationship, a stable emotional element in the midst of ever-changing realities that gradually deepened the mutual trust and affection between us.[9] No less important was the fact that the different interpretations and reactions of children and adults to my changing roles turned out to be an additional source of ethnographic data.

Based on these theoretical and methodological assumptions, Chapter 5 interrogates children's own experiences and peer cultures in each of the social settings analysed in Part One. In negotiating their interactions with missionaries, children's right activists and *farang*, they learnt the humanitarian (and Christian) values of 'rights' and 'victimhood', which they deliberately embodied as a strategic subject position: the 'innocent child', who is a bearer of rights. By engaging in socially-situated performances of 'victimhood', the children thus increased their potential to achieve specific economic, social and affective objectives.

While they are infantilised in the context of Western NGOs, I found that their everyday lives in the slum revealed a strikingly different childhood, a lot less innocent and Thai. In the ethnically diverse context of the slums, indeed, not only does childhood differ from what is expected of children in the West (namely, innocence), but it also contradicts the state-enforced standard of the 'good Thai child'. In Buddhist temples and at school, the children often covered up their anti-normative, 'not-Thai-enough' social status, to camouflage their identity. If they were unmasked by teachers as *dek salam*, they tended then to re-organise

---

9   On the epistemic value of the anthropologist's emotional experience in the field, see Bolotta 2019.

themselves into an 'anti-society' (Halliday 1976: 570; M. Davies 2008: 325) – into self-defence groups of 'bad children'. I will explore the social universe of one such group, the *kaeng dohd diao* ('gang of loners'), examining its (anti-Thai) idiom, its values, gestures and rituals, and looking at its Facebook page and its specific culture. Chapter 5 demonstrates the uncanny capacity of poor children to incorporate, reformulate, contest and deploy multiple childhoods, and to act as social chameleons, disguising or accentuating their bodily, emotional, and communicative expressions of self, according to the situational context in which they are performing at any one time. Their social polyhedrality irreverently challenges the national norm of the 'good Thai child'. It is an 'ambiguous act of agency' (Durham 2000; Bordonaro and Payne 2012) that symbolically threatens the socio-political, religious and ethnic traditional order of Thailand.

While this study is mainly built on distinctively anthropological methods and intellectual preoccupations, my former training and professional commitment as a clinical psychologist continued to inform some lingering questions on the entanglements between power, culture and subjectivity. *Dek salam* in Bangkok were simultaneously being raised by multiple caregivers, in an incredibly varied range of family settings, religious outposts and cultural institutions – a diversity of settings, often structurally imposed, that characterises a large proportion of the marginal childhoods of the world (e.g. Bolotta and Vignato 2017). How did the children understand themselves, as they reflected on their polysemic experience and strove to reach social adulthood?

Deconstructing Western, essentialised – and unitary – formulations of the self, a growing body of scholarship in interdisciplinary fields such as psychological anthropology, sociohistorical psychology, medical anthropology, post-structural philosophy and feminist theory has variously addressed this same question (e.g. see e.g. Biehl et al [eds] 2007; Butler 1993; Hall 1996; Cohen1994; Holland et al 1998). For instance, as Holland et al have rightly pointed out:

> We can discern at least three interrelated components of a theoretical refiguring of the [...] self. First, culturally and socially constructed discourses and practices of the self are recognised as neither the 'clothes' of a universally identical self nor the (static) elements of cultural molds into which the self is cast. Rather, [...] they are conceived as living tools of the self – as artifacts or media that figure the self constitutively, in open-ended ways. Second, [...] the self is treated as always embedded in (social) practice, and as itself a kind of practice. Third, 'sites of the self', the loci of self-production or self-processes, are recognised as plural. (Holland et al 1998: 28)

'Discourses of childhood' reflect and put into action a wide range of ideas about who children are and can be, as well as how they should and could live their lives (K. Smith 2015).[10] Such discourses create particular understandings of what an ideal childhood should be, confining the socialisation of children within specific 'discursive fields' (ibid.). In this regard, it is important to stress that poor children in Bangkok operate within multiple (rather than single) discourses of 'marginal childhood' and that, linked to this, they act out multiple selves. The discourses of missionaries, NGOs, families, monks, teachers and friends on (slum) childhood provide *dek salam* with different 'tools of the self' (Holland et al 1998: 28), affective bonds and role models. The children's constant efforts to fashion their selves are both constrained and enabled by these cultural politics of childhood.

Moving beyond the conventional social sciences focus on structure–agency dialectics, Chapter 6 throws light on 'the psychic life of power' (Butler 1997) as it is expressed in the bodily, cognitive, emotional and motivational aspects of the children's selves. The chapter delves into the biographies of a handful of slum children over a ten-year period – which are punctuated by (at times) radical turning points. It focuses on the children's plural selves as the site where the conflicting cultural politics that confront them are embodied, internalised and subjectively experienced, as a psychological conflict between incompatible concepts of self. It shows how, for most *dek salam*, what has been described as the 'Thai self' constitutes an 'internal persecutor' (Fairbairn 1981), creating an introjected psycho-political process of self-sabotage that generates feelings of social inadequacy, powerlessness and fragmentation. At the same time, the (significantly, 'non-Thai') cultural diversity in which the children are immersed, their cosmopolitan connections with influential *farang*, socially engaged Buddhist monks, and children's rights activists, as well as their digital intelligence, have all equipped some of them with the subjective tools to defuse, neutralise, or reframe the 'Thai self' in politically subversive ways. This chapter also sheds light on how impoverished children experience religions and religious institutions as very serious sources of inspiration and support, despite their hybridity, while at the same time developing a specific ability to make their own way through the ideas and expectations of these agencies.

---

10 In this book I use the notion of 'discourse' as it has been defined by Foucault (1984): a historically contingent and socially-situated way of organising knowledge – ideas, social practices, linguistic facts – about a specific subject. A 'discursive field', in this context, is a system of meanings that has gained the status of truth, and that structures social relations by establishing what can be legitimately thought and said about a specific subject and what cannot. Dominant discourses gain primacy through the exercise of power and through social institutions (e.g. the family or the school) that 'systematically form the objects of which they speak' (ibid.), and thus dictate the ways in which social actors define and understand their sense of self and their social worlds in a specific context.

Their relationship with Father Nicola and the radical Catholicism of St. Jacob's, in particular, has become a self-rehabilitative political and affective reference point for many *dek salam*. As a whole, Part Two unveils the cultural and psycho-political violence that the Thai militarised state exercises on marginalised childhoods that are regarded as 'not-Thai-enough', while also envisioning a possible future that is Thai in a different way, one in which the many *phu noi* – 'small people' – in the country play decisive roles in reshaping the nation.

Ethnicity and the social, religious, political and economic dynamics that flow from notions of ethnicity is, clearly, another deep thread running through this study. Scholars of Southeast Asia have explored the historical tensions between national and ethnic identities in border areas within the region, as well as the complex relationships – economic, political and cosmological – between upland 'stateless groups' and lowland state or state-like societies (e.g. Scott 2009, Thongchai Winichakul 1994). In this book, instead, I explore these tensions in the slums of the Thai capital – the political, religious, and cultural centre of 'Thainess', the Thai national identity.

Thailand is inhabited by a hugely diverse range of ethno-linguistic groups, including the dominant Siamese Tai or Central Thai, the northeastern Thai-Lao, the southern Thai-Malay, the Northern Thai, and the 'tribal groups' of the highlands. Many of these groups belong to the Tai family – Sino-Tibetan peoples, who probably originated in Southern China, and gradually populated mainland Southeast Asia from approximately the 7th century (e.g. Reid 2015). Although politically, socially, and culturally dominant, the Bangkok-based Central Thai do not constitute the majority of the population in contemporary Thailand. Yet, since the Chakri dynasty took power (1782), their language, identity, and 'race' – which define the essence of 'Thainess' – came to form the core of citizenship in the modern Thai nation-state. As a result, Thai citizens of ethnic minority background have historically suffered discrimination, exclusion, and political marginalisation as second-class citizens, who are regarded as 'insufficiently Thai'.

The ethnic profiles of slum children – purportedly 'non-Thai-enough' – are central to the way in which *dek salam* are regarded by the state and by the individuals and organisations they encounter. The paths these children take in life are governed by the ethnic labels that are forced upon them or that they choose. Importantly, unlike previous generations of slum dwellers, many *dek salam* are born in Bangkok and from (Central) Thai families. Yet, the fact that they live in the slums causes state officials and schoolteachers to assume *a priori* that they are ethnic minority children (especially Thai-Lao) and, as a result, to treat them as second-class citizens. 'Thainess', indeed, is not simply an ethnic descriptor, but a historically constructed ideological, political and moral ideology, from which *dek salam* (like their parents) are considered dangerously distant in many respects. Those who do not fully embody 'Thainess' within mainstream Thai society – that is, Bangkok – are thus regarded as 'non-Thai': belittled citizens of loose morals, who need to be realigned to the national norm. *Dek salam* in Bangkok are at the centre of these tensions. The nature of their self, moreover, is increasingly contested as new local and international actors are in charge of their future.

As Comaroff and Comaroff (2005: 22) have noted, in this age of globalisation young people constitute an important 'generation trouble', because the ability of governments and aid agencies to control children's and youth's bodies, energies and initiatives appears to be significantly diminished. As Butler (1990: vii) observes, however, this 'trouble' is not necessarily only negative, for it can also productively destabilise hegemonic epistemic regimes through desire, anger or frustration.

In this era of global uncertainties and diffuse anxieties, formulating hypotheses about the future is a hazardous move, and one that transcends science and requires imagination. The protagonists of this book, Bangkok's 'belittled citizens', like others belonging to their generation across the planet, make me feel hopeful, against all the odds. Childhood is, after all, a powerful trope, even in a country under military dictatorship.

PART ONE

THE CULTURAL POLITICS
OF CHILDHOOD

CHAPTER 1

The Good Thai Child

I t was my first day at Maha Phra Mongkut ('Great King Mongkut') middle school, a large state school in the north of Bangkok. At 8 am schoolchildren and teachers gathered in the main square of the school complex, in front of the flagpole up which the Thai national flag would be lifted. The teachers had scrupulously arranged the students in parallel rows: seniors – *phi* ('elder siblings') – made up the first row (the tallest student at the front, the shortest one at the end of the row). First-year students – *nong* ('younger siblings') – formed the last row. While I stood quietly at the edge of the square, not quite sure where I would fit into the picture, the students in each row mechanically raised both arms to the side in order to check that they were in the correct position – they were meant to be at points equidistant from each other in a straight line. Acting as though they were leading a military operation, the teachers checked the accuracy of the students' positions, repeatedly shouting a mantra – *riaproi luk* ('order, order, children') – which completed the militaristic character of the whole ritual: the ordering of the students into hierarchically organised 'battalions', ready to march. At their teachers' command, the units thus organised walked towards their respective classrooms, taking up predefined positions while waiting for the school loudspeaker, which was synchronised to the same frequency as all other national public institutions, to begin broadcasting the national anthem. Prior to the anthem, a recorded male voice stressed the solemnity of the moment through an exhortatory formula: 'The Thai flag and the Thai anthem are a symbol of "Thainess". We Thai must engage our hearts and stand up to show respect for our national flag, proud of our identity and of the sacrifices of our Thai ancestors'.

The concept of 'Thainess', *khwam pen thai* (the 'Thai mode of being'), was coined by King Vajiravudh (Rama VI) in the early 1900s and is a fundamental dimension of Thai public life. The expression establishes a connection between the ideas of nation and monarchy, prescribing to citizens not only a code involving 'authentically Thai' cultural and religious traits, but also patriotism, pride in the nation's cultural heritage and glorification of the monarchy (Igunma 2006). 'Thainess' is construed, from a historical perspective, as tripartite, with three official dimensions: monarchy (*phra mahakasat*), nation (*chat*) and religion (*sasana*) – namely Buddhism (Reynolds [ed.] 2002). Each of these is associated with one of the colours of the national flag: red for *chat*, white for *sasana*, and blue for *phra mahakasat*. The slogan *chat, sasana, phra mahakasat*, recited daily by Thai citizens as part of a repertoire of nationalistic rituals preceding the start of any activity in a public space, is intended by the state to capture as concisely as possible the collective essence of what it means to be a citizen of Thailand.

While the presidents of the student body, who were standing below the national flag, were raising the sacred symbol of the nation, the teachers were making sure that every child was singing the anthem in tune, paying special attention to the *dek salam* ('slum children'), who are considered particularly undisciplined 'because they come from the slums', as the school principal rather hastily put it. The national anthem was followed by the anthem in honour of the king, celebrated as the nation's father; next was a Buddhist prayer, completing a trilogy of songs celebrating identity and 'Thainess'. A few students in the first row – who had a clean-cut, neater appearance than the *dek salam* – were praised by a female teacher, pleased with the stylistic perfection of their performance: 'Very good! That is how a mother expects good children to behave'.

In order to understand why, at Maha Phra Mongkut middle school, students are 'sons and daughters', expected to honour the king as the nation's father and to make sense of schoolteachers' military zeal and attitude towards those students who do not act (and look) like 'good children' – as the *dek salam* do not appear to do, in their eyes – we must examine how the concept of childhood is publicly articulated within the modern Thai school system.

In this chapter, I analyse, historically and ethnographically, the normative notion of 'Thai childhood', which children are expected to embody in schools in order to be considered 'good children' and citizens. As I will show, this notion of childhood emerged in Thailand as part of early 20th century Thai ethno-nationalism and took its current shape in the context of several waves of (military) government interventions on state education. As a social concept, 'childhood' is a modern political formulation; however, it also encapsulates, symbolically, cultural ideas of hierarchy, power and agency that have deep-rooted political and religious ties with the long history of monarchical Southeast Asia.

I will first discuss childhood as part of Indo-Buddhist doctrines of kingship, which underpin normative hierarchies and the socio-political order in Thailand, and I will highlight the way in which a fatherly notion of monarchy has been instrumentalised and intertwined, historically, with an ethnic conceptualisation of the Thai nation that casts citizens – especially those of ethnic minority background – in childlike roles. I will show how these constructions of childhood have been variably politicised during the creation of the modern school system, to generate the public paradigm of the 'good Thai child'. My ethnography focuses on some of the Bangkok schools that are attended by poor children inhabiting the slums of the capital. Their 'not-Thai-enough' ethno-linguistic, class, moral and aesthetic profiles are seen as political deviations from the purity of 'Thainess', especially since former Royal Thai Army general officer Prayut Chan-o-cha, and his military junta, seized power in 2014.

BIG PEOPLE, SMALL PEOPLE

Before considering how the public notion of 'Thai childhood' has been historically constructed through modern education, and why *dek salam* are a cause of concern for teachers in Bangkok schools today, we first need to examine the conceptual value of 'childhood' within Thailand's traditional social structure and in the context of its enduring cosmology of kingship.

The king is positioned at the top of the Thai social hierarchy as a semi-divine being and is the most exemplary instance of a *phu yai* ('big person'). This conceptualisation of kingship is a prominent feature of pre-modern Southeast Asia's Indo-Buddhist kingdoms, and has been widely described in anthropological and historical literature as the cosmological basis of Thai political power (e.g. Hanks 1962; Tambiah 1976, 1977; Condominas 1980; Keyes 1977; Kirsch 1977, 1978; P.A. Jackson 2002). While scholarship has mainly focused on the monarchy's 'divine fatherhood', I would argue that a full understanding of Thai social order also requires tracing the political concept of childhood that emerges, as a shadow cast by the light from the fatherly monarch. The contours of this shadow, however, can only be inferred by first facing the light source.

As famously argued by Clifford Geertz (1980), Hindu conceptualisations of absolute monarchy as the objectification of a deity were a typical trait of the pre-colonial Indic polities of Southeast Asia as 'theatre states'. These were political formations organised around royal ritual spectacles dramatising the charismatic power and sacred authority of rulers. From the time of the Ayutthaya kingdom (1351–1767) to the advent of the Rattanakosin era, with the foundation of Bangkok (1782), Thai monarchs tied their role to God Vishnu (P.A. Jackson 2010: 36). Rama, Vishnu's seventh avatar in the Thai epic poem *Ramakien* (the local version of Hindu classic *Ramayana*), is the appellation used to designate all of the Chakri dynasty's monarchs. King Vajiralongkorn, heir of King Bhumibol[1] and currently in power, is Rama X. Besides being traditionally

---

1   The late King Bhumibol Adulyadej (Rama IX), the longest-reigning monarch in Thai history, was not only portrayed as a divine being but also as the 'father of all Thais' (de Rooij 2015; Siani 2016). The royal cremation ceremony after his death took place at Sanam Luang, in the centre of Bangkok, on 26 October 2017, after the conclusion of this ethnographic study. The

described as *devaraja* ('God King'), the king also represents the personification of the Buddhist *dharma* (*thamma*): he is a *thammaraja* ('King of Law') – a virtuous being, ruling in conformity with the canon of Buddhist norms known in Thai as *thammasat* (from Pali *dhammasatha*) (Akin Rabibhadana 1963: 49; Anand Panyarachun 1996). As such, the king embodies *barami* (charismatic power) and unquantifiable karmic merit (*bun*).

The metaphysics associated with both the *devaraja* and the *thammaraja* imply a pyramidal and strongly hierarchical cosmological structuring of the socio-political order, within which the monarchy is confirmed in its role as the guide of the universe. As Sinhalese anthropologist Stanley Tambiah (1976) observed, Siamese kingdoms were traditionally organised in a 'galactic' or 'mandalic' configuration (something that is expressed in the centrality of Mount Meru in the Hindu universe), which replicated identical geopolitical patterns radiating outwards from an exemplary cosmological centre – the capital (and at its centre, the royal palace) – to the most peripheral provinces. The latter were in a subaltern (tributary) relationship with the central state, but internally organised on the same hierarchical structure: a palace-city in the middle, site of the governor of the vassal state (often a prince who was a direct relative of the king), with a group of satellite villages.

From an administrative point of view, until the end of 1800 Siamese society was also organised in compliance with a system known as *sakdina*,[2] within which every subject was assigned a numeric code designating his or her rank within the social hierarchy. The king's *sakdina* was considered immense and unquantifiable, and below him *sakdina* ranks ranged from 100,000 for *uparat* (the highest office in the state, generally occupied by the king's son, brother or uncle), 10,000 for a minister, 25–10 for commoners (*phrai*) down to five for a slave. Every *phrai* man and woman outside the *sakdina* system of the nobility was assigned to live under the authority of a supervisor-owner (*nai* or *munnai*), so that the general population was comprised of groups of *phrai* subject to the authority of *nai* (Akin Rabibhadana 1963: 27–28). Hence, the kingdom's geo-political configuration replicated mandalic patterns, and *sakdina* ranks served as the administrative operationalisation of subjects' karmic merit within the moral stratification characteristic of the Thai social pyramid.[3]

---

golden crematorium prepared for the occasion was a 50-metre-high, nine-spired structure representing Mount Meru, the centre of the Hindu universe.

2 The word *sakdina*, composed of the terms *na* (a field dedicated to cultivation, or a rice field) and *sakdi* (power), literally translates as 'field of power'. It refers to what Quaritch Wales (1965) has described as 'seals of dignity', which corresponds to an index of status and prestige.

3 In the Hindu caste system, assignation to a certain caste happens at birth and establishes once and for all an individual's spiritual positioning in relation to others (Dumont 1980). By contrast, as has been pointed out by Keyes (1977) and Hanks (1962), in Buddhism an individ-

As the cosmological heart of Thailand's social body, these complex hierarchies continue to be reflected in public interactions between subjects of complementary socio-moral status, according to a self-replicating pattern: the king–subject dyad defines the extreme and overarching polarity within a moral continuum of dichotomies relating to social categories of decreasing importance (e.g. monk–laymen; teacher–student; etc.). At the opposite end of this continuum we find the elementary unit of the social cosmos – the family – and, more specifically, the juxtaposition of parents and children, and also of elder (*phi*) and younger (*nong*) siblings. All of these dichotomies juxtapose *phu yai* ('big people') with *phu noi* ('small people'): the king is *phu yai* vis-à-vis his subjects, who are *phu noi*; monks are *phu yai* vis-à-vis laymen, who are *phu noi*; teachers are *phu yai* vis-à-vis their students, who are *phu noi*; and parents are *phu yai* vis-à-vis their sons, who are *phu noi*. *Phu noi* must show respect, obedience, and gratitude to *phu yai* as their (paternal and morally superior) protectors (Akin Rabibhadana 1963: 108).

The significance and nature of childhood that is embedded in this cosmological structure comes vividly to the fore here. In the Thai social system, the term *dek* (which we would usually translate into English as 'child') often refers to someone of a lower hierarchical status vis-à-vis another person, rather than to chronological age. The term *dek* and the personal pronoun *nu*,[4] which individuals in the position of *dek* vis-à-vis someone else often use to refer to themselves in that particular context, are socio-linguistic indicators of hierarchical grade. However old the speaker, if their interlocutor is an older person, a monk, a teacher or simply an older friend, the speaker will be considered a *dek* in that context, and, to express this, he or she will commonly refer to himself or herself as either *nu* or *nong* ('younger sibling'), while the interlocutor will be addressed as *phi* ('elder sibling'). Even outside the circle of family relationships, social interactions are mediated by the use of kin terms that establish hierarchical boundaries between *phu noi* ('small people') and *phu yai* ('big people'). As sociologist Hans-Dieter Bechstedt (1991) has made clear:

> As the formal genealogical structure of Thai kin terms demonstrates, there are no equals at all. Pupils in a group on the way to school are expected

---

ual's karmic status cannot be entirely predetermined. In fact, karmic theory, the cornerstone of Thai social hierarchy, presupposes an irreducible margin of indefiniteness, as well as the potential for anyone to improve their own karmic condition through the accumulation of *bun* (merit) in their current life (e.g. Obeyesekere 1968: 21). Such indeterminateness of *karma* (*kam*) should lend dynamism to the possibility of social mobility on the part of individuals. Nonetheless, in the historical context of Thai kingdoms, as can be seen in the *sakdina* system, this indefiniteness of *karma* was merely theorical.

4   *Nu*: literally, a mouse – an animal that was occasionally eaten by the Thai although they did not particularly like it. Tambiah (1969) has suggested the possibility of an analogy between the smallest, most marginal animals and children.

to walk according to their age; likewise, during their morning procession for alms the single file of monks is headed by the most senior one. At a wedding, a funeral, or an official party, all guests set great store on addressing each other according to rank and status. All Thai people, whatever the situation, are fully aware of their own as well as everyone else's position in the social hierarchy, and will reinforce this by appropriate manners and speech. (Bechstedt 1991: 242)

As quintessential *phu noi* ('small people'), children are situated at the bottom of the Thai social hierarchy, with the monarch at its top. The relationship between children and adults can be thus understood as the metonymic base of the Thai social universe: children must interact with adults as Thai subjects are traditionally expected to relate with the king.

With the establishment of Siam/Thailand as a modern nation-state at the turn of the 20th century, this conceptualisation of children as the most exemplary instance of *phu noi* provided the basis for specific understandings of citizenship and state–citizen relations. Notably, citizens came to be regarded as 'children' (*dek*) by virtue of being *phu noi* vis-à-vis state authorities, who are considered the nation's *phu yai*. This played a key role in Thai royalist and military nationalism, especially through compulsory state education.

EDUCATING THE NATION: THE THAI SCHOOL SYSTEM

Until the end of the 19th century, the Buddhist temple constituted the informal venue of Siamese education. In every village (*mu ban*) surrounding a temple (*wat*), monks provided the basic knowledge required to understand Buddhist teachings and local traditions. Temple schools served as the channel for disseminating a vision of the cosmos grounded in the Buddhist religion, generating a rationalisation of the socio-political world through the lens of Buddhist notions such as *karma*, *dharma*, and *nirvana* (Wyatt 1969: 12; Tambiah 1976; Watson 1980: 69–76; Keyes 1991a: 91–92).

With the transformation of Siam into a modern nation-state, the traditional school system underwent radical changes. King Chulalongkorn (Rama V, who reigned from 1868 to 1910), celebrated by authorised Thai historiography as a national hero, considered modernisation and state education necessary to maintain formal political independence in the colonial period.[5] Concerned that

5   While its political independence was formally preserved, Siam could in fact be described as a semi-colonial or 'crypto-colonial' kingdom (Herzfeld 2002). The Siamese ruling elite's negotiations with Western powers in the region resulted in the adoption and local adaptation of 'Western' ways (in relation to art, etiquette, cuisine, science and technology), which led to

the French colonisers of neighbouring Indochina could use the argument that Thai society had supposedly 'primitive' (*bohran*) traits as moral leverage for a potential invasion, Rama V initiated a broad process of reform to introduce 'civilisation' (*siwilai*) to the country and to Westernise it, partly drawing on the British colonial model of Burma (Loos 2006; Anderson 1978). During this phase, Siam went from a galactic political system to a 'radial', centralised polity (Tambiah 1977). The process of reform was based on the centralisation of power in Bangkok and the creation of a bureaucratic, administrative apparatus (capital, provinces, districts and villages) that is in large part still in use. It also included the introduction of a secular school system. The integration of Siam's ethnically diverse population into a uniform national body and within an efficient administrative system was deemed crucial to the creation of a 'modern citizenry': one that was literate and educated in Western skills (Wyatt 1975: 125).

In 1900 three types of school were already present in Siam (Keyes 1991b: 7): traditional monastic schools, Christian missionary institutes, and schools created by Chinese immigrants, especially in Bangkok. Missionary schools were strategically identified as the model to replicate. In 1898, with the Decree on Organisation of Provincial Education, King Chulalongkorn and his advisers promulgated a school policy dictated by the state (Wyatt 1969; Watson 1980). The decree established a continuity between monastic and state education. Specifically, it entailed state education taking place in temple schools and teachers being monks. The latter were expected to provide a new kind of education: lessons must be taught in Thai (the language of the Siamese Tai or Central Thai), the national language, and maths and natural sciences must be added to traditional Buddhist subjects. The school system conceived by Chulalongkorn was, however, only a transitory phase. It was King Vajiravudh (Rama VI, who reigned from 1910 to 1925), the ideologue of 'Thainess', who developed the basis of the school system as we know it today.

Compulsory education in 'Thainess'

King Vajiravudh (Rama VI) committed to the plan to transform Siam into a modern nation-state.[6] At the centre of this project was education, which was identified

---

a Westernisation of 'Thainess'. Especially during King Chulalongkorn's reign, the territorial boundaries of Siam were determined by the British and French, and a series of trading treaties established colonial-style relations between the Buddhist kingdom and the West (Harrison and Jackson 2009: 339).

6   Unlike in other countries in Southeast Asia, in Thailand the 'idea of nation' (Gellner 1983) was created through a monarchical nationalism (Anderson 1978). While in many respects Siam was actually a 'semi-colony' (e.g. Harrison and Jackson 2009), the fact that the Buddhist

as a key tool to propagate 'Thainess' and ensure the nationalistic assimilation of Thailand's ethno-linguistic and geographic margins under the dominion of the monarchy and its Bangkok-centred Thai establishment.

According to Walter Vella, author of an important monograph about Vajiravudh, *Chaiyo! King Vajiravudh and the Development of Thai Nationalism* (Vella 1978), Rama VI conceived the project of building a nation-state that would be both as modern as Western countries and genuinely Thai. The modernisation envisioned by the king has in fact been realised through the adoption of European nationalistic models – among these, the British slogan 'God, King and Country', upon which the core of 'Thainess' has been built (religion, monarchy, nation). At the same time, Vajiravudh was very careful to underline the specificity of Thai nationalism. In the formulation of his project, he envisioned education, both formal and informal, as the basis of national unity (Vella 1978: 160–167). In 1921, with the Primary Education Act, formal education (4 years of primary school) was made compulsory for all children in the kingdom (Wyatt 1969; Watson 1980). Monks were not thought fit to be teachers and were substituted by professionals trained by the state. Although the roles of *sangha* and those of Buddhist monks were profoundly altered by the introduction of a state school system, the Buddhist authorities supported the king's reform, ensuring its success. Vajiranana, patriarch of the *sangha* and Vajiravudh's uncle, followed his nephew's instructions to the letter, and together with Prince Damrong, the powerful Minister of Internal Affairs, contributed to the production of textbooks in which the monarchical Buddhist ethic appeared harmoniously integrated with the curriculum of the secular education system. All texts were written in Thai, the national language. To avoid Christian missionary and Chinese schools channelling ideological diversity, thus hindering ethno-nationalistic homogenisation of the Thai kingdom's subjects under the banner of 'Thainess',[7] from 1918 all schools (both public and private) were mandated to conform to the same curriculum, to teach in the (Central) Thai language and to adopt the same textbooks (Vella 1978: 189–190).[8]

---

kingdom was never formally colonised was used by the Bangkok elite as historical evidence of the monarchy's solidity. As a result, the development of an 'ethnic concept of nation' (Reid 2010) as Thai is deeply entrenched, with grossly exaggerated historical accounts of past Siamese kings' patriotic heroism: the so-called 'standard total view of the Thai monarchy' (Hewison 1997: 266).

7 Vajiravudh's ethnic nationalism has often been characterised as anti-Chinese. *The Jews of the Orient* (Vajiravudh 1917) is a well-known text by the king, in which the monarch supports the thesis of Western anti-semitism and puts forward disturbing parallels between the Jews and the Chinese.

8 In other Southeast Asian countries that were colonised by European nations (for example Vietnam, Burma or Malaya), there was a binary school system ('indigenous' schools, where

An important part of the king's educational project was the progressive militarisation of society. With the establishment of several paramilitary organisations, Vajiravudh identified the prototype of nationalistic loyalty with the figure of the soldier, ready to sacrifice his own life for the sake of the nation. Wild Tigers, the unit in charge of the king's personal safety, was created in 1911. By establishing paramilitary forces made up of civilians, Vajiravudh likened them to soldiers through the use of a warrior paradigm: 'We should understand that although we have two separate names for soldier and civilian, the truth is that we have one name that applies to both, and that is the word *thai*' (ibid.: 31). As well as the Wild Tigers, the organisation of boy scouts (whose Thai name is *luk seua*, 'Tiger Cubs') was also established.[9] This was conceived of as the junior version of the paramilitary organisation, with the same goals as the adult corps. The decree with which King Vajiravudh ordered the creation of *luk seua* stated:

> Boys in their adolescent years should receive both physical and mental training of the sort given to Wild Tigers so that when they become older they will know their proper duties as Thai men. [...] The instilling of the proper spirit must begin when one is still young. A tree that is to be shaped into a pleasing form can be most easily trained when it is young and supple. (Vajiravudh 1911, cited in Vella 1978: 42)

Since its establishment, in 1913, the training of Tiger Cubs has been carried out, unchanged, in all of the schools in the country. King Vajiravudh also established other paramilitary units that copied the original model of the Wild Tigers: Girl Scouts, Tiger Women, the Hunters' Club and the Teachers' Club.[10] During this period, the king introduced rituals, symbols, songs and nationalistic hymns that are still used during extra-curricular activities in schools, as well as team

the vernacular language was used, and 'European' schools aimed at the education of the elites, where classes were taught in English or French). By contrast, in all Thai schools, both public and private, the Central Thai language was the only language used in teaching (Keyes 1991b: 7).

9   It seems that Vajiravudh knew about the English scouting organisation founded by Robert Baden-Powell at the start of the 20th century. While some similarities between English and Thai scouting persist, Thai scouting was largely modelled after the Wild Tigers, in an explicitly nationalistic key (Vella 1978).

10 The historical importance of royalist paramilitary organisations in the articulation of Thai ethno-nationalism is reflected in the birth of far-right groups such as the Village Scouts or the Red Gaurs. These played key roles in the military repression of the communist guerrillas in the 1970s. Such organisations, believed to be close to King Bhumibol (Rama IX), were responsible, with the military, for the massacre of students who were peacefully protesting to invoke the reinstation of democratic regime at Thammasat University in Bangkok in October 1976 (Bowie 1997; Somsak Jeamteerasakul 2001; Handley 2006).

games, which became core elements of youth organisations as well as being part of the school curriculum. As patron of the National Football Association, founded in 1915, the monarch promoted the organisation of tournaments and competitions such as the Warrior's Cup and the King's Gold Cup. Thus, both inter-school sport competitions and the discipline of the Tiger Cubs (*wicha luk seua*) became fundamental parts of the modern Thai school system (Vella 1978: 144–150).

The militarisation of education

In the context of the military nationalism that has shaped Thailand since the fall of the absolute monarchy (1932), childhood has been charged with new political meanings. Children are no longer just *phu noi* – they are also symbolic referents for other citizens. The king, formally devoid of any political power, is regarded as his people's father and as the 'Soul of a Nation' (to cite the title of a popular BBC historical documentary on King Bhumibol).

Especially during the regimes of Field Marshals Phibun Songkran (1938–1944; 1948–1957) and Sarit Thanarat (1958–1963), the school system became the cornerstone of an assimilationist, centralising and mono-ethnic social engineering system at the service of the army, the new total institution at the core of the state's cultural production (Barmé 1993: 181). During these decades, Thai nationalism, fed by Phibun's admiration of the Nazi and fascist regimes in Italy, Germany and Japan, intruded into the sphere of private behaviour; and school, the first manifestation of the state encountered by an individual in his or her life, constituted the public foundation for the 'Thaification' of the citizenry (ibid.: 138).

The objective of Phibun's government was to subject society to a conservative ethics that was generically identified with the concept of an 'appropriate Thai code of conduct' (Thak Chaloemtiarana 2007: 179–186). This code of conduct, known as *khwam riaproi* ('order–discipline'), was inculcated on a large scale between the 1930s and the 1940s, through a number of 'state conventions' (*rathaniyom*), conceived as key to the nation's wellbeing (Barmé 1993:144). The first of these conventions, in 1939, renamed Siam Thailand, explicitly projecting the nation as independent, with a Thai ethnic profile and belonging to the Thai people. The term *watthanatham* ('culture') was introduced in the place of the previous central mantra, 'civilisation' (Thongchai Winichakul 2000b), referring on one hand to the richness of Thai material culture (architecture, arts, cuisine, traditional costumes), and on the other to an unspecified ethical-moral Buddhist core, regarded as essential to the kingdom's stability and progress (ibid.). *Watthanatham thai* (Thai culture) is now one of the main subjects in all of the schools in the country. Other conventions prescribed that all citizens were defined uniquely as 'Thai' (*chon thai*) despite local ethno-linguistic identifications (for example Thai-Lao), that they had to speak Thai, and that they had to embody 'Thainess'.

There were two sets of conventions that had a particular impact on the school system: the prescriptions regarding clothing and those intended to regulate the daily routine of citizens, which had to follow a pre-established model. The former set of conventions prescribed the use of Western clothing, abandoning traditional costumes for civilians and introducing military-style uniforms for all government officers, including teachers.[11] The latter set of conventions aimed to regulate citizens' lifestyles, following an orderly, standardised pattern. Both sets of conventions may be regarded as an attempt to impose a singular, unified order and a standardised vision of society.

During Sarit's military regime, government investment in schools increased tremendously throughout the national territory, including in rural communities.[12] Since the 1950s, virtually every village has been provided with a state school, a new point of reference for the community beside the temple. In 1960, mandatory education was extended to seven years (four years of lower primary school and three of higher primary school) and a number of five-year educational plans began to be developed. In 1977, the school system changed from the format 4 (lower primary education) – 3 (higher primary) – 3 (lower secondary) – 2 (higher secondary) to the current one, 6–3–3.[13]

Under Sarit, childhood became the primary symbol of citizenship, the family became a metaphor for the (militarised) state, and the monarchy's public role registered a new expansion after years of absence. Sarit, whose style of government has been tellingly described as 'despotic paternalism' (Thak Chaloemtiarana

---

11 Uniforms are also mandatory for all students, with few variations from a standard model. The dress code for primary (*prathom*) and secondary (*mathayom*) schools imposes dark blue knee-length shorts, an off-white, short-sleeved shirt with an open collar, long socks and either brown or black shoes for boys. Girls wear a dark blue knee-length skirt, a white blouse, a tie worn loosely, white socks and black shoes. The student's name, matriculation number and school name are often embroidered on the shirt or blouse.

12 Charles Keyes (1991a) has shown how Thai military governments used schooling to reshape the value systems of peripheral rural communities, enforcing a secularised experience of the national cosmos within which a cronometric conception of time (e.g. a bell marking the beginning and end of lessons, the adoption of a school calendar, and so on) and a hyper-hierarchical spatial culture were intended to reflect the developmental mission of the national family of 'Thainess'. See also Uthai Dulyakasem 1991, Chayan Vaddhanaphuti 1991, Gillogly 2005, and Liow 2009.

13 The current school structure is arranged in four main phases: the first three years in elementary school, *prathom* 1–3, are for children aged 6–8; the second level, *prathom* 4–6, is for those aged 9-11; and the third level, *mathayom* 1–3, is for those aged 12–14. The secondary level of education is made up of *mathayom* 4–6, for those aged 15–17, and is divided into academic and professional-vocational streams with different curricula.

2007), reinstated the terms 'Army of the King' and 'government led by the King' and established King Bhumibol's birthday (5 December) as Thai Father's Day. To use Thai scholar Thak Chaloemtiarana's words, the dictator understood that power 'radiated from above, the monarchy, rather than from below, the population' (ibid.), and that 'the one who governs is nothing but the chief of a big family that must look at the population as he would at his children and grandchildren' (Baker and Pasuk Phongpaichit 2005: 176–177).

As political scientist Michael Connors (Connors 2005: 530) has observed, the nationalistic cult of the monarchy has been particularly strengthened by the cultural policies enforced by the Army since the 1970s in response to communist insurgency. After granting amnesty to the former guerrillas of the CPT (Thai Communist Party) in 1981, Bangkok elites adopted new forms of bureaucratic rationalisation of 'non-Thai-enough' rural provinces, moving from a zero-tolerance war strategy to a paternalistic policy focused on the propaganda of 'Thainess' and the promotion of 'development' (*phatthana*) and 'democracy' (*prachathipatai*). The king, presented as a father suffering for the different parts of his family, willing to lovingly assist even those children who have rebelled, assumed the official patronage of these policies and programmes, particularly through the proliferation of royal projects (*khrohngkan luang*) addressing the development of peripheral communities.[14]

The military establishment in Bangkok had two aims: first of all, to reinstate, from an ideological point of view, the parental role of the monarchy, connecting this to development and democracy;[15] and secondly, to expand the meaning of Thai culture and identity so as to integrate wider social forces in more pluralistic notions of 'Thainess' (Connors 2003). This second objective was achieved through the birth of new institutions: The National Commission for Culture (founded in 1979 within the Ministry of Education), the National Identity Board (founded in 1980, as part of the Prime Minister's office), and the Ministry of Culture (founded in 2003). These institutions are particularly active in the

---

14 *Khrohngkan luang* have particularly targeted the Thai-Lao territories of eastern Thailand, where there have been numerous historical attempts to break free from Bangkok (see e.g. Keyes 1977, 1978); and northern Thailand (former Lanna, a vassal kingdom) and its mountains, a no-man's-land area inhabited by 'stateless people' (Scott 2009; Rossi 2012). This created a situation of 'internal colonialism' by the Central Thais, with Bangkok extending its control over other ethnic groups in the border areas of the Thai state – where most of the slum dwellers in the capital originate (Anderson 1978; Chaiyan Rajchagool 1994).

15 According to the 'total standard vision of monarchy' (Hewison 1997: 266), the end of absolute monarchy and the subsequent advent of democracy was promoted by the king (Thongchai Winichakul 2008: 23). The statue of King Prajadhipok (Rama VII) located in front of the Thai parliament in Bangkok expresses 'the essence of such connection between monarchy and the emerging of democracy in Thailand' (Isager and Ivarsson 2010b: 15).

schools of the country. Through the Ministry of Culture, children (understood as both *phu noi* and future citizens) are a prime target for the nationalistic ideology of the state, of which military paternalism is a key element.

Colour-coded politics in the Thai school system

The Thai school system as outlined above remained essentially unchanged until the 1990s, when Thaksin Shinawatra (in office from 2001 to 2006) appeared on the Thai political stage. A telecommunications tycoon, Thaksin was part of an emerging power bloc on the political chessboard of the country (e.g. see McCargo and Ukrist Pathamanand 2005; Pasuk Phongpaichit and Baker 2004). The booming economic-industrial development of the 1960s and the adoption of a free-market economy had led, over time, to the birth of new networks of power outside of Thailand's capital city: a decentralised urban middle-class largely made up of Sino-Thai capitalists – able contenders for political primacy with Bangkok-based royalist and military elites. This may be regarded as the origin of the contemporary political division between the 'yellow shirts' (yellow being the king's colour), standing for the traditional socio-moral order (aristocracy, army, bureaucracy, and royalist Thai groups centred in Bangkok) and the 'red shirts', a movement grouped around Thaksin, which was largely made up of a rural and provincial urban electorate, located mainly in Thailand's northern and northeastern ethnic minority regions.[16]

Aware of the increasing electoral weight of the 'non-Thai' (especially Thai-Lao) element of the population, Thaksin launched a series of populist reforms aimed at favouring the country's rural areas, whose economic exploitation had historically fed Bangkok's 'modernity' and urban development. These initiatives also affected the school system, which was deemed to be second-rate compared with international and regional standards (Prachathai 2014a). Developing the guidelines prescribed in the 1997 Constitution (considered by many the most democratic in the country's history[17]), Thaksin's government urged the decen-

---

16 The royalist 'yellow shirt' movement, also known as PAD (People's Alliance for Democracy) played a key role in the 2005, 2006 and 2008 political crises, backing the army's intervention into politics. The 'red shirt' movement, also known as UDD (United Front for Democracy Against Dictatorship), was created in opposition to military rule, and in support of ex-premiers Thaksin and Yingluck Shinawatra. In May 2010 the Thai military cracked down on pro-democracy 'red shirt' activists in central Bangkok. More than 85 civilians were killed, including 2 foreigners and 2 paramedics (e.g. Montesano et al 2012).

17 The 1997 Constitution was the first to be created by an elected assembly. Considered a definitive step towards democracy, the Constitution established a bicameral system based entirely on elections, processes of state decentralisation and an explicit reference to the respect of human rights. For this reason it has been described as the 'Constitution of the people' (McCargo

tralisation of schools (in parallel with that of the state bureaucracy), empowering local provincial and district offices (Tambon Administrative Organisations, TAOs) in place of the Ministry of Education. The performance of Thai students was substandard at an international level, and this led to the introduction of the so-called child-centred learning method, introduced through the Thai Education Act (TEA) in 1999. This was reformulated under Thaksin, as part of a deliberate attempt to undermine the traditional social order in his favour. The reformulation introduced significant changes in teaching methods (from vertical to horizontal), the introduction of state-of-the-art digital learning tools (tablets and computers), the acknowledgement of ethno-linguistic and cultural regional specificities, and the introduction of an explicit goal of promoting children's critical thinking.[18] These innovations were intended to free education from the shackles of Thai monarchical nationalism, within which students are conceived of and treated as sons/daughters trapped by their moral obligations towards teachers/parents (Bangkok Post 2014a).

Thaksin's controversial project ended with the 2006 military coup. The royalist groups who were supporting the military takeover – the 'yellow shirt' movement – accused the government of corruption (Callahan 2005), and pointed to Thaksin's 'red' electorate as a clear sign of the weaknesses of Thai democracy: illiterate farmers who did not have the intellectual and moral capacity to exercise the 'right' electoral choice (Pavin Chachavalpongpun 2011). The argument presented was that solving the crisis required a cessation of democracy, an interim government appointed by the king (as guarantor of dharmic morality), and 'restorative' reforms, before the electorate was given back their voice. However, despite the military's 'restorative' intervention into politics, in 2011 Thai voters handed the country's leadership back to the Shinawatra family, electing Yingluck, the fugitive ex-premier's sister, as Prime Minister. Even Yingluck's efforts, however, soon collided with Thai traditional establishment. Beginning in October 2013, a series of anti-government protests by royalist groups in Bangkok blocked governmental offices, eventually leading to another military coup on 22 May 2014.

In the current political crisis, the army is once again involved in an authoritarian attempt to restore a form of public morality grounded in the monarchy.

2005). It was later superseded by the 2006 Constitution, following the military coup through which Thaksin's government was overthrown. Thailand's latest constitution (2017), which was largely designed by the military junta leading the country after the 2014 coup, created a permanent place for the military in government and sought to normalise their intervention.

18 On the Thai educational system and the 1999 Thai Education Act, see also Baron-Gutty and Supat Chupradit (2009), and Mounier and Phasina Tangchuang (2010).

The NCPO (National Council for Peace and Order), the military junta that seized power with the 2014 coup, has imposed martial law, tamed the media and journalists, put social media under surveillance and suppressed freedom of speech[19]. The new instructions given to the OBEC (Office of the Basic Education Commission of Thailand) by the junta state that any criticism of the army is banned in schools. Teachers are forbidden to take part in protests or political events. School staff must persuade students and their families of the regime's benevolence as protector of the nation, religion and the monarchy. Every student must complete a 'student's passport of good deeds' every day. Suthasri Wongsamarn, in his capacity as the representative of the Ministry of Education, has declared that these passports can be used as criteria in applications for places in higher education and at universities (Bangkok Post 2014b).[20] OBEC secretary Kamol Rordklai has also announced the revision of history textbooks, proposing to remove references to Thaksin. This is said to be with the aim of reinforcing children's patriotic feelings for the Thai nation (Asian Correspondent 2014b).

In this context, the political relevance of childhood has become explicit: the cult of *phu yai*, of the king as supreme father, and of the junta as the Thai national family's last defence have all led to the strengthening of military-style discipline in schools, with the stated aim of guaranteeing national security through the hierarchical subordination of childhood. 'Thainess', with all its military grammar, is transmitted powerfully in schools, targeting in particular those sections of the population most affected by Thaksin's 'red disease': ethnic minority groups in the north and north-

---

19   The regime's main legal strategy, in neutralising potential dissidents, rests on the arbitrary use of the law of *lèse majesté*, the violation of which can lead to a 14-year imprisonment. *Lèse majesté*, a law that has created many issues within the historiography and analysis of the Thai political system, generating auto-censorship among scholars themselves (Thongchai Winichakul 2008), ensures that the king's grandiose and quasi-divine image is preserved from scrutiny and judgement. After the 2014 coup, there has been a vertiginous increase in the number of trials related to *lèse majesté* (e.g. Sopranzetti 2017a). For a more in-depth analysis of the political usage of law in Thailand, see, for instance, Streckfuss 2010.

20   In order to make access to institutes of higher education 'meritocratic', the Ministy of Education introduced the Ordinary National Educational Test (O-Net) in 2006: a multiple-choice test, standardised nationally. However, as Jennifer Goodman (2013) has observed, the test has become 'the producer and the product of what authors of this tool consider ordinary knowledge in Thailand – the knowledge of the dominant class'. The children of Bangkok's middle classes and of those belonging to the Bangkok elites, to whose world vision the contents of the test refer, score systematically better on a national level. Goodman argues that through the ritual of carrying out the national test on the same date and time in all the schools of the country, students who are located far from the centre are indoctrinated into regarding themselves as situated within 'an imagined community' (Anderson 1983) and convinced of the fairness of the test. In this way, 'through the illusion of objectivity, the test is effective in de-politicising the preferential access to higher education guaranteed to the golden children of Bangkok's middle class' (Goodman 2013: 101).

east and the capital's urban poor. This is the political context in which I explored what was happening in the schools attended by Bangkok's slum children.

LEARNING 'THAINESS'

The Thai education system in the form in which it was first designed by King Vajiravudh, and then put into practice by a series of military regimes, still seems to be operating in the cultural creation of 'Thai children', especially since the NCPO seized power in 2014. In the ethnographic vignette opening this chapter, we saw how nationalistic rituals with a strong paramilitary flavour regulate space and time in schools. Propaganda putting forward the national ideology is also conveyed through the curriculum and through teaching methods.

An example of this can be seen in a *phasa thai* ('Thai language') lesson at which I was present during the time I spent at Thairath Witthaia primary school, a small state school in the northern part of Bangkok. The children in the class were first-year students (*prathom* 1). The children were learning a song – 'For the Love of Thailand' – taken from a ministry-approved Thai language textbook:

> Thai people are good. We are *phi* [elder siblings] and *nong* [younger siblings].

> We love the land of the Thai people.
> Our flag has three colours:
> Red for the nation [*chat*], white for religion [*sasana*].
> And blue for our great Thai King [*phra mahakasat*].
> Thai villages and cities have a long history.
> Traditional heritage, authentic and beautiful, cannot be forgotten
> We have our language to speak: Thai.
> Today Thai children must be good.
> They must be honest, patient and disciplined.
> We will love our nation until the end.
> And we turn wholeheartedly to her.
> (Field notes, August 2013; translation of original Thai by author)

The teacher read out a verse at a time and the students had to repeat each in chorus. The teacher then asked a series of questions, to which there were set answers that the students gave in unison: 'What are we Thai people?' 'We are elder and younger siblings!'; 'Which language do we use to speak?', 'Thai!'; 'What must Thai children be like?', 'Good, honest and obedient!'[21]

---

21 This song has also been cited by Wallace (2003: 7–8) as a paradigmatic instance of the 'ideological' framework of the Thai education system.

The teaching method was as follows: the teacher explained, mostly copying the ministerial textbook word-for-word on the blackboard; the students copied what was written on the board into their notebooks and were expected to memorise it. The teacher (*khru*) addressed the students as *luk* ('sons/daughters') and in effect played the role of symbolic parent, to whom students owed reverence and gratitude. Students were not allowed to comment or to formulate questions; this would have been regarded as demonstrating a lack of respect towards the teacher, who reacted to transgressions using public, and sometimes corporal, punishment (hitting students on the hands or on the bottom with a stick).

I was surprised to observe these teaching practices, since the teaching method officially introduced by Thaksin's Thai Education Act – the child-centred learning method – prescribed, in theory, teacher–student relational equality, and practices of corporal punishment were branded illegal. One 56-year-old English teacher, originally from eastern Thailand and clearly hostile to the military government, expressed her disapproval of the system: 'The only purpose of school is to propagate nationalism, not teaching. They talk about the child-centred method, but we are still using the teacher-centred method. We have started to involve students in our lessons. They are asked to think critically. But children certainly cannot express any critical judgement towards "Thainess" (*khwam pen thai*)'.

The norms introduced by Thaksin's government also had an impact on the curriculum. The curriculum in Thai primary schools (*prathom*) and secondary schools (*mathayom*) has two components: *wicha lak* ('basic subjects') and *wicha phoem toem* ('optional additional subjects'). The latter were introduced after the 2002 National Education Act (No.2). *Wicha lak* subjects include: Thai Language and Literature; Society, Religion and Culture; History; Art; P.E. and lastly *wicha luk seua* – the discipline of the Tiger Cubs, introduced by King Vajiravudh at the start of 1900. These subjects ensure that the pivotal elements of 'Thainess' are conveyed 'correctly'. Maths, Computer Science, Natural Science and English complete the group of *wicha lak*. Subjects such as Society, Religion and Culture (*sangkhom, sasana, watthanatham*) and History (*prawatsat*) are regarded as carrying the highest levels of 'Thainess' (Mulder 1997). *Prawatsat* textbooks propose an authorised version of Thai history, centred on the glorious history of the monarchy. This narrative presents the country's very existence, survival and independence as being dependent on the heroic qualities of the king, who is cast as the pillar of the nation's indissoluble unity and as its moral conscience. This is the 'standard total view of the Thai monarchy' (Hewison 1997: 266). Similarly, 'Society, Religion and Culture' defines what it means to be Thai, and includes activities aimed at promoting the embodiment of 'Thainess'.

Figure 2. Thai traditional salutation training for primary school students. Thairath Witthaia School, Bangkok, August 2013. Colour version, p. 229.

At Thairath Witthaia primary school I observed lessons whose purpose was training second-year students in the correct posture to adopt in approaching *phu yai* (see Figure 2). In one of these, children, kneeling, moved towards the teacher, who waited for them on the other side of the classroom, holding an object. When they got closer, the children, looking down, received the object in their hands, supporting the right one with the left. The difference in level between the adult (high) and the child (low) was even more pronounced when, in the simulation, the adult was a monk. When this was the case, students, kneeling before the 'monk', had to bow three times (the same number as the 'three precious jewels' of Buddhism: Sangha, Buddha, and Dharma). These lessons teach what Marcel Mauss (1936) describes as 'techniques of the body' – patterns of behavioural repetition functional to the production/reproduction of the Thai socio-moral hierarchy.

Wicha phoem toem ('optional additional subjects'), on the other hand, constitute a more useful innovation introduced by the Thai Education Act. The regulations allow schools to adopt additional subjects based on Thailand's different regional cultures, depending on the region in which a school is situated. *Wicha phoem toem* are taught alongside the basic subjects (*wicha lak*). However, as the vice-principal of Maha Phra Mongkut middle school told me, the selection of additional subjects is influenced by financial factors, which are in turn affected by the national system for evaluating schools. The main focus of ministerial evaluations is whether a given school is teaching 'Thainess' correctly. Schools can improve their ranking by obtaining special moral awards, the most prestigious of which is the coveted title 'King's beloved school' (*rohngrian phra rachathan*). Some of these awards are given to schools that win inter-school competitions at district, provincial and finally national level. While competitions may cover a number of subjects, knowledge of *watthanatham thai* is key to success. Students who win these awards are described as 'champions of morality', and their success allows their schools to secure symbolic capital, potentially leading to government funding, increased student enrolment, and the promotion of school principals to higher positions within the school administrative career field (e.g. superintendent or district administrator). This means that additional subjects chosen by schools are generally those related to 'Thainess' (rather than those reflecting the country's cultural diversity), which are more likely to guarantee a more positive evaluation for a school.

'Not-Thai-enough' students

Many of the teachers whom I interviewed told me that poor children ranked lowest in inter-school competitions related to 'Thainess' and national morality.

Dek salam, especially those 'lucky' enough to be accepted by Bangkok's private schools, were said to be *dek deu*, 'obstinate children' – 'not-Thai-enough'. In June 2014 I visited a rather prestigious private school, Phra Mae Marie ('Merciful Mother Mary') – a combined *prathom* (primary) and *mathayom* (middle) Catholic school in downtown Bangkok. Historically in Thailand, private Catholic schools have educated the country's aristocracy and urban elite. Notable alumni of Catholic schools include figures like the late King Bhumibol and former Prime Minister Thaksin Shinawatra. Institutes such as the Assumption College, founded in Bangkok by the Gabrielite Brothers, count among its alumni four prime ministers, fifteen privy counsellors, and some of Thailand's richest citizens – even though all of these alumni are Buddhist. While most of the children at Phra Mae Marie were from rich families, the school had some *dek salam* among its students. The NGO Saint Jacob's Centre, led by Catholic missionaries, had a good relationship with the school principal, and covered their fees, so that *dek salam* could access a 'good education'.

The quality of the school infrastructure was impressive. It was an enormous complex with two main buildings where the classrooms were, a parking lot, an external courtyard, a large canteen, a football field, a basketball field and even a swimming pool. The school was formally Catholic and this was recognisable through the presence of Christian symbols and statues; yet, Phra Mae Marie's Christianity was rigorously anchored in the triad of 'Thainess' and its public iconography. At the entrance, for example, a poster displayed Buddha and Jesus together, with the royal seal above the two. The logic of this is that the (Buddhist) monarchy both protects and is protected by religion. In every classroom, above the blackboard, there was a picture of the king and a Thai flag, either side of a crucifix (whereas in state schools an icon of Buddha is included, completing the nationalistic Thai triad).

In spite of the presence of Christian symbols, 97% of children enrolled at Phra Mae Marie declared themselves to be Buddhist. In fact, what really makes a difference between private Catholic schools and state schools in Bangkok is not religion but the students' socio-economic status. As the mother of one of the students at Phra Mae Marie explained to me: 'We are Buddhist. But that is not a problem. The Christian religion is not taught here. The teaching is identical to that in state schools, but the quality of teachers is quite clearly better!'. Since King Vajiravudh's interventions in state education, in fact, nationalistic rituals, textbooks, and so on are essentially identical in all schools, in compliance with the standardised educational model developed by the Ministry of Education's agencies.

The presence of *farang* teachers and the fact that English teaching is offered are other prominent features of Bangkok private schools. However, as Jeff, an

American teacher working at Phra Mae Marie, complained: 'We *farang* do not get included in school board meetings, nor in decisions concerning teaching. We mainly serve a marketing purpose: we have to welcome students in front of the entrance door, so that parents can see that the school have *farang* teaching English' (Jeff, July 2013).

One expects to find Christian symbols in a Catholic school. Other features of Bangkok's private Catholic schools are rather less what one would expect – a considerable attention paid to staging nationalistic rituals of 'Thainess', an almost obsessive focus on discipline and order, and an emphasis on conformity, among the students, to a particular dress code and to moral conduct grounded in Thai hierarchy. Students from wealthier backgrounds at Phra Mae Marie – who had already had elite etiquette heavily ingrained in them through their upbringing – embodied perfectly the position of *phu noi*, giving elegant and flawless performances. The more students showed themselves capable of submission, reverence and gratitude, the more positively they were assessed, and the more they were rewarded by their teachers, as role models. As the parents' representative, a wealthy engineer, explained: 'Here students become *dek di* ('good children'): they always look tidy and well dressed, and they listen to and respect *phu yai*'.

While students from wealthy families were described as *dek di*, poor children were regularly described by teachers as *kere* ('undisciplined'), *sokaprok* ('dirty'), *mai riaproi* ('untidy-looking') and *deu* ('obstinate'). In schools like Phra Mae Marie, *dek salam* are easily recognised. This is first of all at a concrete level: they arrive at school crowded into the back of dented NGO pick-ups rather than in fancy cars, their uniforms are frequently dirty or not perfectly ironed, and their school stationery is second-hand and often damaged. One Thai history teacher had this to say about them:

> *Dek salam* are different from the others. They do not respect *phu yai*; they are not tidy [*mai mi khwam riaproi*] and they are less intellectually able than normal students. Their problem is that they come from the slums: a dirty, ugly, disorderly environment. They also have problems in their families: their parents do not take care of them, they sell drugs and are separated. We try to explain to them that this is a different environment, one that requires different behaviour.　　　　(Teacher at Phra Mae Marie, July 2013)

Order and discipline (*khwam riaproi*), the code of conduct first established by Phibun Songkran's regime between the 1930s and the 1940s, and now refashioned by Prayut's military government, appeared to inform the way in which the teachers thought of *dek salam*. They appeared to associate *dek salam* with the negative pole within a dichotomous system in which 'Thai' (in other words moral, tidy, disciplined, intelligent, clean, beautiful, well-dressed, respectful, and so on) is in opposition to 'non-Thai' (in other words immoral, untidy, undisciplined, intellectually immature, dirty, disrespectful, etc.). In a private school of the capital, the prototype of 'Thainess' was a rich, Sino-Thai student from what was considered to be a 'good family'. By contrast, 'non-Thai' Otherness was epitomised by children from the slums (populated by internal migrants from Thailand's ethnic minority regions): those whom I am describing as Bangkok's 'belittled citizens'.

Given all of this, *dek salam* risked damaging the commercial image of a school like Phra Mae Marie. On the one hand, the school welcomed them at the invitation of Saint Jacob's; on the other hand, *dek salam* were removed from the school's promotional *mise-en-scène* during events open to the public. Prasit, the head of staff at Saint Jacob's, told me about something that happened to Bus, a seven-year-old *dek salam* supported by the Catholic charity and enrolled at Phra Mae Marie: 'Last year, when government officials were visiting the school, a teacher asked Bus to stay home. The students were performing a show about Thai culture, and the teachers were afraid that the presence of our children would damage Phra Mae Marie's reputation, because *dek salam* are considered impolite, ugly and dark'.[22] As Thai historian Thongchai Winichakul (2000b) has observed, these discourses reflect the history of the country's ethnic, class and geopolitical stratification.

The exclusion of poor students like Bus from their class, on the very day the quality of the school was being assessed by government officials, may have played a role in contributing to its very positive evaluation. In 2013, after the inspection visit, Phra Mae Marie was indeed awarded the 'National Morality Award' (Daily News 2013). The prize was awarded by the Centre for the Promotion of National Morality (*sun khunatham*), a public organisation working with the Ministry of Culture. This organisation has as its main objective to bolster the nation's moral rectitude and to develop 'good people' (*khon di*).[23]

---

22 *Dam* ('black' or 'dark') and *theuan* ('wild') are terms that are typically used to indicate an ugly and/or dangerous individual. Having dark skin is also associated with the rural populations of the south and northeast, who work in the fields, under the sun (Persaud 2005).

23 In 2006 the Centre for the Promotion of National Morality (*sun khunatham*) inaugurated the National Centre of Meditation, whose purpose was to build morality among children through new classes dedicated to meditation in all the nation's schools. In the year that Thaksin's government fell, by military coup, Inspector General Seripisut Temiyavej, interim head of *sun khunatham*, declared that Thai society is declining due to growing materialism, and that people do not develop their minds as they should. As a result, society is experiencing disorientation and confusion. The General reminded the nation of the fact that the Centre of Meditation was founded to help people manage their minds, beginning with children and young people (source: Thai National News Bureau, Public Relations Department – 4 December, 2006).

TEMPLE SCHOOLS, THE KING'S SCHOOLS, SCHOOLS OF THE NATION

> Teachers do the right thing. They are diligent, persistent, hospitable, ideal-
> istic, strong and patient. They are disciplined and avoid illicit activities like
> smoking and drinking. They are also honest, sincere and kind to others.
> They take the middle way. They are unbiased. They are wise, reasonable and
> knowledgeable.   (Bhumibol Adulyadej 1980, cited in Wallace 2003)

In an article published in 2003, anthropologist Merle Wallace underlined the traditional role of teachers in Thailand: to act as 'pillars of morality' and 'moral parents' (Wallace 2003). As parents do, the ideal teacher must mobilise every resource at his or her disposal (lessons, tutoring, and so on) so that children can become 'good people' (*khon di*). As pillars of national morality, teachers have, as a reference point, the supreme symbol of Buddhism: the king.

The moral framework described by Wallace was only occasionally presented at Thairath Witthaia School. Built in the 1950s on temple land amid the paddy fields of a suburban area, this small school operated according to the traditional model of temple schools. A picture of King Bhumibol watched over the school from the main entrance, on which the phrase *khru phaen din* ('teacher of the land of the Thai people') was written. The poor state of the school infrastructure was striking, contrasting sharply with that in private schools: the classrooms were bare, with little more than a blackboard and a few posters, discoloured by dust. A number of students, often poorly dressed, sat on the floor because there were not enough chairs.

The schools of Bangkok's metropolitan area are usually far better equipped than are state schools in rural provinces. Many are provided with IT labs, air conditioning and large sports fields. In small schools like Thairat Witthaya, however, the situation is quite different. The teachers are paid very little, and it is not uncommon for a teacher to have a second and even a third job. Teachers are not motivated to do a good job. They often do not show up at school, and they sometimes indulge in 'immoral' practices while at work. One day, for ex-ample, I was invited to drink whisky during school time by a visibly intoxicated teacher. He explained frankly: 'They pay us a pittance, we have to monitor too many students, many of whom are the children of seasonal workers who will be transferring to another school a month later. We don't have the funding that the big schools receive. We must at least relax a little! Otherwise the time never passes … We just have to ensure that the school presents a good 'face' when there are ministerial inspections [*thamhai na rohngrian du di*].'

There are no entrance tests for Thairath Witthaia School, as is the case in the majority of small state schools. As the principal told me: 'We do not receive funding from the government because we are a small school. Funds come in if the numbers enrolled at the school increase, so we do not have entrance tests (*sop khao*). The result is that those who get in are the students that no one else wants: children from poor families, migrants with a lot of problems. Many children are *dek salam*'. By contrast, the biggest and best state schools regulate enrolment with entrance tests. Upper-class Bangkok families have many strategies to secure places for their children at the most important schools. Bribes, rigged tests, *phu yai* and influential parents' pressure on the school board are extensively documented (Bangkok Post 2003).

For these reasons, the quality of teaching and the level of disciplinary control exercised over students are significantly lower in state schools such as Thairath Witthaia. Teachers are much more permissive and often avoid teaching subjects that are traditionally difficult for young Thai students, especially English. The English teacher at the school, a 55-year-old Thai man with only an elementary knowledge of the English language, told me: 'There is no point working ourselves to death to teach these children English. Because they won't need it. They are not rich, white, beautiful children. Many *dek salam* are *dek lao* [a pejorative term used to describe children of Thai-Lao ethno-linguistic origin from the northeast]. They have to learn to grow crops... What would they need English for?'. At small suburban state schools, children who come from the slums of the capital are the rule, not the exception.

Thairath Witthaia School's finances have improved during the last five years, after the principal decided to make changes to the school's image and teaching methods following the Centre for the Promotion of National Morality's recommendations. The school now formally grounds its teaching in Buddhist meditation principles, and as a consequence it now benefits from significant funding, both public and private, including from ultra-conservative political organisations. Among these is the Thai newspaper *Thai Rath*, the most widely-read newspaper in the country, after which the school is named.

When asked about the elements of the teaching method in his school, the principal's response was rather superficial: 'This school uses Buddhism as a teaching method. Before the lessons, children have to meditate for 10 minutes: they sit in silence in the traditional cross-legged position, close their eyes and focus on their breathing. Children must learn how to cool their hearts [*jai yen*] and accept their own *karma* [*kam*]'. This approach to morality has a role in the conservation of the normative social order: if students know their own position, and behave in accordance with their own *karma*, they will ensure balance and social wellbeing. They must be agreeable, go with the flow, avoid conflict and maintain a neutral attitude towards life. In cognitive terms, it is advisable not to think too much or use up excessive amounts of energy. A simple life, devoid of worries (*sabai, sabai*) is presented as the ideal life (Wallace 2003: 3). The authoritarian regime in Thailand sees these values as the basis of ideal citizenship. It is useful, here, to recall the title of Prayut's campaign of national reconciliation: 'resurgent happiness'. Citizens should not engage with politics, or think too hard. They must cheer up and not become stressed; the military will solve the political problems of the country. In this way, 'happiness will come back to the Land of Smiles' (Prachathai 2014b).

Although the new teaching method based on Buddhist meditation is publicised as central to the way in which the school operates (with posters, plates, etc.), what happens in the classrooms is no different, in fact, from what happens in other state schools. The image presented to me by the principal is projected only at public events and ministerial inspections, when the theatrical deployment of Buddhist morality becomes the school's main fund-raising technique. On these occasions there is discipline and control, students are expected to behave well, teachers are punctual, and Buddhist meditation is practised as though it were always at the focus of classroom routines.

I observed the way in which this image is projected at one school evaluation. Beforehand, teachers and students were busy setting up the school as a *talat pho phiang* ('market of sufficiency'), to honour the royal philosophy of 'sufficiency economy' (*sethakit pho phiang*). This concept was formulated by King Bhumibol in a royal speech in 1997 at a time when Thailand was in the throes of an economic crisis that had affected the entire region. *Sethakit pho phiang* identifies the moral causes of the economic crisis in consumerism and Western capitalist individualism. Turning to Buddhist ideals such as honesty, moderation, and wisdom, the king's philosophy prescribes sustainable development through industrious but modest economic efforts, based on self-sufficiency. After the 2006 coup that overthrew Thaksin's government, the military junta made a great deal of use of *sethakit pho phiang* as part of its royalist agenda, leading to what Walker has described as 'sufficiency democracy' (Walker 2010). *Sethakit pho phiang* was constitutionalised in 2007 as an authentically Thai mode of production, inserted in the tenth National Economic Development Plan. The Crown Property Bureau (CPB), the agency in charge of the monarchy's assets as well as one of the most important mega-corporations in the region (Porphant Ouyyanont 2008), began collaborating with the Ministry of Education to integrate *sethakit pho phiang* into the school curriculum. The National Identity Board created cartoons and comic strips based on King Bhumibol's philosophy, in order to teach morality in schools. For example, these portrayed families involved in work in the fields within a highly romanticised rural environment. Since then, *sethakit pho phiang* has been a central part of the primary curriculum (Ivarsson and Isager 2010a: 232), presenting an 'ethnic ideology of Thainess' that represents the Thai nation as 'a calm and happy village community [...] characterised by fluxes of socio-economic clienteles and familial relationships that are reciprocal, cooperative and intimate' (Kasian Tejapira 1996a: 247).

For the occasion, Thairath Witthaia School was transformed into an open-air market which could be visited by people from outside the school, and students were turned into merchants and cooks: fruit, rice and vegetables were brought in from plots of land near the school, while students were expected to cook traditional dishes using the harvest. All of these activities were thought of as morally appropriate for the *dek salam*. The poor children enrolled at Thairath Witthaia School were, after all, regarded as being destined for an agricultural future.

FINAL CONSIDERATIONS

My examination of childhood in Bangkok had to begin with schools, the social space where the children I met at Saint Jacob's spent most of their time. The particular construction of childhood they encountered daily in this context, the national paradigm of the 'good Thai child', constitutes the overarching (and most intrusive) discourse to which children are subjected in Thailand.

Since the 1921 Primary Education Act, the Thai state's basic method of achieving ethno-nationalistic assimilation and moral domestication of new generations has been developed through school. The ways in which the public concept of childhood is played out in this context reveal the ideological and institutional apparatus deployed by the state in its attempt to construct a desirable childhood. Firstly, children must embody 'Thainess': whatever their ethno-linguistic background, they must speak (Central) Thai, honour the nation, love the king unreservedly, practise Buddhism, and be ready to bravely sacrifice themselves as soldiers. Second, they are inserted into hierarchical (as opposed to horizontal) relationships with adults. They are the passive recipients of the teachers' knowledge and morality, and they must be obedient, polite and grateful. Teachers, in turn, are strategically re-cast as quasi-parents. Through this, they act, symbolically, as an emotional link between the family and the nation-state. If we consider children and adults as respectively symbolising citizens and authority, we can fully appreciate the political implications of such a construction of childhood. The ideal child, like the ideal citizen, should be willing to passively welcome the benevolent knowledge and abilities of his or her 'parents' (i.e. the authority of the state). Only by doing this will each child-citizen fit harmoniously into Thai socio-moral and political hierarchies.

This means that schools are like militarised political laboratories for the creation of child-citizens. Within schools, children practise ethno-nationalistic rituals of hierarchy via top-down teaching methods and by learning moral lessons stressing their status as *phu noi*. However, *phu noi* are not simply children – they are also, more generally, anyone relating to 'big people' (*phu yai*). Children relating to parents, laity relating to monks, and citizens relating to the representatives of the state – all are *phu noi* who must demonstrate absolute loyalty, respect and gratitude to *phu yai*, the highest-level referent of whom is the king.

The way in which concepts of childhood have historically altered is linked to shifts in political and socio-cultural spheres. Even in Thailand, the radical social transformations brought about by fast-flowing processes of modernisation and economic development since the Second World War have paved the way for a new concept of children and their relationship with adults. An outcome of this can be found in the 1999 Thai Education Act and its promotion of the so-called child-centred learning method. This was officially conceived of as recalibrating, in horizontal terms, the relationship between student and teacher, and as emphasising the centrality of children (rather than that of teachers) in the educational process.

The May 2014 military coup, through which former Thai army chief general Prayut Chan-o-cha toppled Yingluck's government, put an end to both the trend towards political democratisation and to that towards the re-interpretation of children as individuals with rights – both of which were, in fact, rather loosely rooted in Thai society. Besides enforcing martial law, summoning activists and academics for 'attitude adjustment' and introducing extensive restrictions to civic and political rights, it is interesting to note that one of the military junta's first official acts was to introduce a new nationalistic ritual for students, to be performed daily in all of the country's schools: before classes, 'good Thai children' (*dek thai di*) have to sing a new national song about the 'twelve key values (*khaniyom*) of "Thainess"' (Asian Correspondent 2014a). The first of the twelve values imposed by the military recommends that good children should preserve and worship the sacred triad of monarchy, religion and nation; another important value, not surprisingly, encourages children to respect *phu yai*.

As Judith Ennew and Jill Swart-Kruger (2003: 3) emphasise, 'the moral normative constructions of family, home, domesticity, and childhood cannot exist in the absence of contrastive constructions of the "other"'. In Bangkok schools, *dek salam* are construed as dangerous deviants, compared to the purity of the ideal Thai child. As descendants of migrants from Thailand's rural provinces and ethnic minority regions, they are commonly described as dirty and dark and as disrespectful towards *phu yai*. Especially in the context of the capital's private schools, they embody the 'non-Thai' Other, and are, as such, targeted by the Thai state's militarised pedagogy with particular emphasis.

CHAPTER 2

On Karma and Childhood

lthough the Buddhist canon does not deal with children directly – for example, there is nothing in it about childhood rituals and ceremonies such as baptism, purification or other birth-related rituals (Sasson 2013: 1–3) – it nonetheless includes a set of complex norms that regulate interpersonal interaction and dictate reciprocal moral obligations between members of the religious community (the *sangha*) and the family. The scholar of Buddhism Alan Cole (Cole 2011) has examined the Buddhist position on childhood and the way in which it expresses symbols or allegories that lay out what are regarded as ideal attitudes in adult believers. In his analysis of Buddhist primary sources and classic literature, he shows that children are commonly conceptualised as needing 'to learn that their own fate is a function of a two-fold submission defined as service to their parents and generosity to the Buddhist establishment' (Cole 2011: 284). Through this, parents and *sangha* are placed on a symbolic-metaphoric continuum, so that 'the private realm of family emotions is being deployed to construct its opposite: the world of invisible public religion, peopled by nonfamily members and their institutional representatives' (ibid.: 285). A number of parent–child narratives also explain what happens to ungrateful sons and daughters: for the smallest impertinence or act of resistance, terrifying punishment awaits children in hell (ibid.). Such texts have the purpose of creating docile children who are careful to conform to parental directives, and of symbolically asserting the moral authority of monks over infantilised laymen.

Children's moral obligation towards their parents is most highly developed in the Chinese Confucian take on Buddhism and in the notion of 'filial piety', re-formulated in Thai Buddhism as *khwam katanyu*: children's debt of gratitude towards their parents. This is what children were taught during a class in Buddhist prayer that I attended in a Bangkok state school in 2013:

> Dad and mum are Buddhist saints for all children. Do not stand in front of
> your parents. Do not dare to argue with them. Pay respect to your parents
> by prostrating yourself and *krap*[1] before leaving. Good children must be

---

1   The *krap* is a gesture of respect normally performed in relation to monks. It involves placing both palms on the ground three times.

selfless and show *khwam katanyu* [gratitude] to their parents every day, because when they are at home their dads and mums stand for *phra* [monks].

(Field notes, July 2013)

The Centre for the Promotion of National Morality has ensured that Buddhist prayers expressing this type of moral behaviour are widely distributed as booklets, flyers and leaflets, which are available in all the public structures of Bangkok: hospital waiting rooms, post offices, public transport, etc. As I have shown, royalist and military elites have drawn widely on (conveniently manipulated) Buddhist teachings and practices as an ethical and moral framework legitimising the enforcement of 'Thainess' in all public spaces, especially schools. In contemporary Thailand, if mum and dad are the *phra* of the household, the king (together with the military) is the *phra* of the nation.

It is worth noting that despite this kind of rhetoric the birth of Buddhism is associated with an act of filial insubordination. As is recounted in Buddhacarita of Aśvaghosa, the Sanskrit epic poem about the life of Gautama Buddha, at the age of 29 the Buddha's 'four sights' (an old man, a sick man, a corpse, and a holy man) marked his decision to abandon royal life and violate his father's expectations. The Enlightened One's stubborn desire to directly partake in the suffering of the world that is recounted in Buddhist scripture problematises notions such as *khwam katanyu*, as well as the patriarchal form in which Thai Buddhism has developed. Nevertheless, the Thai military's royalist propaganda has made extensive use of Buddhist morals, centred on the notion of *khwam katanyu*, establishing a connection between the filial obligations of children and the duties of the citizen – even more so now, with Prayut confirmed as Thai prime minister.

Notwithstanding, the hegemonic Buddhism of 'Thainess' is not the only religious discourse to which poor children are exposed. State Buddhism and the Bangkok *sangha*, patronised by the monarchy, are currently being challenged by several emerging strands of socially engaged Buddhism, regional social movements, and (post-modern) local cults, which have been re-conceiving and re-organising Thai Theravada Buddhism as an increasingly plural, heterogeneous and contested field (e.g. see Taylor 2016; Mackenzie 2007; McDaniel 2011; Pattana Kitiarsa 2012). The majority of children whom I met in the slums of Bangkok were being supported by several local and international aid organisations, including Buddhist charities and NGOs led by 'development monks' (Lapthananon Pinit 2012).

In this chapter I focus on these monks' organisational commitment towards poor children in Bangkok, and I investigate whether (and if so how) their socially-engaged Buddhism qualifies as a counter-position and as a dissonant voice with the potential to disrupt the state monologue of 'Thainess' and its cacophony of moral injunctions. After a brief discussion of Thai socially-engaged Buddhism, I will present two Buddhist NGOs that assist poor children in Bangkok: Saphansung temple, where *phra* Manid carries out 'training and social rehabilitation' activities among children from Khlong Toei, the largest slum in Bangkok; and the Suan Kaeo Foundation, managed by *phra* Payom Kanlayano, who is one of the most popular monks in Thailand.

Phra Manid's and *phra* Payom's doctrinal explanations of the marginal conditions, filial duties and *karma* of *dek salam*, as well as poor children's positions as guests of the NGOs run by these monks, have the potential to provide an alternative view of 'childhood' and of children as part of the 'Thai social body' (Aulino 2014). Adult–child relationships are analysed here as the symbolic proxy for competing politico-religious discourses. As I show, this conflictual debate on childhood, children's moral obligations and parental authority voices Thai society's meta-reflection on (and, sometimes violently, confronts) its own cosmological, socio-political, and inter-ethnic structure.

THAI ENGAGED BUDDHISM: BUDDHIST NGOS FOR BANGKOK'S POOR CHILDREN

As both Tambiah (1976: 288) and Wyatt (1994: 207) have documented, Buddhist temples have, historically, served both as a refuge for orphans and disadvantaged boys and as the only path to socio-economic mobility available to them. Unable to provide for their offspring, poor families used to view temples as places where male children could acquire merit and receive room, board and basic education as 'novices' (*nen*) or 'temple children' (*dek wat*) in the service of the monastic community. Excluded from monkhood, female children had instead to repay their 'debt of gratitude' to parents, who brought them into this world, through alternative sources of merit-making, notably lifetime filial service in the parental household (e.g. see Swearer 2010: 53; Lindberg-Falk 2007).

Buddhist charity towards underprivileged (male) individuals was, in the past, usually exercised passively, rather than being organised through formal strategies and administrative structures explicitly designed to promote social development. However, this has changed significantly in recent decades. Reflecting dramatic transformations in the political, socio-economic and cultural structure of Thai society, as well as global innovations such as the transnational discourse of human rights, a number of Buddhist monks have, doctrinally and institutionally, reformulated their roles and now see themselves as facilitators of both worldly and other-worldly liberation from 'suffering' (in Pali, *dukkha*). They have channelled this renewed interest in mundane affairs into humanitarian engagement and development work. 'Development monks' (Lapthananon Pinit 2012) are now involved in a wide range of aid initiatives: community development, care of people who are HIV positive, treatment of drug addiction, environmental activism – and humanitarian initiatives focused on children. Since the 1960s and 1970s, largely as a result of the proliferation of foreign and international aid organisations in Thailand (e.g. transnational development agencies, INGOs, missionary organisations), Thai Buddhism has undergone a process of mimetic re-configuration, bureaucratisation and rationalisation through the establishment of Buddhist foundations, NGOs and socially engaged projects specifically oriented towards the country's minorities and aimed at revitalising the traditional role of the temple as the main agent of social mediation (e.g. see Seri Phongphit 1988; Essen 2005; Lindberg-Falk 2010; Darlington 2000, 2012). The emergence of child-focused Buddhist NGOs in the slums of Bangkok is, thus, an expression of the contemporary diversity of Thai Buddhism, and an indication of the increasing importance of socially-engaged Buddhism throughout Southeast Asia.[2]

In their co-edited book *Engaged Buddhism: Buddhist Liberation Movements in Asia*, Christopher Queen and Sally King (1996) have drawn on the idea of 'engaged Buddhism', applying it to contemporary 'Buddhist movements of liberation' in the region, as well as to the religious engagement of Buddhist monks in terms of socio-political activism.[3] In the editorial introduction to the book, Queen (1996) emphasises the doctrinal innovations brought about by engaged Buddhism in orthodox Buddhist teachings and practices. In its classic form, Buddhism is conceived of as a philosophy, an individual ascetic and meditative practice of liberation from suffering deriving from *samsara* (a Pali term referring to the cycle of repeated births), with *nirvana*, as the 'otherworldly' objective, achievable by pursuing detachment from the illusionary world of phenomenal

---

2   The term 'engaged Buddhism', sometimes associated with so-called 'Protestant Buddhism' (Obeyesekere 1972), was coined by the Vietnamese monk Tich Nhat Hanh in reference to the Buddhist monks who set themselves on fire during the Vietnam War, as an extreme act of protest and self-sacrifice.

3   'Buddhist movements of liberation' (Queen and King 1996) include: Thich Nhat Hanh's 'socially engaged Buddhism' in Vietnam; Ambedkar's mass movement of the 'untouchable' converted to Buddhism in India; the Sarvodaya Shramadana movement and its Buddhist rural development plan in Sri Lanka; the Dalai Lama's Tibetan liberation movement; and the movement of Asian women actively involved in the attempt to re-establish the Order of Buddhist Nuns (*bhikkhuni sangha*).

desire[4] (Gombrich 1988: 72). By contrast, in engaged Buddhism the focus of liberation moves from the otherworldly to the worldly here and now: *nirvana* must be sought in *samsara*. This means that social movements drawing on engaged Buddhism share 'a profound change in Buddhist soteriology – from a highly personal and other-worldly notion of liberation to a social, economic, this-worldly liberation' (Queen 1996: 9–10). This implies a two-fold phenomenology of suffering: the traditional focus on *karma* and rebirth fades into the background, while reflections on the suffering of the poor – understood as victims of unequal economic and socio-political systems – come to the fore. This 'mundane awakening' (in Pali, *laukodaya*) (ibid.) expresses a new awareness of the social, economic, political and institutional dimensions of *dukkha*. This awareness translates into new organisational strategies for addressing poverty, injustice and intolerance. Buddhist NGOs and charities for poor children constitute examples of these kinds of strategies.

In Thailand, socially-engaged Buddhism is a relatively recent phenomenon that has resulted from the doctrinal fragmentation of the national religious rhetoric. Since the fall of absolute monarchy in 1932, industrialisation, urbanisation and the considerable expansion of the market economy have brought significant social change and have had a dramatic impact upon all aspects of everyday life. Competition among increasingly diversified secular institutions, along with the progressive erosion of village-based subsistence and rural lifestyles, have profoundly destabilised the integrity of Thai Buddhism. These changes have led to criticism of central hegemonic Buddhism, which is regarded as having succumbed to the pressure of the inexorable processes of Westernisation, modernisation and secularisation. In recent decades, this criticism has precipitated a doctrinal division of Thai Buddhism into different socio-religious movements.[5] While the authority of the central *sangha* remains formally undisputed, on the fringes of contemporary Thai Buddhism there are alternative and competing visions of childhood, the family, political life and the socio-moral order.

In a country where politics and religion are indistinguishable and are mutually constructed, several scholars have noted that these distinct socio-religious movements within Thai Buddhism are at opposite ends of the Thai political

---

4   The heart of Buddhist teaching corresponds to the 'Four Noble Truths': life is suffering, the origin of suffering is desire, desire can be eradicated and the path to eliminate desire corresponds to the 'Noble Eightfold Path' (Gombrich 1988: 62).

5   Among the most popular are the Suan Mokkh progressive movement; the Dhammakaya temple movement, which Satha-Anand (1990: 400) has described as 'consumerist and neo-liberal Buddhism'; and the extreme traditionalist Santi Asoke movement, whose members declared their independence from the Thai *sangha* and its 'Council of Elders' in 1975.

spectrum (e.g. Seri Phongphit 1988; Keyes 1989; P.A. Jackson 1989; Swearer 1996). Peter Jackson, a specialist in Theravada Buddhism, has pointed out that exegetical divergences within Buddhism provide the symbolic and moral bedrock upon which Thai political conflicts are built (P.A. Jackson 1989: 3). Specifically, this relates to the distinction between hyper-royalist, neo-tradition-al and/or right-wing Buddhist movements on one side and progressive, liberal movements on the other.

Perhaps the most renowned exponent of right-wing Buddhism is Kittivuddho Bhikkhu: a monk who went down in history for having declared in the 1970s that killing communists was not a sin (P.A. Jackson 1989: 147–158). Within pro-gressive Buddhism, the figure of Buddhadasa Bhikku[6] (1906–1993) – the most prolific monk-scholar in the history of Thai Buddhism – stands out as a source of inspiration for many local activists. Repeatedly accused of sympathising with Communism during the military regimes of the 1960s, Buddhadasa is known for having criticised the decline of the Thai *sangha* and of Thai society, and sav-age industrialisation; for having rationalised and demystified Thai Buddhism; for having promoted lay people's access to spiritual education; and for having contributed to the development of monastic education. It is widely recognised that Thai socially-engaged Buddhism is the result of Buddhadasa's progressive reformism. For example, the Thai scholar and activist Sulak Sivaraksa,[7] who founded the INEB (International Network of Engaged Buddhists), a transna-tional network connecting a number of forms of socially-engaged Buddhism in Southeast Asia (Swearer 1996), was deeply influenced by Buddhadasa's thought.

While the centralised state Buddhism of 'Thainess' permeates institutions and public spaces such as state schools, some child-focused Buddhist NGOs op-erate on the basis of Buddhist conceptualisations of childhood, *khwam katanyu* ('gratitude') and *karma* that contest the moral paradigm of the 'good Thai child'. Over the course of my research, I did fieldwork within two Buddhist charities catering for the *dek salam* of the capital: Saphansung temple, led by *phra* Manid; and the Suan Kaeo Foundation, whose head is *phra* Payom.

---

6 On the historical, political and doctrinal role of Buddhadasa in Thailand, see for example P.A. Jackson 1987 and Gabaude 1988.

7 Sulak Sivaraksa was charged with *lèse-majesté* in 1984, imprisoned for 4 months, and subse-quently forced into exile for having criticised the monarchy and General Suchinda Kraprayoon. He has argued that Thai Buddhism has been turned, for political reasons, into a chauvinistic civic religion, at the expense of 'non-Thai' minorities (Sulak Sivaraksa 1989, cited in Swearer 1996). In 1994, he was nominated for the Nobel Peace Prize. The Thai Criminal Court revoked all *lèse-majesté* accusations against him in 1995. The activist's supporters, including represent-atives of the 'Assembly of Small-Scale Farmers of the Northeast', attended the reading of his sentence, to support him (ibid.).

Phra Payom and *phra* Manid lead religious institutions committed to improving the lives of deprived young people and children. Together with a number of other socially-engaged monks, they have experienced at first hand the damaging effects that uncontrolled industrialisation and neoliberal developmentalism can have on minority groups and rural communities. *Phra* Manid is an ex drug addict born and bred in the slum of Khlong Toei; *phra* Payom, the son of poor peasants, grew up in Nonthabury, previously a rural area and now a fast-growing industrial suburb of Bangkok.

Saphansung temple: Dharmic teachings for poor children

In Bangkok city centre, at *wat* (temple) Saphansung, *phra* Manid coordinates social rehabilitation services and spiritual training, mostly aimed at the *dek salam* of Khlong Toei, the largest slum in the capital, where the monk himself grew up. *Phra* Manid has been influenced by socially-engaged Buddhism and is referred to as *phra nak phatthana* ('development monk'). As part of his this-worldly commitment, he collaborates with the Thai Ministry of Social Development and Human Security's Department of Social Development and Welfare and he is a lecturer in the Department of Buddhist Studies at the monastic University of Maha Chulalongkorn Rajavidyalaya.

In August 2012, while I was conducting fieldwork focusing on the monk's social development projects, *wat* Saphansung hosted training sessions in meditation, under the broad rubric 'Dharmic Teachings for Drug Addicts and Poor Children', which entailed a religious conflation of poor children and destitute junkies, as spiritually immature individuals in need of Buddhist formation.

Sessions took place in the main prayer room of the temple, and included activities intended to 'cool the heart' (*jai yen*) and promote self-awareness and concentration (*sati*) through *anapanasati* meditation, also known as 'mindful breathing' (Figure 3). There were about forty participants, male and female, aged between nine and 16, all from Khlong Toei slum. They were dressed in white, the colour of purity and religion, which laymen are expected to wear during the practice of *dharma* (*thamma*). They walked slowly with their eyes closed, in a perfect line, following the rhythmic instructions of *phra* Manid, who sat on an elevated stage and addressed them as *luk* ('sons and daughters'). At *wat* Saphansung interactions between monks and children were, as they are in schools, mediated through the use of kin terms.

I stood next to the prayer room, to gain a panoramic view of all the participants. While most of the children were fully engaged and focused, some noticed my presence and furtively exchanged conspiratorial looks and smiled at each

Photo: Kochphon Onshawee, Wikimedia Commons.

Figure 3. Thai students practising Buddhist meditation, October 2014. Colour version, p. 230.

other in amuseument when they thought the monk was not watching, until *phra* Manid suddenly boomed out: 'Those who don't close their eyes will miss the meal!' A boy of about ten, caught red-handed, instantly half-closed his eyes, reverently apologising: 'I am sorry, *luang* [a title used to address senior monks or royals] *pho* [dad]'. *Phra* Manid briefly frowned, annoyed, and then persevered in his efforts to guide the meditation.

During a long interview, *phra* Manid told me that children must be trained in discipline and self-awareness, which are regarded as essential to attaining mindfulness. 'Children must walk, sit, eat, speak and think, paying attention to their breathing, with focus and awareness, in accordance with Lord Buddha's Eightfold Path: correct understanding, correct thought, correct speech, correct action, correct livelihood, correct effort, correct mindfulness, and correct concentration'. For *phra* Manid, more importantly: 'Discipline is the prerequisite for responsibility, and it is of crucial importance in the education of children [...] If soldiers were not able to agree on communal rules, they couldn't fulfil their duties efficiently!' – which struck me as a view I had also heard many times in Thai schools.

As well as discipline, the notion of 'gratitude' (*khwam katanyu*) also plays a key role in *phra* Manid's spiritual pedagogy for poor children: 'Gratitude towards parents, who gave us life, is the core attribute of a 'good person' [*khon di*]. Those who show gratitude and are able to be grateful demonstrate their capacity to act as respectful members of social groups and societies'. When I broached the possibility of the concept of *khwam katanyu* being politically instrumentalised to naturalise the moral obligations and related structural subalternity of minority groups, the monk pondered the question for a while and then introduced a politically-charged variation on the Buddhist theme of gratitude:

> *Khwam katanyu* is not a unilateral force. It is rather everyone's moral duty as part of reciprocal and interdependent relationships grounded in compassion. *Khwam katanyu* presupposes parental compassion, that is to say parents providing children with gratuitous love. Being aware of having been loved, taken care of, and protected, children will be grateful. Divergent interpretations of *khwam katanyu* are distortions produced by politics. The correct conception of family is, in fact, based on compassion, not on the exercise of power. Those who exert authority for their own interests are not acting as parents. (*Phra* Manid, August 2012)

To deserve the gratitude of 'small people', therefore, 'big people' – including rulers – must prove they are true parents, providing love and rules for compassionate reasons, solely in the interests of their children. If we follow this line of reasoning, *khwam katanyu* ('gratitude') is not, then, mandatory but conditional.

Phra Manid also drew attention to the importance of education as part of children's spiritual maturation: 'Children should be trained to develop awareness, avoid immoral lifestyles and cultivate moderate attitudes. Education is indispensable for moral development [*phatthana*]'. This conceptualisation of children as spiritually incomplete individuals is often linked to the idea of upbringing as a prerequisite for enlightenment (Gross 2006: 411). Although some classics, such as the Buddhacarita, cited above, underline Buddha's 'godly child' status and emphasise the fact that his supernatural attributes manifested themselves even before his birth, the majority of commentaries in the Theravada tradition give an account of the Buddha's gradual development (from initial darkness to enlightenment), establishing a staged pattern of maturation for all practitioners (Cole 2011: 280). It is worth noting that, according to *phra* Manid, poor children have more potential for moral development than do the high- or middle-class youngsters of Bangkok. Due to the material deprivation they have undergone, they are likely to be more accustomed to coping with (not satisfying) desires, whereas children from wealthy families may lose their ability to control their impulses because their parents promptly satisfy their every whim. In this respect, the monk – a former drug addict and slum dweller in Bangkok –

challenges normative assumptions about Thai society's class structure, inverting the moral relationship between the wealthy and the urban poor.

However, when I asked him what he thought, as a monk, about Thai society's enormous socio-economic inequalities, he reverted, to some extent, to a standard position – that poverty is due to bad (although not insurmountable) *karma*:

> If you act in a good way, you get good things. *Kam* [*karma*] is action. If you are born poor, you still have time to behave in a correct way in order to emerge from your marginality. You can study, work, be committed and persevere in order to reach your goal. This good conduct will progressively improve the karmic condition you are in at the beginning of your life. You don't have to wait for your next life to reap its fruits!   (*Phra* Manid, August 2012)

The monk's words cast material poverty neither as a karmic final sentence nor as a static cage, but rather as an adverse starting position that can nonetheless be overcome through moral effort and meritorious action, that is to say Buddhist practice. The solution is down to an individual's personal commitment.

After talking to *phra* Manid and attending his 'Dharmic Teachings for Poor Children', I was somewhat puzzled by his socially-engaged Buddhism. While several elements of his child pedagogy were seemingly at odds with dominant religious and public discourses, others fully embraced the militaristic nature of state education, making it rather difficult to fit the monk's religio-political orientation into a binary classification. My questions were not easily answered at the Suan Kaeo Foundation, either.

The Suan Kaeo Foundation: 'Dharma for everyday life'

Phra Payom is the abbot of *wat* Suan Kaeo and head of the homonymous Suan Kaeo Foundation, whose headquarters are located within the main complex of the temple, in Nonthabury province. Suan Kaeo Foundation hosts several social development programmes: the 'Centre for occupational and work training', the 'Shelter for people in need', the 'Campaign for the education of the illiterate', and a programme for the 'Promotion of employment for poor gifted students'. The official purpose of the Buddhist NGO is to alleviate hunger and poverty for parts of the population that have been most affected and damaged by industrialisation and the processes of development.

I decided to select the Suan Kaeo foundation as an ethnographic case study of Thai socially-engaged Buddhism for several reasons: first of all, a number of the slum children whom I met in Bangkok had previously found shelter at *wat* Suan Kaeo; and secondly, *phra* Payom, popular nationally, is a professed disciple of Buddhadasa Bhikku.

The first day I went to the Foundation, *phra* Payom was keen to stress the special nature of his temple. The monk proudly stated that, unlike other urban temples, *wat* Suan Kaeo was built on the model of *wat* Suan Mokkh ('liberation garden'), founded by Buddhadasa Bhikku in the southern Thai province of Surat Thani, where *phra* Payom had spent several years before ordination as part of his own spiritual formation. As does *wat* Suan Mokkh, *wat* Suan Kaeo openly takes inspiration from the tradition of 'forest temples' (*wat pa*). These were particularly widespread in Thailand before King Chulalongkorn's 1902 Sangha Act, which formalised the Buddhist ecclesiastical system and Buddhist education under the centralised authority of the (royally endorsed) *sangha*.[8]

Following the tradition of forest monks, *wat* Suan Kaeo is built in a style that can be described as eco-architecture, prioritising nature over bricks: the main prayer hall of the temple is on a raised platform, surrounded by lush vegetation in which statues of the Buddha and magnificent centuries-old trees stand. Dharmic precepts are displayed everywhere on plaques posted on tree trunks. The small wooden houses of the monks and of Buddhist laywomen (*mae chi*)[9] are spread at regular intervals throughout the forest–temple.

Wat Suan Kaeo also includes a large orchard (with bananas, mangos, papayas and pineapples among the species grown) and a rice field, and also grows other crops. The Foundation has a number of community members (unemployed peasants, urban poor, unregistered migrants), who produce food in the orchard and fields. Within the temple complex, there are also areas dedicated to courtyard animals and what can be described as a 'dog condo', which provides shelter for the strays of the city. Next to the main entrance is a recycling station, where garbage and damaged objects (including computers, televisions, etc.) are

---

8   In 1902, King Chulalongkorn and Prince Wachiraya passed the Acts of the Administration of the Buddhist Order of the Sangha of Thailand. While Thai monastic education was previously neither formal nor centralised, with the 1902 Sangha Act those who lived in a monastery were put 'at the nation's service'. The details of this law in large part lay out administrative norms that divide the Buddhist clergy into formal ranks, replicating the rising nation-state's bureaucratic-administrative structure and creating national, provincial and district religious bodies, which were placed under a Council of Elders and the authority of the supreme Patriarch, who was appointed by the king. With the creation of new ecclesiastical ranks, textbooks printed in Thai characters (in the central Thai language) and formal systems of monastic examinations, Bangkok consolidated its control over Siam's peripheral vassal states (see e.g. Keyes 1971, 1989). Regional and local cults were labelled superstitious beliefs that undermined orthodox Buddhism. Northern, northeastern and southern monks were forced to study in the newly established monastic universities in Bangkok (Maha Chulalongkorn Rajavidyalaya and Maha Makut Universities).

9   *Mae chi* are positioned somewhere between ordinary lay people and ordained male monks. While they are not formally recognised as *bikkhuni* (nuns) in Thailand, they devote their lives to Buddhist practice, and take the Eight or Ten precepts, including celibacy (see e.g. Collins and McDaniel 2010; Lindberg-Falk 2008).

sorted, repaired, re-assembled and then converted into reusable materials and goods, to be sold cheaply at *talat suan kaeo* (Suan Kaeo market). Drawing on King Bhumibol's *sethakit pho phiang* ('sufficiency economy'), the Suan Kaeo Foundation is thus designed as an ideal self-sustaining community.

Phra Payom has become a national celebrity because of his public speaking skills. The monk's biography has even been the subject of a TV series. Punctuated by funny jokes, street-level slang, and narrative vignettes of the lives of the lower classes, the monk delivers his sermons in a wide range of contexts, from schools and universities to companies, YouTube and pop concerts. The Suan Kaeo Foundation has its own radio and website and a private TV channel. The monk's particular style of preaching, known as '*Dharma* for everyday life', makes use of humour and popular language rather than Pali (the liturgical language of the Theravada Buddhist canon), putting across Buddhist social teachings through vitriolic remarks on the contemporary socio-economic and political situation. For these reasons, scholars of Thai Buddhism such as Seri Phongphit (1988: 9) and Santikaro Bhikkhu (1996: 179) have credited *phra* Payom with having made Buddhadasa's intellectual doctrines accessible to the urban poor, especially to young people and children.

Over time, the Suan Kaeo Foundation has benefited from a lot of funding, both public and private. *Phra* Payom has developed doctrinal innovations that give religious legitimacy to the projects of his own NGO. The traditional Buddhist notion of merit-making (*tham bun*) has, for example, been reinterpreted here in relation to the idea of financial transactions: to support the Suan Kaeo Foundation's social development programmes financially is to gain both merit and 'secular happiness' at the same time (Pitch Pongsawat 1994). In this context, *phra* Payom's role has been recast and his leadership has been expanded to include spiritual guidance, administrative responsibilities, the use of media, fundraising and financial affairs, highlighting the relations between Theravada Buddhism and development in contemporary Thailand (Bolotta 2018a; Feener and Fountain 2018).

A number of *dek salam* from Bangkok have found refuge at the Suan Kaeo Foundation as 'temple children' (*dek wat*).[10] During my time there, I stayed in the same building that housed the boys: a three-storey edifice located in the middle of the very large orchard. I followed the daily routine of the *dek wat* and helped them carry out their various duties. They slept together, crammed close together on the dirty floor in a bare space with no furniture other than an old bookshelf leaning against a wall covered in scratches. On the bookshelf were a

---

10 Although *wat* Suan Kaeo was home to many *mae chi*, which might suggest that *phra* Payom has a progressive stance on the role of women in Buddhism, the 'temple children' (*dek wat*) hosted at the temple were all males, as per tradition.

number of religious comics and cartoons about the life of the Buddha, all created and published by the NGO led by *phra* Payom. The children at the Suan Kaeo Foundation owed much of their knowledge of Buddhism to these comic strips, which they found much more interesting than the traditional dharmic lectures delivered by monks at the temple or by teachers at school.

The *dek wat* at the Suan Kaeo foundation came either from the slums of the capital, were orphans and/or were immigrants without residence permits. Once they arrived at *wat* Suan Kaeo they were granted room, board and primary education. In exchange, they were subject to strict discipline and intensive labour: they rose every morning at 5 am and, before school, followed the monks when they went out for the daily collection of alms (*binthabat*). After school, they were expected to perform many tasks, and to help the community members of the temple in various ways: cutting grass, working in the fields, feeding animals, cleaning rooms and generally providing help to any adult who requested it.

After just one week at the NGO I was exhausted. The boys woke me at 4:30 am with amused compassion; in the afternoon they taught me the ropes of work in the fields. We only had one meal per day, and in the evening I could barely stand, even though the less onerous jobs were set aside for me. The majority of the work at which the *dek wat* toiled was in the orchard. The monks of *wat* Suan Kaeo considered agriculture to be the heart of human work. During one conversation, *phra* Payom emphasised the value of agriculture with these words: 'If you cannot plant a tree, you cannot live in Thailand!', expressing his attempts to revitalise the purportedly original Buddhist community: small, self-sustaining and based on industrious cooperation and reciprocal solidarity between people. This is a romanticised Buddhist rural community that has, in the monk's eyes, decayed because of modernisation.

Dek wat were also trained in the tenets of *dharma* and Buddhist meditation. Following Buddhadasa's teachings, *phra* Payom has granted full access to cultural and spiritual education to laymen, laywomen, and especially to poor boys: 'Religion mustn't be reserved for older people, who aren't able to have an impact on the present or the future any more, but it is especially for children, who will become tomorrow's adults, that Buddhism needs to be taught in simple terms'. *Phra* Payom's educational philosophy integrates the classic teaching of *nirvana*-oriented *dharma* (liberation to be achieved in the otherworldly realm) with his 'Dharma for everyday life', which is focused on the here and now. Children were trained in *dharma*, thus conceived, through the pragmatism of daily work and meditation.

By offering poor boys material assistance as well as spiritual formation, the ideal that *phra* Payom pursues is promoting the democratisation of *dharma*. According to *phra* Payom: '*Dek salam* must be thought of as the ill-fated result of savage capitalism, Westernisation and hyper-individualism, rather than as karmic outcomes of immoral behaviour in previous lives'. In the monk's opinion, democratic access to *dharma* and Buddhism rests on material equality, which he views as the pre-condition for *nirvana* (*nipphan* in Thai). Suan Kaeo Foundation's development projects, which aim to disseminate *dharma* as widely as possible, are thus based in ensuring that food, shelter and jobs are available, which are regarded as fundamental requirements for spiritual maturation. *Phra* Payom's social activism, following Buddhadasa and revealing his mentor's openness to the Sino-Tibetan Mahayana tradition of Buddhism (P.A. Jackson 1987: 228–229), strives to actualise the principle of *nirvana* in *samsara*: salvation must be achieved in this world rather than being sought through world refusal.

Although these doctrinal, social and organisational efforts to address poor children's marginal position appear to substantiate *phra* Payom's progressive perspective and views, his apparent collusion with the orthodox authority of the central *sangha*, as well as some of the elements of his pedagogy, suggest that *phra* Payom's reformism is actually rather nuanced, and even that it is unclear and controversial. At times, for example, his educational attitudes towards the *dek wat* restated the centrality of moral hierarchy, the obligations of children, and the different status of parents and children, which are part of more conservative formulations of childhood and the proper social order.

Phra Payom's '*Dharma* for everyday life' teaching is focused on three main themes: family, young people and children, and work (Pitch Pongsawat 1994). The first two are particularly important here. While he points to benevolent compassion (as opposed to authoritarianism) as the cornerstone of Buddhist parenthood, the notion of 'small people' (*phu noi*) needing to show diligence, self-discipline, and especially gratitude (*khwam katanyu*) towards 'big people' (*phu yai*) is emphatically reiterated as paramount in the education of children.

Smoking, drinking alcohol and gambling are strictly forbidden at the temple. If these rules are broken, immediate expulsion follows. Children are expected to interact with monks and other adults in the community with absolute reverence. They must not speak unless they are spoken to and they must comply with requests from adults promptly. Some of the boys hosted by Suan Kaeo told me that *phra* Payom even used to entrust the task of instilling self-discipline in *dek wat* to Thai soldiers volunteering at the temple, so that they could inculcate a sense of common purpose, hierarchy and the respect due to superiors in the children's minds and bodies. In line with the *sangha* in Bangkok, *phra* Payom's pedagogy and educational practices seem here to reflect the strongly hierarchical and masculinist script of royalist state Buddhism, although it is de-mythologised and anchored in the materiality of this world.

The political ambiguity of *phra* Payom's socially-engaged Buddhism is also illustrated by the ambivalent public stance that he has taken in relation to recent political crises. During the May 1992 political rallies, when anti-military protesters were demanding democratic elections, the monk backed the army's instructions, suggesting that Buddhist citizens stay neutral in order to ensure the nation's economic stability (Payom Kanlayano 1992: 11–14). On the other hand, in November 2008 it was *wat* Suan Kaeo that was chosen by the pro-Thaksin 'red shirts' movement – hostile to the army and to the Bangkok-based royalist elite – as the ideal site, from a moral perspective, for a political demonstration which they called 'the truth' (*khwam jing*) (Matichon 2008). This involved sharp criticism of the military government, its 'yellow shirts' supporters and the royalist establishment. After this, *phra* Payom was linked by the media to Thaksin's anti-regime forces.

BEHIND THE 'GOOD THAI CHILD' MASK

During my time at the Suan Kaeo Foundation, *phra* Payom placed me in the care of Bank, a 17-year-old orphan and senior 'temple child' (*dek wat*). The boy was found abandoned at the age of two near a Buddhist temple in the northern province of Chiang Rai. Without a birth certificate, Bank could not obtain Thai citizenship and has therefore been deprived of the basic rights granted to nationals: free healthcare, regular employment and access to higher education. Until the age of six, he was raised by a Buddhist laywoman (*mae chi*) living an ascetic life at the temple, and he was subsequently entrusted to a travelling monk who, after some years of wandering, left him at the NGO run by *phra* Payom. As one of the long-standing *dek wat* at Suan Kaeo, Bank is now in charge of all the boys being helped by the NGO, including several *dek salam*.

Bank embodied the position of *phu noi* ('small person') flawlessly. When I first met him, he carefully avoided eye contact, performed reverential *wai*, and made sure that my every need was promptly met. I was embarrassed at being waited on hand and foot by children who appeared to me to already be worn out by daily hard work. A few days into my stay, attempting to build a less ceremonial relationship with Bank, I asked him if it was possible to break the one-meal-per-day rule. 'I'll get you whatever you want outside the temple. There are many cheap food spots around,' Bank replied shyly. Around 3 pm, we enjoyed some noodle soup, which I insisted on paying for. Staring at his empty bowl, with an absorbed look, Bank started talking about the value of food, weighing each word as he spoke: 'For many years I suffered from hunger. Here at the temple, *phra* Payom has taught me to appreciate our sacred relationship with food. Even when I drink a simple glass of water, I do it meditating [*dohi samathi*]. Water gives us life and when we drink that glass of water, we are taking in something that allows us to survive!'

I was struck and fascinated by the boy's arguments, but not entirely convinced by his apparently incorruptible moral rectitude. I knew that Bank and other *dek wat* smoked in secret. I had noticed them hastily hiding an ashtray while tidying up the room where I slept. In Thailand, smoking is a habit attributed to 'bad' (*mai di*) children, particularly if they are girls, a moral position that is clearly expressed in the media and in public discourse. Since we were outside the temple, I decided to bring up the topic with a smile: 'We share a nasty habit. I smoke too, and we both know this is forbidden in the temple. Watch yourself or you'll get caught with your hands in the cookie jar'. Bank seemed amused but unfazed.

The next day *phra* Payom left the temple, to return a week later. The evening he left, Bank revisited the topic. In the presence of other *dek wat* – who listened intently – he asked me defiantly whether I smoked. I answered that unfortunately I did; I had been stupid enough to start as a teenager, had become addicted, and that from then on I had not succeeded in quitting. I saw the excitement of the group. Revealing a new side of himself, Bank addressed another forbidden topic, asking if I had ever played videogames. I replied that as a boy I had used to go crazy for them. Overcoming some hesitation, he disappeared, returning with a PlayStation console that the boys had hidden somewhere. Some friends of Bank's joined the party soon after, bringing along spicy fried pork and a few beers. I was unsure how to behave. While I was glad that the youngsters felt comfortable about sharing their secret social world, it was not my intention to undermine *phra* Payom's authority, and I was also afraid that the *dek wat* might be discovered and severely punished.

One of the following evenings, disturbed by these thoughts, I asked them: 'Do you really feel good here? How do you imagine your future?'. Smiling, looking almost resigned, Lek – a 10-year-old boy who had been living in the temple for years – spoke up: 'We're *dek wat*, there's no place for us outside. We're not even *khon thai* ['Thai citizens'] for them [i.e. Thai people]'. As the group spokesperson, Bank added:

> Life here at the temple is really hard, sometimes soldiers even come and train us to be good children, and it is not fun! The monk [*phra* Payom] is very strict, but we do respect him, he's the only *phu yai* who has really helped us. He's not like other monks and we owe him gratitude [*katanyu*]. He helps the poor and, in his way, he loves us all. Here, we also acquire merit [*tham bun*]. One day, maybe, I'll become a monk like dad [i.e. *phra* Payom]! We need people like him in Thai society.
>
> (Bank, September 2012).

Bank embodies perfectly the habitus of the 'small person' and the 'good Thai child'. While his position as 'temple child' prevents him from accessing the middle-class opportunities of Thai urban society, he owes his life to the very moral system that underpins his subaltern status: it has been Thai Buddhism that has saved this youngster, abandoned as a small child on the doorstep of a temple.

Boys are resigned when they say: 'We're *dek wat*, there's no place for us outside'. Bank and his friends' peer-to-peer transgressive subculture does not openly challenge the policy of the temple. It operates more as a hidden, cathartic social space in which the 'good Thai child' mask can be temporarily stripped off. *Phra* Payom, a socially-engaged monk devoted to the urban poor, and to those regarded as 'non-Thai' in mainstream Thai society, is a model with whom the *dek wat* can identify emotionally, because he both opposes normative Thai Buddhism – 'He is not like other monks!', as Bank commented – and is also aligned with orthodox Buddhism. The religiopolitical ambiguity of *phra* Payom's approach, in between traditionalism and progressivism, seems to reverberate with the children's self-ambivalence, caught as they are between their frustration at being 'temple children' and their ambition to become monks.

On the day that *phra* Payom was expected to return, I was astonished at the way in which the boys synchronised and coordinated their movements. The youngest child (described as *nong*, 'younger brother') stood on guard at the main entrance of the temple; another boy stood about 100 metres from him, at the entrance to the courtyard. The chain of surveillance set up by the children ended in their room, where Bank and other boys were getting rid of crime-scene evidence. Eventually, Lek excitedly announced the arrival of *phra* Payom. He came into the boys' room with a scowl on his face, complaining about the *dek wat*, describing them as 'noisy slackers'. I looked at him and recognised the hint of a knowing smile in his frown. The monk was, in fact, only pretending to be unaware of what happened during his absence. One day he made this quite clear when he said to me: 'They think I'm a fool but I know them well. Sometimes I let them have their fun but it is important that there are strict rules. I'm here to represent them for their own good'.

BUDDHIST COUNTER-NARRATIVES
OR NEO-TRADITIONALISM?

Phra Payom's Buddhist pedagogy, like that of *phra* Manid, sheds light on the politically ambiguous position of Thai engaged Buddhism, weaving together seemingly contradictory notions of childhood, poverty, hierarchy, and the Thai social body through newly-fashioned organisational strategies that lie at the crossroads of religion and development.

In directing their social engagement primarily towards slum dwellers, the two monks implicitly underline contemporary Thai society's moral failure. By focusing their work on children, both re-address conservative Buddhist constructions of childhood and family, and advance politically-loaded doctrinal innovations such as 'nirvana in samsara' and 'Dharma for everyday life'. Through revised readings of Buddhist notions such as bun ('merit') and kam (karma), they also attempt to re-position the (political) futurity inherent in childhood, as well as its current significance, within an ideal framework of what they regard as true Buddhism – an imagined religious realm whose original purity they seek to restore through worldly social activism. In opposition to these innovations, however, both monks' educational methods confirm the inherently subordinate role of children as spiritually incomplete subjects, and thus the cosmological validity of traditional Thai socio-political stratification.

Some of these contradictions can be traced back to Thai commentary on the Pali Buddhist canon. In the philosophy of Buddhadasa, phra Payom's mentor, the concept of dharma (thamma in Thai) corresponds to that of nature (thammachat), understood as the system of mutual interdependence among beings. Buddhadasa's 'dharmic socialism' (Buddhadasa Bhikkhu 1986) prescribes the universal equality of all living creatures as a structural dimension of 'natural reality'. Even in Buddhadasa's thought, however, this utopian vision, which would imply a democratic form of political organisation, is in conflict with the theoretically different moral status and karmic condition of individuals. Granting equal rights of speech to enlightened and spiritually incomplete subjects would lead to a social catastrophe. It thus appears preferable to adopt a pyramidal social structure, led by the individual who represents the highest expression of dharma, in other words the virtuous king (thammaraja) (and the virtuous parent). As the elementary unit of the social macrocosm, the family stands as the prime metaphor for the moral order of the whole of society: parents – the phra of a family, as stated in the pamphlet on khwam katanyu ('gratitude') analysed at the beginning of this chapter – are called on to embody Buddhist morality and to channel the principles of dharma to their children. The latter, in turn, are expected to show obedience and respect to phu yai. Although on the one hand this perspective is fully aligned with the paternalistic rhetoric of 'Thainess' (as expressed by the Thai school system), on the other hand both monks insist that true phu yai (whether the king, parents or the state) are not tyrannical, despotic or authoritarian, but compassionate and fair. With respect to the state, this

important point shifts the focus from children's duties to parents' moral obligations, thereby acknowledging the right of 'small people' to question the integrity
and sacred status of 'big people'.

The equivocal polysemy of Thai engaged Buddhism is not significant only
in relation to exegetical controversies over the interpretation of scripture; it is
also profoundly related to, and nourished by, political divisions in society. Like
Bangkok-based royalist scholars, *phra* Payom and *phra* Manid attribute the dete-
rioration of Buddhism to Western capitalism, consumerism and individualism.
Embracing King Bhumibol's 'sufficiency economy' (*sethakit pho phiang*), both
monks advocate a return to an original self-reliant community, grounded in
subsistence farming and Buddhist morality – a position that clearly echoes what
is put forward by conservative political groups, which associate Thai economic
crises with the 'Thaksin system's' persistent toxic influence – despite the fact that
the neoliberal turn in Thailand has been endorsed, historically, by the US-backed
military regimes with which those conservative political groups are associated.

Asian 'development monks' have been described as brokers of social change
as well as prominent leaders of anti-caste, 'liberation' social movements. In
Thailand, however, the boundaries between socially-engaged Buddhism – including its progressive fringes – and the hegemonic state religion of 'Thainess'
come across as being far more blurred. As a matter of fact, when applied to
the Thai political arena, Western political labels such as 'progressivism' and
'conservatism' are often interwoven and co-present. I would argue that this
religiopolitical ambiguity is related to the core symbolic role that the monarchy,
and consequently hierarchy, plays in all strands of Thai Buddhism.

While *phra* Payom's and *phra* Manid's development projects imply a harsh
criticism of Thailand's political economy and related socio-economic inequalities, their child-focused pedagogy reaffirms (royal) parenthood as the moral
lifeblood of Thai society. Although with different emphasis and purpose, both
state Buddhism and its socially engaged counterpart agree in their positioning
of (poor) children as spiritually incomplete, and thus hierarchically subaltern
subjects, and cast *phu yai* (parents, soldiers, monks and the king) as dharmic
lighthouses called upon to illuminate the children's karmic path.

Bank has lived at *wat* Suan Kaeo for as long as he can remember. Other boys,
by contrast, have spent shorter periods in the foundation established by *phra*
Payom, returning home to their families after a period there, or entrusted to
other NGOs after they leave the Buddhist foundation. In the context of what
may be described as a 'humanitarian economy of deprived childhood', poor families choose to move children between aid agencies as part of the livelihood and

survival strategies that they develop. Children's circulation through ideologically diverse institutions and environments provides poor youngsters with alternative possibilities for self-identification and growth. In the Catholic NGO on which I will now focus, the Saint Jacob's Centre, Bangkok's *dek salam* encounter very different religiopolitical perspectives on childhood, family, ethnicity, gender and urban poverty from those linked to the 'good Thai child' narrative.

CHAPTER 3

God's Beloved Children

Atypical day for *dek salam* at the Saint Jacob's Centre is quite structured. At 5 am, they are awoken by a bell, signalling the start of morning activities. After showering, children put on their school uniform, which they will have washed and ironed the previous day, and head to the pickup truck bound for the canteen, while the NGO's head of staff, who is going to be driving the vehicle, honks furiously to hurry stragglers. One minute before 6 am, piled into the back of the overloaded vehicle, the children, still sleepy, count the seconds down to the hour, announcing the imminent departure of the pickup. Whoever is there is there. The others will have to walk and give up their daily allowance.

Once at the canteen, the *dek salam* line up in tidy rows, awaiting their meal. Before breakfast, as before all meals, the children – although they are all self-declared Buddhists – recite the Thai version of the Our Father prayer together. At 7:30 am, the NGO vehicles take them to their respective schools. Older children (described as *phi*, 'elder siblings') fight over the only two seats next to the driver, while the others elbow their way to the back of the pickup, singing, reading Japanese manga or listening to music on their iPods. They will return to the Centre at around 4 pm.

Before dinner (at 6 pm), the Thai staff at Saint Jacob's announce upcoming activities, publicly reproach children who have misbehaved, issue reminders of upcoming birthdays, and finally start the collective prayer preceding the meal. The 7 o'clock mass, which all those who are guests of the NGO are expected to attend, closes the activities of the day.

The Thai staff's assiduousness in maintaining discipline and adherence to formal rules is regularly put to the test by the NGO director's unpredictable intrusions. One afternoon in April 2011, while the head of staff at Saint Jacob's was coordinating the children's daily chores – sweeping, mopping, cleaning, cooking and so forth – Father Nicola appeared in the doorway of the children's house. The Thai staff looked concerned, and the *dek salam* stopped what they were doing. Full of unbridled enthusiasm, they ran towards the Catholic missionary, yelling in unison '*Pho! Pho!*' ('Father! Father!'). Some climbed up his legs and on to his shoulders, messing up his hair; others jumped up and down as though they had been electrocuted, ready to sneak inside the writhing mass of bodies circling around the priest. Father Nicola, smiling, announced: '*Luk* [children], forget about housework for today! Let's cook something together and have a picnic in the garden!'. The Thai staff, disoriented, weakly attempted to complain: 'But Father, sir... the children still have to finish cleaning everything here...'. The missionary, half-jokingly, reminded them who is really in charge at Saint Jacob's, saying: 'Look at how happy they are. In these children's smiles we encounter Jesus Christ. There is always time for work. After all, it is we who are serving them. They are in charge'.

Together with Buddhist temples and foundations, Christian NGOs such as Saint Jacob's are at the forefront of humanitarian endeavours to address poor children's marginality in Bangkok. Although they are often below the public radar, these organisations play a significant role in (re)framing public notions of childhood, parenthood, poverty, gender, and ethnicity from a religious perspective, sometimes against all the odds, as Father Nicola's behaviour suggests.

The Saint Jacob's Centre provides residential care, scholastic support and spiritual formation to *dek salam* from five to 18 years old. In this chapter, I investigate how 'childhood' is thereby constructed, focusing in particular on the Catholic missionaries who lead the NGO. I will examine these missionaries' mimetic strategies of adaption to the Thai context, and their efforts to reformulate and contest dominant discourses on 'Thainess', through what may be described as a 'political theology' of childhood.[1] I will demonstrate that this underpins their critique of both state Buddhism and Thai (royalist) Catholicism, as well as their attempt to introduce a new way of indigenising the Gospels in favour of Thailand's ethnic minorities and '*phu noi* cultures'.

CATHOLICISM IN THAILAND: THE THAIFICATION OF THE GOSPELS

The presence of Catholic missionaries in Siam can be traced back to the sixteenth century, when the first Portuguese Dominican missionaries of what were described as 'Christ's caravels' arrived in Ayutthaya, then the capital of the Siamese kingdom. These Portuguese missionaries were followed by Jesuits and by the French missionaries of the Missions Etrangères de Paris (MEP), who operated in Siam from 1662 onwards (van der Cruysse 1991: 149–192). Despite this long, uninterrupted effort, the Thai Catholic Church and Protestants together

---

1   On the concept of 'political theology' and the intersection of religion and politics in contemporary Asia, see Bolotta et al (eds) 2020, and de Vries 2006.

represent a minority religious group of about 1% of the national population.[2] It is only among the 'non-Thai' mountain groups (*chao khao*, 'hill tribes') in northern Thailand that Christians have had conversions in recent centuries.

Charles Keyes (1993) has suggested that Thais are not Christian because Buddhism is so closely associated with Thai national identity – so that being Thai means being Buddhist. I want to push Keyes' argument further, suggesting that Thais are not Christian not only due to the secular nationalisation of Buddhism but because (at least in the case of Catholicism) Christianity has been accommodating in its attitude towards the national concept of 'Thainess' (Bolotta 2018b: 142). I would argue that this can be described as a 'Thaification' of Christianity, which has been promoted, historically, through 'secular collaborations' between Thai monarchical elites and Catholic missionaries in course of the building of the modern Thai state (ibid.). Let me take a brief look at the most significant phases of this historical collaboration.

Exchange between Catholic missionaries and the Thai monarchy in the secular fields of science, art, architecture, medicine, and printing techniques is historically well documented (Wyatt 1969; Watson 1980; Bressan 2005; Bressan and Smithies 2006). Education was at the forefront of these joint modernising efforts. In 1659, the Congregation for the Doctrine of the Faith – the Vatican department that has coordinated Gospel-related activities since 1622 – formally instructed the apostolic vicariates of China and Southeast Asia, stating: 'You must build schools everywhere with great care and diligence, for the children of Christians but also open to non-Christians' (Bressan 2005: 10–11). French Jesuits in Ayutthaya responded to the Vatican's instructions by establishing institutions for the education of 'children beloved of His Highness the King' (ibid.). This was the beginning of a close link between Catholic missionaries and the kings of Siam that would grow stronger in the following centuries, especially after the capital shifted from Ayutthaya to Bangkok and the Rattanakosin dynasty took power.[3] Under King Mongkut (Rama IV)[4] and

---

2   Bressan and Smithies (2006: 1) give the following statistics: 300,000 Catholics, 400 Thai priests, about 250 foreign missionaries, mostly Western, 1,500 nuns, and 120 consecrated laymen. The Thai Catholic Church is divided into ten dioceses and 500 parishes distributed throughout the national territory.

3   For an exhaustive report on the activities of Jesuit and MEP missionaries in 17th and 18th century Siam, the period preceding the advent of the Rattanakosin kingdom and Chakri dynasty, see e.g. Alain Forest (Forest 1998).

4   On the bonds of friendship and collaboration between Rama IV – the Thai king who liberalised foreign trade in Siam, signing trade treaties with the British Empire under Sir John Bowring (Governor of Hong Kong and Britain's envoy) in 1855 – and the apostolic vicar in Siam, Jean-Baptiste Pellagoix, see, for example, Bressan and Smithies (2006: 3).

King Chulalongkorn (Rama V), the position of Christian missionaries within the court grew stronger.

With the establishment of Catholic schools, missionaries had the opportunity to expand their evangelisation activities, which had previously been limited to 'non-Thai' ethnic minorities in the north (e.g. see Kammerer 1990) and to elite groups in central Thailand, even though these activities were supposed, officially, to be primarily secular. Through modern education, missionaries hoped to slowly promote favourable conditions for conversion within Thai elite groups. Their strategy recognised that, given the pyramidal Indo-Buddhist socio-political structure of Thai society, the king's conversion might catalyse the conversion of the entire population.

However, what actually happened was that what was brought in from the West by the Catholic missionaries was appropriated by the Siamese kings to enforce Buddhist and monarchical Thai ethno-nationalism. First of all, as Keyes (1993) has pointed out, the Catholic Church's centralised organisation may well have inspired the reforms of Thai Buddhism brought in by Rama IV and Rama V. The 1902 Sangha Act passed by Rama V organised the *sangha* within the framework of the administrative structure of the state, placing Buddhism under royal patronage and political control. Moreover, as already mentioned, missionary schools have been used as ideal models for the establishment of the modern Thai school system.

Since the early 20th century, missionaries working in secular institutions, such as schools and hospitals, have chosen to interact closely with the national culture of the Thai state, thus producing the theological and political conditions for what can be described as a progressive 'Thaification' of institutional normative Catholicism (Bolotta 2018b). In order to understand the religious and political context in which contemporary Catholic NGOs operate, it is essential to take a closer look at the characteristics of this Thaified Christianity as it is now represented by the local Catholic church, especially in the Archdiocese of Bangkok, and its private Catholic schools.

The indigenisation of Thai Catholicism

The Thaification of Catholicism was officially sanctioned after the Second Vatican Council (1962–1965) with the foundation of the Catholic Bishops' Conference of Thailand (CBCT) and the appointment of Thais as bishops instead of foreigners. The link that had already been established between Catholicism, monarchy and 'Thainess' became explicit with the guidelines laid out in Vatican documents such as *Gaudium et Spes, Nostra Aetate* and *Ad Gentes* (1965), which marked a substantial shift in missionary efforts from a conversion-based approach to what was described as the 'inculturation' of the Gospels, to fit in with local cultural contexts.[5]

The recommendations of the Second Vatican Council emerged from the Roman Catholic Church's critical awareness of the historical role that Christianity had played in supporting Western deculturising practices of power (e.g. Comaroff and Comaroff 1986). Nevertheless, as the Italian anthropologist Flavia Cuturi (Cuturi [ed.] 2004) has observed, these recommendations did not provide definitions that would enable 'culture' to be distinguished from 'religion' in non-Catholic contexts, nor did they address problems or questions related to 'adaptations of the Gospels' (liturgical arrangements, communication strategies, daily life, theories of preaching) to local cultures. As a result, as noted by the Jesuit Michael Amaladoss (2000: 23–30), the inculturation of Christianity became a vehicle for dominant cultures in a number of contexts, including in Asia. Jesuits Francis Xavier (in India, Malaysia and Japan) and Matteo Ricci (in China) adapted strategically to aristocratic societies and to hierarchical rituals and customs central to local civil and religious life (e.g. the tea ceremony). In fact, in these hierarchical societies the poverty and sacrifice epitomised by Christ's crucifixion actually aroused suspicion and hostility (Di Fiore 2001).

Amaladoss' point regarding the way in which 'inculturation' was utilised by dominant cultures is also pertinent to the story of Thai Catholicism after the Second Vatican Council. I would argue that in Thailand – the only country in the region to have developed a monarchical (as opposed to a popular and anti-colonial) nationalism (e.g. see Anderson 1978) – the 'inculturation' of the Christian message has taken place in the context of a desire to ensure a continuing harmonious political relationship with the Thai monarchy.[6] The supposedly 'local' culture that was accommodated within Catholicism was consistently identified in the reified, ahistorical, and mono-ethnic (i.e. Central Thai) construction of *watthatham Thai* ('Thai culture') that had been developed a decade earlier by Phibun Songkhram's military regime. In the selection of the vernacular language to be used as a vehicle of the Word, the choice thus fell on central Thai,

---

5 The theological term 'inculturation' gained growing acceptance at the time of the 32nd General Congregation of the Society of Jesus (December 1, 1974–April 7 1975) (Roest-Crollius 1984). It was intended to be an adjustment of the concept of 'adaptation' that had emerged from the statements of the Second Vatican Council (Buono 2000: 151).

6 The fact that Thailand became a hostile territory for Christian missionaries during the years following the fall of the absolute monarchy (1940-1944) and the king's disappearance from the Thai political scene is significant (Strate 2011). After the Second World War, when Thailand was repositioned geo-politically as a key American ally in Southeast Asia and the monarchy was reinstated at the centre of the Thai political arena, Christian missionaries operating in the country enjoyed, once again, safety and political protection.

the national language. Buddhism, the religious component of 'Thainess', was re-conceptualised as a respectful local philosophy, whereas local cults (such as the belief in spirits, the cult of amulets, divination, etc.), which are particularly significant among the 'non-Thai' ethnic groups of the north and northeast, were labelled primitive superstitions (Bolotta 2018b: 147).

Catholicism reproduces 'Thainess' through two channels in particular. The first is related to the liturgical management of the king's image. As they are in Buddhist temples, government buildings, shopping malls and private homes, grand images depicting the king and members of the royal family are displayed on all Catholic buildings (churches, schools, universities and hospitals), alongside traditional Christian icons. The faithful, when they enter the church, are expected to take off their shoes as Buddhists do in temples; and the *wai*, the Thai traditional salute with folded hands (as opposed to the handshake common among 'hill tribes') must accompany every 'Amen' during the liturgy. Furthermore, during all Catholic celebrations – including Christmas and Easter – the liturgy includes prayers in praise of the King (ibid.).

According to some priests I interviewed, the king is included in the Catholic liturgy as a secular element of the local culture, in the same way that heads of state are mentioned by name in prayers in the liturgical context of Catholic masses in the West. However, His Majesty is far from merely representing a constitutional head of state for Thai Catholics. He is publicly portrayed as the incarnation of the Hindu God Vishnu and as the supreme embodiment of Buddhist dharma.

The second central channel through which Thai Catholicism reproduces 'Thainess' is via the embodied rules governing the relationship between clergy and laity. Laymen should pay respect to priests (often called *phra* – the same word used to designate Buddhist monks) according to the ritual relational praxis that already shapes the normative relationship between laymen and Buddhist monks and, more broadly, between *phu noi* and *phu yai*. By sticking to this relational model, not only do clergymen secure a privileged position with respect to laymen; they also confirm, in a bodily fashion, the political validity of the Buddhist stratification of the cosmos as based on merit and *karma*.

This royalist inculturation of the Christian message as the 'Thaification of the Gospels' is, however, increasingly being challenged by new actors on the fringes of the local Catholic movement. Several foreign priests and nuns I met during fieldwork belong to a new generation of Catholic missionaries who were sent to Thailand after the 1960s, officially to support the local Thai church and to carry on humanitarian interventions based on Christian charity. Some of them described, with great disappointment, the theological and pastoral approach of the Thai priests in Bangkok, which are mainly vertical, exclusively other-worldly, and are grounded in a retributive logic of salvation that reflects, both politically and from a religious perspective, Thai elitist interpretations of *karma*. Unlike the Thai clergy of Bangkok, these missionaries are now working in the most marginal areas of the capital as 'development missionaries' and as heads of officially secular child-focused NGOs.[7] They position themselves at the crossroads between local and global change in both the secular and the religious spheres, and act as translators of a counter-indigenisation of Thai Catholicism that I describe as 'de-Thaification'.

Together with a significant number of 'non-Thai' religious actors (mainly Thai-Lao and *chao khao* priests from the northeast and the north of the country), these missionaries feel deeply uncomfortable within the local Thaified church that was created in earlier centuries by their Western predecessors. They do not recognise a deified king as a cultural element compatible with Christianity, and they are very critical of the military promulgation of 'Thainess'-oriented interventions, which they view as exacerbating the political and economic oppression of 'non-Thai-enough' marginal groups (Bolotta 2018b: 150). Among these 'development missionaries' are Father Nicola and Sister Serafina, the heads of the Saint Jacob's Centre and the House of the Little Ones respectively.

FATHER NICOLA: GOD'S BELOVED CHILDREN

Father Nicola, a 72-year-old Italian missionary, began his work in the 'tribal areas' of Thailand in 1978, during the years of communist guerrilla warfare. At that time, the US-backed Thai military state governed the country's 'non-Thai' insurgent peripheries through strategies of suppression, surveillance and agricultural development (e.g. Rigg 1995; Haberkorn 2011). Reforms in the farming sector, together with fast-moving technological advancements in cultivation techniques, made a large part of the rural workforce redundant. Many farmers were victims of these policies, and a mass of unskilled ex-peasants migrated to the capital in search of job opportunities. Since he had access to considerable funding, Father Nicola decided to buy plots for sale in ethnic minority villages in northern Thailand, to then return them to local villagers – 'their rightful owners', as he said – in order to protect indigenous communities' resources and territory and to prevent land grabs and market speculation.

In his evangelical approach, Father Nicola has been influenced by liberation theology, once marginalised as a Marxist deviation of Christianity by the Vatican

---

7 As I have analysed in detail elsewhere (Bolotta 2018b), these 'development missionaries' are, following shifting global trends in vocation callings, increasingly represented by Latin American and African priests and nuns rather than solely by Europeans and Americans, as was the case during previous centuries.

and now apparently rehabilitated by the geopolitical and theological re-structuring of the Roman Catholic Church's centre since the appointment of Latin-American Pope Francesco Bergoglio (Francis I). His approach is grounded on a 'preferential option for the poor' and for all who are marginalised in society. During my conversations with Nicola, the missionary argued that the 'inculturation' of Catholicism should be carried out in the context of Thailand's marginalised ethnic minority cultures rather than being placed at the service of the militarised and monarchical construct of Buddhist 'Thainess', as it has been, historically, in the context of the Thai Catholic church.

What may be described as Father Nicola's 'evangelical activism' in the 'red' villages of Thailand's northern and northeastern ethnic minority regions has not gone unnoticed. In July 1980, while celebrating mass in a parish in the northern province of Chiang Mai, two young government officials, wearing military uniforms, appeared at the ceremony: 'After mass the soldiers tried to dissuade me from working in tribal villages. They claimed these were infected by the communist disease, populated by dangerous people, by terrorists who would pose a threat even to me'. Recalling these experiences, the missionary smiled.

Not only did Father Nicola oppose the military's veiled intimidations, determined as he was to act in those very villages, which were being oppressed by the Thai army's suffocating repression, but he also took the opportunity to catechise the young soldiers: 'Now *luk* [children], sit down and listen to your father!' he commanded. Fluent in Thai and aware of Thai hierarchical norms, the priest cleverly took advantage of local social rules that imply the superior moral status of religious actors as *phu yai*. Disoriented by the missionary's charisma, and unwittingly turned into *phu noi*, the soldiers ended up learning how much the Christian God cares about those who come 'last' (in Thai society).

However, the pressure placed on him became more aggressive, and Father Nicola was eventually relocated by his superiors to Bangkok in 1987. Here, in stark contrast to the local clergy, he decided to direct his mission towards the urban poor, the inhabitants of the Bangkok slums. Father Nicola became particularly active in Akhan Daeng, a densely populated slum in the north of Bangkok where the priest lived for years, taking care of the disadvantaged youngsters in the community.

During many conversations, Father Nicola pointed to state violence and what he described as the 'political ideology of *karma*' as the deep-set causes of Thailand's socio-economic inequalities, of which urban slums are inevitable corollaries. In his view, the imitation of Christ is the salvation-related solution to slum children's suffering:

> *Karma* is a power encompassing the whole Thai society. Slum children are frequently abandoned. If a mother dies during childbirth, it is the baby's

Photo: Giuseppe Bolotta.

Figure 4. Reproduction of the painting Hapag ng Pag-asa ('Table of Hope') by Filipino artist Joey Velasco (1967–2010), displayed at the Saint Jacob's Centre. Bangkok, August 2008. Colour version, p. 230

fault. The law of *karma* solidifies this destiny, thus transforming it into an unequivocal, dead-end path. From this point of view, Christ represents the possibility of liberation. I love poor children unconditionally, I would die for them, I am not afraid to be contaminated by their negative *karma*, just as Christ died to save us all. The suffering of poor children is connected to one original cause: a lack of belonging, which with Christianity we try to transform into belonging. According to Buddhism, merit-making can improve one's *karma* in one's current lifetime, but the starting point of these children [i.e. poverty, political marginalisation, state violence, etc.] makes it impossible for them to do good. Slum inhabitants are not living in conditions that impact positively on their karmic position. It is not their fault, nor the fault of their *karma*. Their marginality is due, rather, to those political and economic processes that have segregated them at the margins of Thai society.   (Father Nicola, August 2013)

Based on this analysis, Father Nicola established the Saint Jacob's Centre, an NGO that is officially secular and that is devoted, formally, to promoting the rights of children. The activities of the NGO include both material and spiritual assistance to Bangkok's *dek salam* (Figure 4).

Since its foundation in 2005, the Saint Jacob's Centre has provided scholarships for about 800 slum children, health assistance to elderly and HIV-positive inhabitants of the slums, and – through the *fai phatthana chumchon* ('community development team') of the NGO – projects related to social development and the improvement of livelihoods, such as the 'slum housewives' club'. These all have a cost. Every month Saint Jacob's spends between 1.5 and 2 million Thai baht (30–40,000 euros). This money is spent on a wide range of things: the rental of buildings in the slums; food, board, medical, and school expenses for the children hosted in the NGO foster homes; salaries for the NGO staff and reimbursement of their expenses; recreational activities and sports; administration expenses and stationery. As an NGO promoting children's rights that is formally secular, Saint Jacob's is financed through donations from both religious and secular sources and from both local and international donors, although most of the funding is from Caritas.[8] The priest clarified: 'We do not want to proselytise or to promote conversion at any cost. We want to share, especially through praxis and by example, the love that the Lord has for us all, particularly for those who come last in this society – slum children'.

Dek salam are the symbolic centre of his mission. The priest explicitly grounds his work, his words and ultimately his perception of his own role as Christ's servant in the profound significance of 'childhood' in the Gospels. In Father Nicola's view, poor children are the prime representatives of the Lord. Because they are the last in their society, they are 'God's most beloved children'. 'In the relationship with them one has the opportunity to meet Jesus Christ, a God who is almost feared by the powerful because of his identification with the dregs of humankind'.

Metaphorically linking the oppression to which ethnic minorities from the north and northeast are subjected to 'Thainess' and to children's normative position as *phu noi*, Father Nicola elaborated: 'Those considered *phu noi* by the Thai state are the closest to God's truth. The sacred elements of childhood and poverty coincide in the condition of slum children. They must be taught this so they can proudly claim their identity, against social injustice'.

At Saint Jacob's, seminarians from the ethnic Thai north, under Father Nicola's pastoral guidance, are encouraged to consider *dek salam* as their own teachers. As Father Nicola put it: 'It is the children, as manifestations of the divine, as subjects intuitively able to recognise the Truth, who are able to bring about the revelation of Christ in seminarians. Only those who demonstrate passion and participation in the service of the last [Saint Jacob's *dek salam*] will continue their spiritual journey towards ordination'.

As demonstrated in the ethnographic vignette that opened this chapter, Father Nicola's theological-political construction of *dek salam* is also embedded in his affective and relational attitudes. When he visits the slums, a swarm of joyfully

---

8   Caritas International is a confederation of over 160 Catholic relief, development and social service organisations operating worldwide. It is the most important arm of the Catholic church devoted to charity and is one of the most important development organisations in the world. It has a delegation at the United Nations headquarters in New York City.

squealing children, all vying for his attention, announce his arrival. Carrying a boy on his back, holding another one's hands, Father Nicola would spend entire days playing with the children. Rather than acting as a *phu yai*, as Thai priests and Buddhist monks alike are expected to (be recognised) in relation to laymen, he hugs dirty slum children, holds little girls (whereas Thai Buddhist monks are not allowed to touch or be touched by women), sits at the children's level during meals and uses impolite slum dialect – in short, he challenges all the embodied dimensions of 'Thainess' and overturns the normative social hierarchy with the enactment of a bottom-up engaged Catholicism.

As Part Two of this book will show, poor children, *phu noi* by definition, are able to find in Father Nicola an alternative model to emulate, a different model from the one they have in family members, schoolteachers or Buddhist monks. As a *phu yai* who does not view them as *phu noi*, the missionary equips 'his children' with anti-normative ideological tools to craft their sense of self. But let me first step back to examine how this priest's religiopolitical approach to childhood interacts (and clashes) with Thai dominant social norms in public contexts, including Catholic private schools. Thai Mother's Day (*wan mae*) provides a very good example of this.

The Virgin Mary and the Queen: Mother's Day at Saint Jacob's

Wan mae is celebrated in Thailand on 12 August, Queen Sirikit's birthday. This is a public holiday dedicated to mothers and, by symbolic extension, to the queen, the 'nation's mother'.[9] During *wan mae* public spaces are decorated with lights, garlands, banners, and flags, all in light blue – the Queen Mother's colour.[10] Enormous portraits of the monarch are displayed everywhere, while national events providing visual evidence of the loyalty of subjects to the 'nation's mother' are feverishly organised, especially in the areas surrounding Bangkok's palaces of power. On the morning of 12 August, a procession intended to be representative of all sectors of Thai society (the government, the army, the school system, etc.) marches solemnly up to the royal palace, where flowers

---

9   The birthday of Queen Sirkit, now the Queen Mother of Thailand, is still celebrated as Mother's Day in Thailand, although in 2019 – after King Bhumibol's death in 2017 – Queen Suthida, the fourth wife of her son, King Vajiralongkorn, became the new Queen of Thailand.

10 Light blue, Queen Sirikit's colour, is part of a national code of colours, each corresponding to a different day of the week (Monday: yellow, Tuesday: pink, Wednesday: green, Thursday: orange, Friday: light blue, Saturday: purple, Sunday: red). This is based on an astrological calendar, probably of Khmer origin, that identifies a Hindu deity as patron for each day (Pasuk Phongpaichit and Baker 2008). The colour of each day matches that of its deity. Queen Sirikit was born on Friday, so her colour is blue, while King Bhumibol was born on Monday and his colour is thus yellow.

are presented to the queen's delegates. Thai public media broadcasts images of jubilant crowds and deeply emotional ordinary citizens, in tears listening to the song 'Mother of the Nation'.[11]

The royal symbolism pervading the iconography of Mother's Day is inter-woven with a highly dramatised and spectacular representation of the ideal relationship between mothers and children, meant to be archetypal of Buddhist compassion (e.g. see Keyes 1984). Public celebrations of the queen are juxta-posed in rather a disturbing way with acts of filial 'gratitude' (*khwam katanyu*) on the part of children. On their knees, carrying garlands made of white jasmine (the emblem of motherly love), sons and daughters bow in front of their mothers and are granted their blessing. Soon after, the same ritual sequence is jointly played out by each mother and child in front of an image of the queen, in a move that projects both as 'children' relating to the 'mother' of all the citizens of Thailand. Parades of this kind are held in all public institutions, especially schools. The standardised celebration of *wan mae* is not optional, nor are the modalities of its performance discretionary. Thai institutions must follow the ritual protocol as defined by the Ministry of Culture.

In July 2014, while I was carrying out research at Phra Mae Marie ('Merciful Mother Mary'), one of the Catholic private schools attended by the children of Saint Jacob's (see Chapter 1), the teachers were preparing the children for Mother's Day. Although many of the *dek salam* at Saint Jacob's had never met their biological mothers, they were nonetheless expected to take part in the national celebration as Thai citizens. In their case, this entailed singing songs and writing poems praising an unknown mother, and finally acknowledging their own debt of gratitude to the queen, mother of mothers. When I rather sarcastically asked the school principal, a Thai Catholic nun, whether the *dek salam* at Saint Jacob's would bow down before an empty chair, I discovered that female schoolteachers were to serve as replacements for the children's absent mothers.

For *wan mae*, a row of chairs for the students' mothers was set up on a raised platform in the auditorium of the school – a proscenium stage facing the audi-ence, behind which a giant image of the queen had been placed. Each student would kneel in front of his/her mother, to complete the *mise-en-scène*. Saint Jacob's children, confined to the two ends of the stage out of the audience's sight,

---

11 The strong association between the symbols of mother and father on the one hand and those of the king and the queen on the other has always been exploited by Thai military governments as the moral source of their political legitimacy. In the 1960s, Sarit's government made King Bhumibol's birthday (5 December) Father's Day for Thailand. Mother's Day in Thailand was initially established on 15 April 1950. In 1976 (a year mainly known as that of the massacre at Thammasat University) Mother's Day was moved to coincide with Queen Sirikit's birthday.

were visibly uncomfortable. Expressionless, they mechanically executed the expected act of reverence before strict teachers, who acted as sort of 'vice-mums'. They were clearly concerned that the 'uneducated' *dek salam* would sidestep the protocol and so ruin the school's reputation in the presence of the wealthy parents of the 'normal' students. In the middle of the stage, the mothers of the other students were smiling, trying to hold back tears, deeply moved by their children's performances.

At the end of the ceremony, I came across a few *dek salam* sitting on the sidelines. They were crying. The very next day, they would attend another, very different, *wan mae* event, this time at the Saint Jacob's Centre. However, Mother's Day as envisioned by Father Nicola was quite a different story. First of all, *wan mae* at the Catholic NGO revolved around the figure of the Virgin Mary. The mother of Jesus replaced Queen Sirikit, taking up the symbolically central position in the scene. Over the course of the activities organised for the occasion, furthermore, orphans were assigned leading roles. For Father Nicola, Mother's Day had the primary purpose of comforting those children who were not able to receive a visit from their mother. It was these children who were chosen as the main characters in theatre performances featuring both Christian and ethnic traditional plays, applauded by a generous crowd – instructed to be enthusiastically responsive – awarded with gifts, and entertained by Western volunteers.

For Father Nicola, *wan mae* constitutes an evangelical and political opportunity to de-Thaify Catholicism. At Mother's Day at St. Jacob's, the entanglement between the collective mother of the Thais (the queen), the individual mothers of the children and the supernatural mother of the Catholics (Mary) generates a symbolic triangle of great emotional impact, which appropriates the core Thai premise of royal nationalism, attempting to reroute its semantic connections into new pathways. Mary is presented here not only as a divine mother, the mother of mothers (including the queen), affectionate, loving, and able to compensate for the emotional void caused by absent individual mothers. Mary's motherly love is also embodied and materialised in the charitable actions of the Catholic NGO. As Father Nicola told me at the end of the celebration, the intention on the part of Saint Jacob's is to transform *wan mae* into a demonstration of his Catholicism's (counter)parenthood, formulated as privileged attention to those in whom God is most present: poor children. In his view, reparative experiences of this kind will empower *dek salam* – the 'last' in Thai society – to overcome socio-political and economic exclusion through spiritual means.

SISTER SERAFINA: (CATHOLIC) NGOS AND
THE 'DE-THAIFICATION' OF CHRISTIANITY

Sister Serafina, nurse and Italian missionary of the Xaverian Society of Mary, is one of Father Nicola's closest aides. She leads the House of the Little Ones, a branch of the Saint Jacob's Centre, which offers day-care assistance programmes to disabled slum children. Like Father Nicola, Sister Serafina regards Christian spirituality as primarily oriented towards serving the 'last' (the poor), whose socio-economic and political marginalisation she regards as constituting a 'structural sin' and a violation of God's plan.

When Sister Serafina first came as a missionary to Thailand, in 2000, she was involved in conflict with the Catholic Church in Bangkok, as she perceived the Church as being 'a very hierarchical, wealthy and pro-monarchical community, wrapped in the distancing mechanism of liturgy, in the context of which nuns are exclusively expected to run high-class private schools' – institutions that she described as 'neo-liberal enterprises aimed at high-class Thai Buddhists, where the teaching of Christian religion is forbidden'. Used to working with and for the 'last', Serafina found the Thai clergy's attitude towards the urban poor intolerable. She lamented that Thai priests would spend their time in their 'gold-plated churches', surrounded by obsequious servants and rich parishioners, rather than reaching out to the poor.

In 2002, disregarding the recommendations of the Thai clerical authorities, Sister Serafina decided to leave the well-established church to which she had been originally assigned and switched to a shack in one of the largest slums in the capital, where she joined Father Nicola. Here, the two missionaries laid the foundations of the Saint Jacob's Centre, which was registered in 2005 as an NGO officially recognised by the Thai government.

In this context, it is important to provide a brief description of the policies of the Thai state with regard to foreign non-governmental organisations. In Thailand, NGOs are officially treated as secular, apolitical entities, defined in terms of international law as 'having the objective of providing assistance to or promoting the development of a person, a group of persons or a juridical person and/or a government agency or a state enterprise, in conformity with the development policy and security of Thailand' (Ministry of Labour and Social Welfare of Thailand 1998). That is, NGOs are supposed to have nothing to do with either missionary proselytism or politics. These legal definitions do not include religious NGOs or faith-based organisations as specific sub-categories. Christian and Catholic NGOs can be recognised as such only through their names. On paper, all aid organisations are listed under the same secular labels, *ongkon* ('NGO') or *munithi* ('foundation'). Accordingly, organisations such as Saint Jacob's are grouped with non-religious NGOs in a category defined in pseudo-legalistic terms, such as: 'charitable foundation providing social relief services to disabled children and promoting children's rights'. In specifying limits and defining boundaries in this way, the Thai state has attempted to implement specific 'techno-politics' (Ferguson 1994; Li 2007; Feener and Scheer 2018) – to turn political and religious elements of potential interference into a technical, inert matter. However, NGOs such as Saint Jacob's actually do far more than simply assist underprivileged children (Bolotta 2018b).

As Sister Serafina explained, there are a number of reasons why Catholic missionaries are increasingly turning to the aid sector, adopting organisational forms that are nominally secular: 'The first reason that we asked to be recognised as an NGO was in order to have legal protection. We deal with children here. Should a tragic event occur, we would be exposed to serious risk and would have no legal recognition. Secondly, this allows us to access the benefits that Thai welfare grants to humanitarian organisations according to international law'. Being recognised as an NGO – a secular organisation without any official religious connotations – gives missionaries legal, economic, political and religious advantages. Having the status of child-focused NGO means that as well as receiving donations from religious and missionary related channels, Saint Jacob's and its House of the Little Ones is eligible to apply for public funding and international donations from secular organisations. Since Nicola's and Serafina's mission has been labelled 'humanitarian', funds from religious sources have been supplemented by funds from secular sources.

Running an NGO promoting children's rights in a generic sense has also generated both political and religious benefits. Firstly, it has allowed Nicola and Serafina, who are Catholic missionaries, to have free access to the pastoral care of the Buddhist poor in Bangkok. As in other Asian contexts where the presence of foreign Christian missionaries is prohibited by law,[12] the technical transnational language of rights and the status of NGO provides missionaries with a legal and institutional umbrella that allows them to circumvent state regulations and enter political arenas that were previously not 'missionable'. Moreover, the label of 'NGO' has made it possible for Nicola and Serafina to reposition themselves not only in respect to the Thai state, but also in relation to the Thai clergy, thereby gaining an autonomous space to articulate the specific ethics of their Catholicism,

---

12 This is the case in the communist countries of China, Laos and Vietnam and in countries where Buddhist politics take particular forms that restrict missionary activities, such as Bhutan, Sri Lanka, Myanmar and Cambodia.

which contrast with the pastoral guidelines and 'Thaified' approach of the Catholic Church in Bangkok.

For Father Nicola and Sister Serafina, the language of children's rights which their NGO officially espouses represents a technical and juridical evolution of Christian charity, an evolution that, in Serafina's words, lacks 'soul'. Father Nicola and Sister Serafina challenge Thai normative Catholicism by taking shelter under the NGO system's secular umbrella, while simultaneously infusing its mechanistic and technical clockwork with their political and theological 'soul'. For both missionaries this is embodied by *dek salam*.

Poor children as the cross of Christ

Like Father Nicola, Sister Serafina does not just provide medical care to disabled children. While the heart of the work done at Saint Jacob's is the spiritual formation of *dek salam*, the House of the Little Ones' endeavour is what may be described as the 'religiopolitical conscientisation' of the mothers of disabled children. As she explained:

> We work as a family here! This is based on the Gospels. We're all God's daughters. If I only provided disabled children with medical care, that would just be passive assistentialism. It is, rather, the spiritual formation of mothers that is at the core of the House of the Little Ones. That is its fuel. I do not force my religion upon others. I do not bind them with chains. If it is of any advantage to them, as humans, to reflect on the Word, my mission is accomplished.
> (Serafina, September 2011)

Serafina engages the mothers of disabled children in daily Bible-study sessions focused on 'childhood' and 'poverty', encouraging collective reflection upon the evangelical meaning of these notions in the context of Buddhist Thailand. Serafina's central aim is to promote a semantic re-conceptualisation of childhood, disability and poverty, from 'embodied evidence of bad *karma*' to what she describes as the 'incarnated evidence of God's love'. Slum women with disabled children face triple discrimination because of their status as the mothers of disabled children, slum dwellers and women, but Sister Serafina tries to prove them that their condition is actually particularly sacred, that their children are God's gifts rather than a curse, and that they have the right to claim dignity for themselves and their children.

For Serafina, the role of children is pivotal to the Christian concept of salvation. As the 'last' in Thai society, as 'Christ's Cross' – which is how the nun describes them – disabled children benefit especially from God's emotional attention and love. Serafina works every day with mothers on the (re)signification of childhood and disability, along these lines: 'These children may be handicapped in our eyes, but in God's eyes they are beloved. Jesus identifies himself in children, in the poor. That's why He scares powerful people'.

Serafina aims to frame the social problems associated with the conditions in which disabled children live in the slums as shaped by broader economic, political and religious worldly dimensions:

> The real problem these women have to cope with is not their children's disability. It is rather the secondary cascade of effects produced by the discrimination they face as poor slum mothers. In the slum, a child's disability becomes an issue because of the low level of economic assistance they receive from the state and because of the political and economic factors forcing peasants from the north and northeast to migrate to Bangkok slums in order to survive. In the context of Thai monarchical Buddhism they were already at the bottom of the social hierarchy well before getting pregnant. Their children's disability just worsens their socio-political and economic marginalisation and it is not surprising that this is explained by Thai rich urban Buddhists in distorted religious terms – by referring to a law of *karma* that preserves their own privileged social status. I do not necessarily want to convert them. They can still be Buddhist if their Buddhism is a good form of Buddhism. But I want them to feel liberated from the oppression of the state Buddhism of 'Thainess'. (Serafina, September 2011)

Her harsh criticism is aimed not only at the Thai state's religiopolitical strategies of poverty governance; it also hints at mainstream, Thai Catholicism, regarded as a variation of the former. Serafina contrasts royalist state Buddhism and 'Thaified' Catholicism with poverty-oriented Christianity and Buddhism, which she regards as authentic, good forms of the two religions. This important distinction is also echoed in Father Nicola's words:

> We foreign missionaries are the only ones dealing with poor, miserable people in Bangkok. Catholic schools for rich Buddhists are almost always headed by Thai manager-nuns, while most Thai priests' perception of the urban poor is that they have merited the consequences of their own sins [in Thai language *bap* – the same word is used to refer to the concept of Buddhist demerit]. Even though they sometimes collect money for the poor, the latter are still viewed as inferior sinners. There's a lot of work to do here. (Father Nicola, July 2012)

In their criticism of the Thai Catholic Church, the two missionaries highlight the historical contradiction between the sacralisation of poverty in the Gospels and the Church's immense wealth. There is a potentially relevant analogy here, between the recommendations for a 'sufficiency economy' (*sethakit pho phiang*) made by an extremely rich Buddhist monarch and the hypocritical praise of the ennobling qualities of poverty put forward historically by the Vatican.

However, despite Nicola's and Serafina's religiopolitical ardour, even the Saint Jacob's Centre exemplifies those same theological-political tensions that their invectives call out. On closer inspection, their Catholic NGO works as a channel for royalist Catholicism focused on 'Thainess' as well as for a political theology of childhood revolving around the sacred primacy of *dek salam* in the Heavenly Kingdom. Following a directive from the Archdiocese of Bangkok, the headquarters and foster homes of Saint Jacob's are located, institutionally, within a very special Catholic parish, Our Lady of Refuge, which is considered by the local faithful – mostly royalist, middle-class, Sino-Thai citizens – to be a 'monarchic church', blessed by none other than the recently deceased King Bhumibol (Rama IX).

OUR LADY OF REFUGE: A MONARCHIC CHURCH?

Our Lady of Refuge, a concrete building in the shape of a cross that awkwardly adapts a Romanesque form to Thai traditional architecture, is led by Father Paul, an American missionary known for his conservative position, one that is not controversial as is Nicola's and Serafina's barely-concealed critical orientation. Coexistence between the parish priest, as the Thai clergy's man on the spot, and Saint Jacob's radical missionaries is not easy. As NGO directors, however, Nicola and Serafina have a degree of autonomy.

The church of Our Lady of Refuge boasts an exclusive relationship with King Bhumibol (Rama IX). Indeed, when the parish was first consecrated in 1974, Rama IX oversaw the ritual, as 'protector of all religions'. The church has both paintings, sculptures and artistic themes from Catholic imaginaries and iconography and also decorative elements that evoke King Bhumibol's participation in the opening ceremony (*phithi poet*), both inside and outside the church. In the lateral nave, a gigantic portrait immortalises a young Rama IX on the church altar, mysteriously illuminated by golden light. Behind him there is an enormous crucifix. In the garden facing the main entrance of the church are two spectacular trees that King Bhumibol planted. These are Bodhi trees – the tree beneath which (Thais believe) Lord Buddha meditated and received enlightenment.

In February 2014, on the 40th anniversary of the founding of the church, Father Paul decided to make the royal association of 'Our Lady of Refuge' even more obvious: he had pieces of marble placed all around the two Bodhi trees to form sacred enclosures. Within these enclosures, a plate was fixed on each tree trunk. The plates had blue backgrounds (the colour of the monarchy) with an inscription on each in golden letters stating clearly that: 'His Royal Highness Venerable King Bhumibol planted this tree on 16 February 2517 [1974]'. Catholic materiality is here expressed by, and encapsulated in, royal symbolism, which represents the fundamental basis of 'Thainess'.

In the eyes of Thai Catholics, Our Lady of Refuge is therefore a 'monarchic church', a doubly sacred place where Catholic and Indo-Buddhist cosmologies converge, reinforcing each other. Thai parishioners revered Rama IX with near religious devotion. Some of them created household altars at home, where they worshipped icons of Jesus alongside Chinese and Indian gods, Buddhist monks and Thai kings, especially Bhumibol and Chulalongkorn (Rama V) – a common practice in Thai popular religion (see e.g. Pattana Kitiarsa 2005). Away from the church, it was common for many to trade crucifixes, holy pictures and statues as magic charms, analogous to Buddhist amulets – a practice that demonstrates that even Catholic objects and symbols have been absorbed into an amalgam of hybrid, decentralised supernatural beliefs, economies, and expressions which echoes what some scholars have referred to as 'marketised religiosity' or 'commercialised religion' (P.A. Jackson 1999; Satha-Anand 1994; Pattana Kitiarsa 2005). More importantly, I often heard Thai parishioners at Our Lady of Refuge presenting Jesus Christ and Rama IX as equal symbols of divine morality (*khunatham*), sacrifice (*sia sala*), and charismatic power (*bun-barami*).

Father Paul, like most people in Thailand, was aware that the Buddhist King held a sacred place in his parishioners' hearts, but he tended to turn a blind eye to beliefs and practices that orthodox Catholicism might interpret as idolatry, in order to avoid promoting what one might describe as 'cosmological competition' between the Christian God and the Thai monarchy. He regarded this undesired competition as an uphill struggle that could cause the Thai Catholic Church to lose its already exceedingly small number of followers; and it might lead less mindful priests to walk the tightrope of Thailand's *lèse majesté* law, which is among the strictest in the world (e.g. Streckfuss 2010).

The Thai faithful encountered the *dek salam* living at Saint Jacob's at the weekly Sunday mass. Their attitude towards the guests of the Catholic NGO was quite different from that of Father Nicola and Sister Serafina. Children who are 'not properly dressed, always unkempt [*mai riaproi*], dirty, undisciplined and constantly giggling', to quote a Thai deacon at Our Lady of Refuge, should not, in their view, be allowed to enter holy places. Their regular participation in the mass upset Thai churchgoers, who made a formal protest about it to the church's pastoral council. Since then, the Thai staff at Saint Jacob's have been instructed to place the *dek salam* in an isolated area of the church, separated from the rest of the faithful: a women's gallery over the side nave – an architectural element originally intended to accommodate cloistered female communities, which is accessible only by an independent, lateral staircase. In this way, removed from the sight of other churchgoers, the 'thugs of Saint Jacob's' are tolerated, once a week, by the wealthy parish community.

In 2013, the charitable work done by the Saint Jacob's Centre with *dek salam* was mentioned in a popular prime time Thai TV show broadcast weekly on Channel 9[13] called 'I love Thailand' (*chan rak meuang thai*). The pastoral council at Our Lady of Refuge benefits from the membership of a retired, high-ranking Thai military man. Thanks to this man's influential connections, the Catholic NGO was selected by the show director as a virtuous example of foreign dedication to the Thai kingdom. Father Paul seized this opportunity. It was no coincidence that Father Nicola was on leave at the time – and although she did not have her mentor to rely on Sister Serafina had no choice but to accept, with some resentment, Father Paul's decision. During the filming I was carrying out research at the Centre, which – for the occasion – was set up to convey a sense of patriotism and national loyalty, as evidence of the trans-confessional and trans-cultural validity of 'Thainess', which was presented by the national media as a moral model that was globally relevant and from which even Catholics draw inspiration. The *dek salam* of Saint Jacob's who were involved in the shoot had been prepared by the NGO workers to present traditional Thai dances, music, cookery, and Buddhist meditation sessions (*nang samathi*), with no reference to Christianity, nor to the Catholic rituals (prayers, mass, etc.) they were usually involved in.

Halfway through the film, Father Paul leads the film crew to the church. It is a pivotal, startling moment. As the camera lingers on an intimate close-up of the painting of the king – an irrefutable sign of the association between the monarchy and the church – Father Paul makes haste to remind the audience of the royal status of his parish: 'This church holds the proud distinction of having been inaugurated by King Bhumibol. His Majesty is an example of moral rectitude and mercy, a role model and a source of national cohesion for the Thai people'.

I was quite troubled by the enormous gap between this representation of Saint Jacob's and the place where I was actually doing my research. This echoed the feeling of having a split self that I had often encountered in my young informants – forced to conform to a public identity that contrasted sharply with their own private sense of self, which needed to be carefully concealed behind the 'good Thai child' mask. The footage ended with the host of the TV show making an ironic comment about himself: 'After getting to know Father Paul and

---

13 Channel 9 is managed by the Mass Communication Organisation of Thailand (MCOT), a public broadcaster running several TV and radio stations.

the Saint Jacob's Centre, I feel very embarrassed. He is definitely more of a Thai than I am myself!'.

Our Lady of Refuge's Thaified Catholicism is therefore the ideological and institutional framework within which the more critical religiosity of the Saint Jacob's Centre sits rather uncomfortably. The intimate relationship between Father Nicola and the *dek salam* would be likely to spark outrage and generate disorientation among the Thai parishioners at Our Lady of Refuge. 'Priests should not let girls touch them!'. 'It is inappropriate [*mai mosom*] for *phra* to stoop to the same level as children! Father Nicola should make the *dek salam* more disciplined!'– comments like these were often made by the faithful during the weekly Sunday mass. While for Father Nicola and Sister Serafina the *dek salam* embodied God's divine spirit, for wealthy Catholics and Buddhists alike they were just sinful 'thugs' who needed to be re-aligned, to transform them into 'good Thai children'.

POLITICAL THEOLOGIES OF CHILDHOOD IN THAI CATHOLICISM

The relationship between childhood and religious morality has long been hotly debated. Clearly, interpretations of children as inherently sinful subjects are not a prerogative of Thai Catholicism. Similar theories have informed the education of children for a large part of European history, at least until the advent of the 'innocent child' in the Romantic period (Cunningham 2014). Theologians have traced these theories back to Saint Augustine's arguments about the peculiar salience of sin during childhood (e.g. Bunge 2001). As Bunge and Wall (2011: 89) argued: 'Augustine unites a sense of human sinfulness [...] with Plato's view, articulated in his *Republic* and *Laws*, that children are primarily unruly and irrational animals in need of civilising. Augustine thus defines infancy, childhood and adolescence as prime (though not exclusive) exhibits of human original sin'. Historian Colin Heywood (2001) further observed that this definition of childhood emphasises not only children's 'depraved and impulsive' nature but also the imperative of their unconditional submission to parental authority, especially that of the father. The idea that parents must discipline their children, because they are bearers of sin, mirrors power relationships between the clergy and the laity in society, with the parent–child relationship exemplifying God's moral control over the lay faithful (as God's sinful children). This religious formulation also has direct political implications for monarchic political theory: the triangular sacralisation of God, King (God's representative in the world) and

Father (God's representative within the family) served as the symbolic basis of *ancien régime* Catholic absolute monarchies (e.g. Monod 1999; Strathern 2019).

As I have shown, an 'inculturated' (Thaified) version of this Catholic approach to childhood found particularly fertile ground in the Buddhist Thailand's fatherly royalism. Consider how the director of Phra Mae Marie private school, a Thai Catholic nun, articulated her thoughts on the *dek salam* of the Saint Jacob's Centre:

> Some Catholic private schools refuse to take these children [*dek salam*] because the majority of our students are well-off, and rich children do not usually want to mix with slum dwellers – they cause too much trouble, are dirty and undisciplined. Our school has nevertheless welcomed a few from Father Nicola's Saint Jacob's Centre. Even *dek salam* are God's children, although the presence of sin is more evident in them. *Bap* ['sin'] has hit *dek salam* more than others. While this is not a reason not to help them, Father Nicola should be much stricter with these kids.   (Sister Na, June 2014)

This Thai nun's Catholic interpretation of human sin overlaps with the Buddhist notion of 'demerit' – *bap*, indeed, is the Thai term used in reference to both concepts. While in (Buddhist) state schools the situation in which *dek salam* find themselves is often explained as based on their negative *karma*, in Catholic private schools they are seen as embodying sin, which is hypostasised as, and demonstrated by, the poverty and improper conduct of slum dwellers. Both perspectives on *dek salam* regard children's social status as being a consequence of their supposedly congenital spiritual impurity. These religiopolitical elaborations of sin and *karma* thus converge in de-politicising poor children's marginality, while at the same time providing moral arguments in support of their inferior position within the Thai social body.

By contrast, Father Nicola's and Sister Serafina's theological-political constructions of childhood see *dek salam* as the 'last' in (Thai) society, and therefore as being 'God's beloved children' who need to be liberated, an approach reflecting the historical transformations that Catholicism has itself undergone in its expansion, indigenisation, and decentralisation, especially after the Second Vatican Council. The 'Christian seed' planted in the Global South during the colonial period has in fact produced hybrid fruits:[14] contextualised and indigenised re-inventions of Christianity, often in conflict with the Vatican centre's dogmatic purity, as is the case for the various messianic and millenaristic movements that have emerged in opposition to colonial and post-colonial regimes across the world (see e.g. Lanternari 2003). A range of liberation theologies, including Latin-American

---

14 On Asian transformations of Christianity, see for example Zupanov (1995), and Young and Seitz (2013).

liberation theology, have taken shape in association with these movements.[15] Within this broad and diversified exegetic framework, neoliberal capitalism, socio-economic inequalities and undemocratic practices have been theologically contested as violations of the Divine Plan (e.g. Gutiérrez 1981; Boff 1977), while human liberation has been conceptualised as requiring the political 'conscientisation of the poor' (e.g. Freire 2011). It is in the context of this theological-political bedrock, embodied – in the view of many analysts – by the current head of the Catholic Church, the Argentinian Pope Francis,[16] that conceptualisations of marginal childhood such as those of Nicola and Serafina have arisen.

Father Nicola's political theology of *phu noi* ('small people') has been gaining particular traction among second and third generation 'non-Thai' Catholics and 'development missionaries' engaged in humanitarian work in the north and northeast of Thailand.[17] Take the example of Father Niphot Thienvihan, born in the north to a Catholic–Buddhist mixed couple, and currently leading the Interreligious and Cultural Affairs department of Chiang Mai Diocese. The priest has been working with *chao khao* ('hill tribes') for decades, based on Paulo Freire's 'pedagogy of the oppressed' (Freire 2011), and he is now attempting to revitalise what he calls the 'wisdom' of ethnic minorities (rice rituals, local cults, and subsistence lifestyles) as 'an antidote to modern Thai society's political economy, ethnic nationalism, and materialistic world-views' – with the aim of 're-enchanting' relationships between humans and nature (Niphot Thienvihan 2016). In an interview, Father Niphot stressed the importance for *phu yai* to learn from (ethnic and generational) *phu noi*: 'So-called *phu yai* – priests, monks, activists and state officials – should approach the wonderful wisdom and ways of life of the ethnic minorities humbly. Thai adults should do likewise with children, God's beloved sons. They'd learn a lot that way'.

These development missionaries' discourses about, and behaviours toward, *dek salam* are radically different from those poor children are exposed to in their

---

15 Other politically-engaged theological reformulations of Christianity include, for instance: the 1960s worker–priest movement in Western Europe; Martin Luther King's black theology (Gibellini 1978); Filipino Charlie Avila's farmer theology (Avila 1976); and emerging strands of feminist theology (Russell 1974; Miller-McLemore 2001).

16 During an exclusive interview with the Italian newspaper *Il Messaggero* (Il Messaggero 2014), Pope Francis declared: 'Marx did not invent anything. Communists stole our flag'. Themes related to liberation theology, such as 'neoliberal capitalism as the economy of exclusion' and 'the privileged place of the poor among God's people' have been also widely addressed by Pope Francis, in documents such as the apostolic exhortation *Evangeli Gaudium* (2013).

17 'Counter-indigenisation' trends on the part of local clergy and communities in reaction to 'vernacularisation' work driven largely by European missionaries is not specific to Thailand (e.g. Brown and Feener 2018).

public interactions with Thai (both Buddhist and Christian) *phu yai*, generating destabilising micro-political effects on dominant Thai social and ethnic hierarchies.

FINAL CONSIDERATIONS

The close historical link between Catholic missionaries and the Thai monarchy has caused normative Catholicism to be adapted and 'inculturated' according to the officially secular concept of 'Thainess', making the local Catholic church a pro-monarchy, semi-capitalist institution ruling prestigious hospitals and private schools attended by upper-middle class, Buddhist citizens. Nevertheless, with the advent of the humanitarian post-Second World War era of development Thai Catholicism has been pluralised by the activities of 'development missionaries' working in the country's most marginal areas, as heads of formally secular NGOs such as the Saint Jacob's Centre. These are mostly foreign missionaries or newly ordained 'non-Thai' priests from Thailand's northern and northeastern regions who, like Father Nicola and Sister Serafina, take advantage of the NGO system's techno-political framework to acquire a religious and political space in which to operate with respect to both the Thai state and the Thai Catholic clergy. By doing this, they are presenting a theological challenge to Thai Catholicism and politically contesting the national Buddhist discourse on the 'good Thai child'.

As suggested by anthropologist Louise Burkhart, 'the missionary is not only dialoguing with those who want to convert, but he is himself "missionised", he builds a strong bond with the natives against the settlers and the church hierarchy and assumes the natives' point of view while still keeping to the purpose of his mission' (Burkhart 1989: 15, cited in Cuturi [ed.] 2004: 41). Interaction with the Christian world can, indeed, teach not only submission but also resistance and dissent. The fact that Catholicism contains both these possibilities may be observed in other missionised Asian contexts. David Mosse (2012), in his study of Christianity and caste society in India, for instance, has explored the historical genealogy of the Tamil Nadu Dalit's 'Brahmanic Christianity'. Mosse highlighted the conflict between high society 'Hinduised' Catholicism (which was accommodated to the caste system culture by the first 17th century Jesuits) and the anti-caste political movement of contemporary Dalit Catholicism, stating that: 'Even while the Church tolerated or helped reproduce hierarchical orders of caste, participation in Christian religion (a realm that tutored explicit meaning and symbolic association) inculcated capacities for the manipulation of symbolic meanings or transactions that would be used (alongside political action) by subaltern groups' (Mosse 2012: 20).

In Thailand, however, there is not, as yet, an organised anti-structural move-ment of 'non-Thai' Catholics. Elements of dissent are expressed, instead, by 'development missionaries' working within the global dynamics of NGOs, devel-opmentalist and humanitarian interventions (e.g. Bolotta, Fountain and Feener 2020; Scheer, Fountain and Feener [eds] 2018; Clarke 2012; Fountain, Bush and Feener [eds] 2015).

Even within Thai Buddhism, despite the centralised Buddhist *sangha*'s pro-'Thainess' position, a number of socially-engaged Buddhist monks have been working with local communities against state-led development projects, putting forward worldly interpretations of salvation that emphasise the socio-political and economic causes of *dukkha* (grief) and the necessity to democratise *nirvana* by promoting social justice. Scholars have pointed to clear parallels between Christian liberation theologies and Asian Buddhist movements of liberation, as both envision soteriology as a predominantly mundane affair (e.g. Queen and King [eds] 1996: 5; Bobilin 1988). Somewhat along the same lines, Thai activist Sulak Sivaraksa has recognised socially-engaged Buddhism and Leonardo Boff's theology of liberation as sharing very similar convictions (Swearer 1996: 221–222). If we follow this argument, we may decide that just as Father Nicola's theological-political approach is critical of the Thai Church's royalist Catholicism, so *phra* Payom's socially-engaged Buddhism may also be regarded as being critical of 'Thainess' and state Buddhism. However, as I have shown, these distinctions are not necessarily obvious, as the boundaries between the two are blurred.

I would argue that the emerging polarisation that characterises both Cathol-icism and Buddhism actually reproduces, in religious terms, the political divide that exists in Thailand, which is itself an outcome of historical disputes between Bangkok and the rural periphery; between (Central) Thai and 'non-Thai' groups; and between monarchy and democracy. During 'yellow' protests against Yingluck Shinawatra's government, a number of Thai nuns in Bangkok took the streets alongside royalist groups in support of a military coup. However, in con-trast to this, in February 2014 the Catholic Bishops' Conference of Thailand, through Joseph Chusak Sirisutil, Bishop of Nakhon Ratchasima in the Thai-Lao northeast, implicitly opposed further military intervention in democratic poli-tics by encouraging Catholics to exercise their right to vote (Prachathai 2014c). This is the complex context within which Father Nicola and Sister Serafina stubbornly persist in pursuing their child-focused mission.

The *dek salam* of the Saint Jacob's Centre are well able to recognise ideologi-cal and behavioural discrepancies between the various *phu yai* with whom they interact. These differences in the positionalities of their caregivers pluralise poor children's experiences of socialisation. While some of these experiences confirm the urban poor's socio-economic, moral and ethnic subordination, others open up a space for criticism and for the construction of a particular kind of political subjectivity in the shadow of the Thai state hegemonic structures.

Saint Jacob's Centre provides *dek salam* in Bangkok with an alternative education setting. The affective bond between the children and the Catholic charity's radical priest can permit the *dek salam* to experience their selves in a way that is distinct from the stigmatised view of the ethnic poor promoted by the Thai state. Before progressing to the heart of this matter, however, we still need to examine yet another social context that has a significant influence on public discourses about 'Thai childhood' and poor children's social experiences: the Bangkok slum into which they are born.

CHAPTER 4

Slum Children as Victims

At sundown, after the day's work, the railway tracks became a meeting point for the inhabitants of the slum (Figure 5). One evening, Fon, an intelligent six-year-old girl, was standing nervously in front of a group of women, like an actor on stage waiting to perform. Affectionately holding her aunt's baby, she suddenly spoke: 'My life's really hard. I have many problems at home. I am not happy. I have nobody to play with and nobody to take care of me. I'd like to go to Saint Jacob's Centre!'. To my surprise, the women in the audience, including her mother, responded to her solemn declaration of discomfort with amused expressions and satisfied smiles, accompanied by laudatory comments such as: 'Look how good she is!' The women's compliments seemed to please the girl, who was now radiant, encouraging her to reproduce the same *mise-en-scène* of 'victimhood' in progressively convincing ways. Fon was evidently following a script she had long been rehearsing in preparation for what would amount to an audition with those running Saint Jacob's, who were coming to the slum the following week to evaluate her application. Fon actually had many friends in the slum. In most situations, she would never have dreamt of complaining like this to the *phu yai* ('big people') in the slum. These complaints were uniquely reserved for the *farang* (white people) – a lesson Fon had learnt by observing her (beloved) mother's and other women's interactions with NGO workers in the slum.

This chapter examines the multiple theories of childhood to which *dek salam* are exposed in today's Bangkok slums. As I will demonstrate, a vernacular conceptualisation of children as *phu noi* ('small people') coexists with government stigmatisation of *dek salam* as a social danger. At the same time, children are politicised, from a humanitarian point of view, as 'victims' whose rights must be protected. Since the 1980s, NGOs have enriched the social environment in which *dek salam* live with new socio-political discourses, transforming city slums from allegedly closed communities of rural-to-urban migrants into transnational settings of development and child protection where local, national and global interests over land and property converge and clash. I would argue that humanitarian representations of childhood suffering are at the core of this conflict.

After briefly giving some context relating to the slums of Bangkok, I will focus on domestic child-rearing and parenting practices in Akhan Daeng, the slum from which most of the children I met at Saint Jacob's came. These practic-

Photo: Giuseppe Bolotta.

Figure 5. Life along the railway tracks. Bangkok slums, April 2013. Colour version, p. 230

es are embedded in matrifocal networks of communal childcare and informed by parental cultural beliefs that reflect the rural and ethnic origin of many slum dwellers. I will then discuss how the 'children's rights' policies of NGOs have been reconfiguring the (local) political economy of motherhood in the slum, generating an (international) moral economy that revolves around humanitarian constructions of slum children's (alleged) suffering. I will argue that thanks to their ability to engage productively with the humanitarian representation of their children as 'victims', mothers are becoming the new political 'brokers' (Lewis and Mosse [eds] 2006: 11) of the urban poor. Childhood constitutes, in fact, symbolic and political capital – not only for the Thai state, for socially-engaged Buddhist monks, for Christian missionaries and for NGOs, but also for slum dwellers themselves, especially the children's mothers.

THE SLUMS OF BANGKOK: A BRIEF HISTORY

The key processes that have shaped Bangkok's contemporary social and spatial organisation began soon after World War II, known as Thailand's 'development boom' season. In the midst of the Cold War, Thai military regimes received a

great deal of economic support from the US and from international organisations including the World Bank and the United Nations (UN). This caused the
country to become known in the 1990s as the 'East Asian miracle' (World Bank
1993: 138–142). Peasants from Thailand's rural areas (*khon ban nok*[1]) began
moving to the capital, seeking job opportunities in the ever-expanding economy
of the big city. For many, migration to Bangkok was their only chance of survival
in a country where the urban-rural gap remains a major problem, both economically and politically.

Between 1984 and 1994, Bangkok experienced the fastest economic growth
in the world (Unger 1998: 1).[2] With its international airport and port, and
containing as it did the headquarters of key financial institutions, international
companies, and most of the Thai industrial sector, the city aspired to overtake
Singapore and Hong Kong as Southeast Asia's regional economic centre (Askew
2002: 86–90). At the same time, economic inequalities increased substantially,
both within the city and between the capital and the rest of the country.[3] It was a
time of tremendous transformation, which turned Bangkok from a 'canal-based
settlement' into 'a key industrial city, a city of the poor, a city of the middle
classes and a tourist city' (Askew 2002: 49), and 'the world's most congested,
sprawling and polluted city' (Rimmer and Dick 2009: xvii).

Landowners played an important role in the creation of slums.[4] Some
landlords, both private and public, held on to their land instead of selling it to al-

1   *Khon ban nok* ('people from rural areas') is the term used by urban residents (*khon meuang*)
    to describe rural-to-urban migrants, including slum dwellers. The dichotomy between *khon
    meuang* and *khon ban nok* reflects perceptions of class and ethnic stratification in a rapidly
    developing Thai society.
2   In 2002, according to official statistics (which are underestimates), the total population of
    Bangkok was 6,320,174 people, 10.4% of the whole Thai population (Source: National
    Statistical Office 2000). In 2010, 17.5 million people resided in the metropolitan region of
    Bangkok, about 28% of the total population of the country. It is estimated that the proportion
    of the population living in urban areas in Thailand will grow from 32.3% in 2005 to 40% in
    2025. The population of Bangkok is expected to reach 30 million by 2025. The United Nations
    has estimated that by around 2050 the urban population of Thailand could be greater than
    43 million (United Nations 2009). Since Bangkok is the main urban centre of the country
    (the second-largest city based on demographic density, Chiang Mai, has a population of only
    142,000 inhabitants), these estimates anticipate a near future in which Bangkok becomes one
    of the most densely populated megalopolises in the world.
3   Statistics regarding the internal distribution of GDP (Gross Domestic Product) demonstrate
    these inequalities very effectively: in 1986 only 46.8% of the Thai GDP was in Bangkok, while
    in 1990 the percentage in Bangkok grew to 52.6% (Source: Office of the National Economic
    and Social Development Board statistical data bank).
4   The UN identifies a slum household 'as a group of individuals living under the same roof in
    an urban area lacking one or more of the following: 1. Durable housing of a permanent nature
    that protects against extreme climate conditions. 2. Sufficient living space, which means

low infrastructural development (Sopon Pornchokchai 1998: 424–425). Those who had suitable land built small wooden houses, renting out cramped quarters to migrants coming into the city looking for affordable housing (Askew 1994: 102). In the 1970s, public authorities such as the National Housing Authority (NHA) and the Community Organisations Development Institute (CODI) were established to tackle the problem of these informal settlements, generating an increasingly bureaucratic rationalisation of the urban fabric (Johnson 2006: 89). Paradoxically, state initiatives aimed at infrastructural development, the drainage of degraded areas, and urban relocation were implemented in conjunction with increasing evictions (Somsook Boonyabancha 1983). In 1981, at the initiative of the NHA, the word *salam*, derived from the English word 'slum', was replaced with the less loaded term *chumchon aeat* ('crowded communities') (CDO 2002). This semantic redefinition was part of an attempt on the part of the state to conceal and subsume its strategies of urban poverty governance under the official heading of 'development policy' (see e.g. Boonlert Visetpricha 2008; Elinoff 2014; Herzfeld 2003, 2016).

A 2007 survey by Bangkok Metropolitan Administration (BMA) showed that there were 1,944 slums in Bangkok, with a total population of two million individuals – approximately 20% of the entire population of the city (BMA 2007).[5] The uninterrupted growth of *chumchon aeat* is linked to the inability of the government and the market to provide low-income populations with adequate housing. Policies on slum relocation and eviction have proven ineffective. Furthermore, slums are essential to the urban economy in terms of providing micro-businesses, informal labour and minor services (these range from food vending to small scale manufacturing; from waste recycling to transport services; and from the provision of financial credit to illegal activities such as drug dealing, gambling and prostitution) (e.g. see Askew 2002; Sopranzetti 2017b).

Slums are publicly described as places of degradation and criminality, and as a threat to urban and national security. In fact, the demonisation of city slums, as places that are inaccessible to state surveillance, constitutes a widespread rhetoric across the Global South and serves to justify massive eviction campaigns

---

not more than three people sharing the same room. 3. Easy access to safe water in sufficient amounts at an affordable price. 4. Access to adequate sanitation in the form of a private or public toilet shared by a reasonable amount of people. 5. Security of tenure that prevents forced evictions' (United Nations Habitat 2006).

5   In Thailand the percentage of slum dwellers is lower than other Asian countries, for example, Bangladesh, where 70.8% of urban residents live in slums (United Nations 2010). However, in rough numbers Bangkok is the city with the highest number of inhabitants residing in slums in the world, more than Kolkata (1,490,811), and double compared to Chennai (747,936) (Office for the Registrar General of India 2001).

officially rationalised as measures to fight criminality and restore the 'beauty' of cities (Davis 2006). In this context, slum children occupy a special place: they are depicted either as victims or as a danger to society.

In public discourses, including within the Thai academic world (e.g. Withitan 2004; Somphong Čhitradab 2007), *dek salam* are associated with certain fundamental traits: drug abuse; uncontrolled and precocious sexuality; criminal behaviour; and gangs.[6] It follows from these narratives that if *dek salam* are not protected from negative influences, they are likely to become immoral and dangerous citizens, deprived of a 'natural childhood' – in other words, 'insufficiently Thai'. According to this analysis, school and a 'healthy' family life (contrasting with children's lives in the slum and with their peer groups) emerge as the only solutions for the promotion of children's social and emotional health (e.g. Burman 2017; Bloch 2003; Canella and Viruru 2004). NGOs, together with (or in opposition to) state agencies such as CODI, thus became major actors in the effort to turn *dek salam* into healthy and happy 'Thai children'.

Despite these accounts of slum children's alleged unhappiness/dangerous nature, I myself found, during my explorations of the Bangkok slums, that the children seemed perfectly comfortable in their home environment, which – despite its material poverty – presented a level of social cohesion that the outside world of the metropolis lacked.

MATRIFOCALITY, COMMUNAL PARENTING, AND CHILDREN'S (IN)DEPENDENCE IN AKHAN DAENG

Beginning in 2009, I carried out field research in Akhan Daeng, one of the oldest slums in Bangkok. Located in the north of the capital, Akhan Daeng hosts about 4,000 residents. It is bordered by the northern branch of the national railway to the north, east and west, and lies on one of the many canals (*khlong*) that run through Bangkok. The name of the slum (*akhan daeng*, 'red building') is drawn from a series of brick-coloured buildings that rise on one side of the railway track, originally destined for the railway employees who maintained the steam locomotives. In the years after World War Two, the railway provided local inhabitants with employment and a large number of people settled in and around this area, giving birth to Akhan Daeng.

---

6   As Mahony (2018: 32–36) has demonstrated, research published in English (often psychological, medical or epidemiological studies) also focuses mainly on the relationship between poor or ethnic minority children and socially deviant behaviour (see e.g. Cash 1999; Allen et al 2003; Morrison 2004; German et al 2006).

Photo: Giuseppe Bolota.

Figure 6. Akhan Daeng, May 2013. Colour version, p. 231

The sludgey marshland on which the wooden and tin-plated houses of the slum sit is visible on both sides of the sheds and cement paths built in the 1980s by NHA to promote internal mobility (Figure 6). Most of the houses are formally registered, and are supplied with water and electricity; however, the sewers are filled with rubbish and waste materials and are a vehicle for severe illnesses and bacterial infections. The general morphology of the settlement (houses next to each other, wooden or metal dividing walls, etc.) means that the stereotypical description of slums as 'urban villages' is quite a good one (see e.g. Korff 1986; Berner and Korff 1994). Here everything is audible, everything is public. During my stay in Akhan Daeng I was aware of conversations, movements, even of my neighbours' most intimate and private activities, as if they were taking place in the same small house I was in.

Most residents of the slum are ex-farmers from the north and northeast of Thailand, where matrilineal and matrilocal kinship patterns are deeply rooted, historically, among local ethnic groups (e.g. see Bowie 1992, 2008; Pairin Jotisakulratana 2012). Households very often included grandmothers, mothers, a large number of grandchildren, and foster children, with matrifocal families as the most common form of household.[7] Compared to rural villages, there is a marked

7   The concept of matrifocality has been used in different ways (e.g. R.T. Smith 1973; Tanner 1974; Pairin Jotisakulratana 2012; Vignato 2020). Here I follow Tanner's definition of matri-

absence of men in urban slums and the bond between mothers and children is privileged. Men in the slum are often described as unreliable providers, violent, and likely to spend all their time and money with friends (e.g. see Thorbek 1987).

According to anthropologist Mary Beth Mills (1999), migration to the city destabilises the normative village-based gender division of labour: while in rural villages needs were usually met through household-based cooperative production, in the city needs are met through wage labour. However, the work that is available in the city is mainly low-level service jobs and it is men and young unmarried women who find employment in these sectors. Therefore, in the context of Bangkok's urban economy, it is quite difficult for unskilled mothers to find employment and affordable accommodation. These ex-farmers are destined for the slum, the main source of labour for the informal economy within the big city. They can make money here, have a cheap place to live together with their children, and rely on motherly networks of female solidarity.

In Akhan Daeng, as in other places inhabited by ethnic minorities in Thailand, the care of young children was primarily communal. Children moved from house to house, cared for by the women of the neighbourhood, in order to suit individual needs. (Foster) mothers, grandmothers, sisters or neighbours covered newborns in baby wraps, worn on the back, or rocked them on fabric hammocks precariously hung from the ceiling while continuing their usual housework. Within the house, older siblings are the primary carers of babies, even while they are still very young themselves. Through these coordinated and collective activities, childcare is incorporated into daily routines.

This kind of parenting is not only a strategy for coping with poverty but also implies a vernacular and specific 'parental ethno-theory' (Harkness and Super 1992; Harkness and Super [eds] 1996; Levine 2003; Levine and Norman 2001). As some women in Akhan Daeng argued: 'It's fundamental that children do not attach themselves only to their mothers [*tid mae*]. They must not develop an exclusive dependence on their mothers, but must learn to socialise with everybody and with the wider social environment'. On the one hand, this view articulates memories of a rural sociality in which vis-à-vis relationships among individuals sharing a localised 'cultural intimacy' (Herzfeld 1997) were supported by communal management of the group's resources (including children). On the other, it refers to the Buddhist concept of attachment as the leading cause of suffering. Such a parental ethno-theory is perfectly adapted to the slum context, promoting children's flexible attachment to family configurations that are of

focality as a 'structure of feeling', an openness towards woman-centered social arrangements that are not necessarily connected to matrilineal kinship structures, although in the context of the north and northeast of Thailand these are prevalent.

necessity precarious, uncertain and scattered. It also shapes the children's selves within a social framework that is much wider and more emotionally diverse than the nuclear family, as the children develop multiple affective bonds within and outside their network of biological kin.

As a result of the way in which they grow up, children come to be engaged in activities usually considered appropriate for adults: collecting and recycling waste, selling food, even drug dealing. A 15-year-old boy called Dan told me candidly: 'Children are good at selling drugs because they are less subject to checks and run faster than grown-ups'. The autonomy that children have vis-à-vis adult caregivers was expressed in the central significance of friendships and of the peer group, collective formations that are commonly labelled 'gangs' in the wider world.

In Akhan Daeng, *dek salam* did not come across as innocent children who were particularly dependent on adults. Instead I, supposedly the 'adult', needed to learn from the 'children' in order to move around in their world, the slum.[8] During the first month of my stay in Akhan Daeng, I would have been lost without them. It was the children who taught me how to survive in the slum, teaching me small things that were mammoth tasks for me. When a moped approached at breakneck speed down an extremely narrow alley, for example, I was taught to simply enter the nearest house without knocking, to avoid being run over. I was also taught to equip myself with a stick, especially at nightfall, in order to fend off stray dogs attempting to assert their dominance. These were automatic gestures that the children made casually but that I had to learn, and it took a long time for me to adapt to them.

I found that the children saw the slum as a place without formal rules, unlike institutional contexts such as school and public spaces. In the maze of alleys that form the labyrinthine slum, they ran around barefoot, often scantily clad, independent and confident. As Phud (10 years old) put it: 'There aren't the rules that we have at school here. We are free to dress as we wish, to run and to play. Children living in the city outside the slum aren't free as we are here'.

However, even in Akhan Daeng children had to adjust their behaviour in the presence of adults (especially their mothers), in order to play the part of *phu noi*, although they did this in a strikingly different way here than in more public places. The dynamics of the relationship between *phu noi* and *phu yai* are rather unusual in the slum, and this deserves closer attention.

---

8   The level of autonomy enjoyed by the children living in the slums of Bangkok is not unusual; there are many examples of similar levels of autonomy in other parts of the world to be found in anthropological literature. As David Lancy has pointed out (2008), in Western hyper-industrialised countries children are effectively infantilised and childhood is progressively and indefinitely lengthened, while it is common in the Global South for childhood to be much shorter.

Reconfigured hierarchies: 'Non-Thai Tainess'

At first glance, even in Akhan Daeng, adults' attitude towards children seemed to reflect the same *phu yai–phu noi* role dynamic which is observable in public contexts, and that is prescribed by the 'good Thai child' state discourse. For example, Luam, a 65-year-old grandmother who had been living in Akhan Daeng for decades, claimed that: 'Children must listen to and help their dads and their mums, and other *phu yai*; they must obey them and respect them. Children who behave in that way are good children'. On closer inspection however, it was clear to me that inter-generational relationships within households in Akhan Daeng had certain specific characteristics, typical of private/informal spaces and common across Asia, that do not fully express the kind of adult–child relationship that is prescribed by the Thai state.[9]

There was gratuitous affection and behavioural flexibility in *phu yai–phu noi* relationships in the slum. These are totally absent in public contexts, where interactional ranks are fixed by official regulations that dictate mechanical, compulsory, even martial, behaviour. In Akhan Daeng, although there is certainly a recognition of the respect owed to *phu yai* and children behave differently when adults are present from when they are not, the relationship between *phu yai* and *phu noi* is not organised according to military-style discipline: children do not express systematic submission whenever they interact with adults whom they know, such as parents, other relatives or neighbours. When children meet adults, they do not always pay respect with the *wai* as they must when they meet teachers at school. They can also transgress their role as *phu noi* through irony (for example by affectionately teasing an adult, or using informal speech) without this type of behaviour being regarded as a serious violation of the moral order to be publicly sanctioned (as happens at school). Children are also permitted to experiment with adult roles, under supervision – something that would be impossible in a public context, where individuals are expected to conform to the prescribed hierarchy without any latitude for self-expression. In order to distinguish between *phu yai–phu noi* role dynamics in public contexts on the one hand, and in the slums on the other, I describe the latter as 'non-Thai Tainess' – a term that evokes the shared history and popular culture of Tai ethnic minorities prior to their political assimilation into the Central Thais' national culture (that is, 'Thainess').[10] During my stay in Akhan Daeng, I was

---

9   Similar adult–child relationship patterns have been described across Asia and express a cultural model of hierarchically-ranked relationships that is different from the usual pattern of hierarchical relationships in middle-class urban environments, especially (but not only) in Western countries. See, for example, Bambi Chapin's analysis of attachment in rural Sri Lanka (Chapin 2013).

10   As mentioned in the introduction, Thailand is inhabited by many ethno-linguistic groups (Thai-Lao, Northern Thai, Thai-Malay, etc.) who belong to the larger Tai family. The term

personally involved in the vernacular intimacy of this 'non-Thai Tainess', as Pan's *luk bun tham*[11] ('adopted son'). Pan was a 52-year-old single mother who had been living in the slum since the age of 30. She came from the Thai-Lao northeast, from Sisaket province on the Thai–Cambodia border, and had raised her five children on her own. Sympathetic to my research and – most likely – to my clumsy attempts as a young *farang* to adapt to slum life, Pan invited me to stay in her humble house. She worked very long hours in order to send her children to school. Acknowledging the sacrifice that their mother had made and was still making, the way in which Pan's children behaved in interactions with their mother was very much that of *phu noi* vis-à-vis *phu yai* (listening without breathing a single word, not bothering their mother with inappropriate requests, etc.), whereas they hardly performed as 'good Thai children' when they were with schoolteachers, whom they considered unworthy of respect. Over time, I myself came to be the subject of Pan's motherly concern: I felt it my duty to ask for her permission to go out, I helped her with the housework, and I accepted her rebukes without replying. On the other hand, she made sure I never missed a meal, and my belongings in her house never went unattended. When I ended up in hospital with dysentery, she stayed by my side, together with her children, sleeping on a chair for two nights. By the time I was discharged from the hospital, I had a true understanding of the meaning of 'filial gratitude'. I bowed down before her, touching her feet, embodying the position of *phu noi* unhesitatingly. Pan replied: 'We're here for you, my son'.

Children's gratitude towards parents is not only publicly prescribed; it is a moral feeling, which arises spontaneously in response to parental sacrifices and loving care. In the slum, it is these sacrifices and this loving care that are considered to be the true basis of the status of *phu yai*: the authority of caregivers is recognised as long as they prove their moral worth. When they become adults, it is up to children – especially daughters – to close the cycle, devoting themselves to their parents, who by that time are elderly and probably do not have a pension. If parents have proved to be 'true' *phu yai*, as Pan does, this role reversal occurs

---

'Tainess' is here used in reference to this common ancestry, and in contrast to 'Thainess', which was imposed by the Bangkok-based hegemonic group of the Central Thai as Thailand's national identity. Most slum dwellers in Akhan Daeng originate from the country's ethnic minority regions, and they are, therefore, of ethnic (especially Thai-Lao) minority background.

11 The term *luk bun tham* refers to a practice of informal adoption, intended as a compassionate and praiseworthy act that results in the acquisition of karmic merit for the adoptive family. Numerous authors (e.g. Goody and Tambiah 1973; Carsten 1991) have documented this kind of practice in other parts of Southeast Asia: it is not uncommon for children to be raised by parents other than their biological parents, especially if the latter are too poor to take care of their offspring, or because a family that has many children decides to give some to childless families.

almost without conscious awareness on the part of the individuals concerned. In this case, children's gratitude towards *phu yai* arises spontaneously, not as a mandatory duty – as happens in the politicised context of schools.

However, there is not always family harmony in the slums. We can see this, for example, in Heather Montgomery's (2001) ethnography on child prostitution in Thailand. She relates how a number of slum children explained their decision to give themselves to *farang* adults as based on their filial obligations; they felt that they had to fulfil their parents' requests for financial support as 'good children should'. Montgomery explains this moral distortion of parenthood as a side effect of Thai monarchical paternalism. The vicious instrumentalisation of the state-enforced, royalist cult of *phu yai* is a fact that can occur not only at a political macro-level, but sometimes also at a micro-level, within the family. People in positions of power – either soldiers or parents – can, in fact, abuse their higher rank in order to justify violence on, and subjugation of purportedly ungrateful 'small people' (e.g. non-compliant citizens and/or children). In Akhan Daeng, however, as far as I could gauge, adults' cultural formulation of children as *phu noi* was embedded in emotionally balanced and relationally flexible inter-generational relationships, providing opportunities for children to make their own choices while encouraging age-appropriate agency. Children's own perception of their homes as affective spaces free of formal rules indicates that this is the case.

On the other hand, from the perspective of the state the relationships that *dek salam* have with adults are abnormal, and their privileged attachment to peers is regarded as a potential threat to Thai society's hierarchical structure, as well as being a dangerous political deviation from the standard of the 'good Thai child'. In the view of city district and CODI development officers in Akhan Daeng, slum children's low adherence to formal hierarchies of seniority was linked to 'the immoral caregiving that *dek salam* had received from their parents', which itself was regarded as a consequence of slum dwellers' 'backward traditions': 'parents are irresponsible, thoughtless or they ignore the correct way to build relationships with children'.[12] Such explanations entrench the state rhetoric on urban slums as a danger to society, while legitimising corrective governmental intervention. The aim of this intervention is to attempt to restore 'Thainess' by

---

12 The mindset that leads to the stigmatisation of 'street children' is not only found in Thailand (see e.g. Glauser 1997; Young, 2003; Honwana and de Boeck [eds] 2005; M. Davies 2008; Scheper-Hughes 1992). Across the world, the 'street child' is commonly construed as the supreme symbol of the immoral, undisciplined, dangerous subject, deprived of a 'natural childhood'. In Thailand, however, references to *dek salam* ('slum children') as a social danger have a specific ethnic dimension: their deviance is ultimately conceived to be a moral violation of 'Thainess'.

prescribing a new and superior model of Buddhist parenthood – namely the *phu yai* cult, which has at its apex the nation's father – the king.

However, the state is not, as I have shown, the only institutional actor involved in these children's lives. Since the 1970s, various international NGOs, religious charities, and other development actors have begun to operate in the slums of Bangkok, with a range of different political, economic and social motives. Many of these organisations focus on a transnational discourse centred on children's rights, and are specialised in assisting 'disadvantaged' categories of children such as 'street children', HIV-positive children, and specifically *dek salam*. NGOs such as the Saint Jacob's Centre, in particular, have precipitated substantial changes in the socio-political and economic landscape of the capital's urban poverty, and have provided *dek salam* with a new social stage, on which they perform the role of 'victims', as we saw above with Fon.

HUMANITARIAN LANDSCAPES: MOTHERHOOD AND THE POLITICISATION OF CHILDREN'S RIGHTS

The proliferation of child-focused NGOs in the slums of Bangkok is part of the broader modern endeavour to 'save children', which gained transnational traction with the 1959 UN Declaration on the Rights of the Child. The image of suffering children captures the moral imperative of humanitarian intervention as founded on what Didier Fassin (2005) has called a 'compassionate ethos': an extreme attention to human suffering produced by the continuous staging, production, and circulation of discourses and images evoking grief and pain. Media representations of vulnerable children are particularly effective in activating public emotion and religious values. They also activate strong, shared feelings that assume a collective intervention to help these 'innocent victims' to be inevitable, legitimate, and urgent (e.g. see Malkki 2015; Hanson and Nieuwenhuys [eds] 2013; Bornstein 2011; Jenks 1996).

Deeply entangled as it is in the civilisational trajectories of Western modernity, however, the discourse of children's rights sets out a Eurocentric standard of childhood, as a romantic time of innocence, dependency, and enthusiasm (e.g. Boyden 1997; James and Prout [eds] 1997; Hoffman and Zhao 2008; Rosen 2007). This Western, middle-class representation may well conflict with local cultural and political conceptions of 'childhood' and 'adulthood' elsewhere, despite the emerging juridical definitions produced by the Thai government in an effort to conform to the global mainstream.

Child-focused NGOs have modified the socio-political and economic positioning of childhood in the slums. By facilitating the opening-up of the slum and increasing the mobility of its young residents, often hosted in NGO-run venues, they have also increased children's agency, principally in terms of access to new physical and symbolic spaces. Very often, it is through children that alliances between slums and NGOs, or other international agencies, can be established. The malleable nature of children – in that they are willing to accommodate themselves to moving from the slum to the context offered them by an outside agency; and to redefine and reconceive of themselves in a way that matches the representation of 'childhood' that is prescribed by that agency – is central to the initiation of the economic relationship that is set up with the NGO (which provides for the child, and sometimes also for his or her family), and this gives children much more contractual power in their inter-generational relationship with adult authority.

There is also the potential for the humanitarian construction of *dek salam* as 'victims' to be effectively instrumentalised by slum residents as an economic and political resource. Before addressing this crucial issue, it is important to be aware of the particular nature of child-focused organisations within the broader NGO sector in Thailand. Not all NGOs have, historically, taken up the political position that Saint Jacob's does.

As Shigetomi et al (2004) have observed, NGO activism can be documented in Thailand from the 1970s onwards. After the 1980s amnesty, it was through the back door of NGOs that former militants of the Thai Communist Party re-entered the Thai political arena (Kanokrat Lertchoosakul 2012). Channelling the discontent of rural communities and of the urban poor vis-à-vis the Bangkok establishment's political and financial power, NGOs initially facilitated connections between what might be described as Thai society's 'internal and external ethnic margins' (Bangkok slums and the peripheral rural regions of Thailand, respectively), contributing to the genesis of popular social movements representing the interests of marginalised communities at a national level (Baker 1999). However, this grassroots activism has not wakened military and royalist groups' grip on power, which has left room for elite capture in NGO development projects.

As Thai academic and activist Giles Ungpakorn (2009) has argued, NGOs gradually became a new vehicle for 'Thainess'-oriented royalist politics. Walker (2010), has argued that the supposedly localist, anti-capitalist and environmentalist turnaround of monarchic rhetoric, which included the promotion of *sethakit pho phiang* ('sufficiency economy') in 1997, ensured the passage of several NGOs from left-wing progressivism to the king's and the military's eco-Buddhist conservatism. Today many NGOs, especially in the 'tribal' north, effectively act as local development agents of centralised 'Thainess', while in the slums of Bangkok there are CODI-led aid projects with the same goal (e.g. see Elinoff 2012, 2014).

In this context, NGOs like the Saint Jacob's Centre deserve a particular mention, as do local foundations and religious organisations that are formally focused on children's rights and wellbeing. Because they are commonly thought of as purely philanthropic in nature, charities supporting children are less feared by state authorities than more politically sensitive organisations that address environmental and economic issues explicitly. For this reason, child-focused NGOs are subject to less government scrutiny and manipulation. Organisations of this kind have received priority access to the capital's poorest districts since the 1980s, transforming city slums into heterogeneous social arenas where the protection of children is 'an opportunity, a profession, a market, a bet, a strategy' (de Sardan 2004: 11).

I have shown above how the missionaries of Saint Jacob's make use of the secular framework of children's rights to advance their politicoreligious mission. Here, I will focus on how this transnational agenda is appropriated by slum residents, particularly the children's mothers. Compared to slum men, who are frowned upon by NGOs, women are better positioned to capitalise on the humanitarian politicisation of their children, becoming the most reliable reference points for NGOs within the slum. By appealing to the matrifocal characterisation of local family structures and to their privileged relationship with children, slum mothers can enter NGO national and international networks, significantly increasing their leadership both in the slums and in the wider context of the Thai capital's political structures.

To demonstrate this, I will now focus on two specific ethnographic case studies. The first takes a look at Prateep Ungsongtham, the famous (female) Thai activist who, during the 1980s, founded the first politically-relevant aid organisation for slum children, in Khlong Toei, the biggest slum in Bangkok to have successfully resisted eviction. The second case-study investigates the collaboration between Pan, the slum woman we met earlier in the book, with child-focused NGOs in Akhan Daeng.[13] Both women are at centre stage of humanitarian concerns arising from the idea that *dek salam* are victims to be saved.

A fairy godmother

In the 1970s there were massive protests against eviction in Khlong Toei slum, and this was a key historical moment in the collective imagination of Bangkok's

---

13 In discussing these two cases, I draw on and develop further some of my earlier reflections on motherhood, NGOs, and women's emerging leadership in the slums of Bangkok (see Bolotta 2017b).

slum dwellers. During these events, one young woman had a central role, together with the children of the slum.

Khlong Toei was first established in the 1950s. Migrants from rural and ethnic provinces in the country moved in and illegally occupied land belonging to the Port Authority of Thailand, finding manual jobs linked to the construction of the port of Bangkok, popularly known as Khlong Toei port. Here they built what was to become the largest slum of the megalopolis (DPF 2013). At the time a young woman living at Khlong Toei, Prateep Ungsongtham, was keen to find a solution to the problem of slum children's education. In 1968 she decided to open an informal school in her parents' home. The Chumchon Muban Phatthana School ('community development school') that she set up led to the Khlong Toei slum becoming a politicised community.

In 1971 the Port Authority of Thailand threatened slum dwellers with forced eviction. The local school created by Prateep, who was by that time addressed as 'teacher' (khru) by all the slum residents, became a meeting place and the symbolic focus of the first anti-eviction assemblies (Asia 1981). Prateep's neighbours finally asked her to put their case to the landowner, the government, and the news media. Although Chumchon Muban Phatthana School was initially declared illegal, the dramatic picture of the children's living conditions in the slum provoked national and international sympathy, with khru Prateep being identified as the motherly leader of the residents of Khlong Toei: a 'fairy godmother for Bangkok's slum children' and 'the angel of the slum' (ibid.), as she was portrayed by both local and international media.

Under pressure from public opinion, the government finally recognised both Prateep's school and the demands of the slum dwellers. Khru Prateep received a number of awards related to international children's rights. In 1978 she received the Ramon Magsaysay Award for service to the public. Two years later she was the first Asian woman to be awarded the John D. Rockefeller Youth Award, for her contribution to humanity. With the prize money she established the Duang Prateep Foundation (DPF 2013). This was one of the first NGOs focusing on the needs of slum children. It was not long before NGOs focusing on slum children were established in all of the capital's slums. In many of these slums, children started to move from charity to charity, with their mothers acting as reference points on the spot for the agencies that were involved.

The local and international support that enabled the inhabitants of Khlong Toei to successfully oppose eviction was a clear response to the media construction of slum children as 'victims'. Coincidentally, the name Duang Prateep refers to a source of light, a guide. Its symbol, a flame, represents children (ibid.). Since its establishment, the DPF has financed a number of child-support programmes in

Khlong Toei, while at the same time developing strong links with the media and with Thai politicians, among them Suwit Watnoo (Askew 2002: 156). Suwit was one of the college students involved in the 1973 pro-democracy rallies. He was a prominent figure in the movement and spoke at protests in October 1976, when he witnessed the terrible massacre of demonstrators by the Thai army and allied right-wing paramilitary groups before his own eyes. Suwit survived the massacre and went into hiding in the forest, joining the Communist Party of Thailand. He was only able to return to public life after the amnesty, through the support of Prateep's DPF, which eventually became a hub for many of the so-called 'ex-Octobrists' (Nitirat Sapsuntorn 2007; cf. Kanokrat Lertchoosakul 2012: 175).

Working with the NGOs operating in the slums, Suwit helped slum dwellers develop political consciousness, using his skills, his knowledge and his networks both to negotiate between slum networks and private sectors for structural change, and to push slum issues onto the national agenda (Nitirat Sapsuntorn 2007). Out of these activities the Four Regions Slum Network (*khreua khai salam si phak*) was born, an organisation that connected slum inhabitants and the so-called 'poor' from the country's four regions and that was involved in public movements agitating for housing rights and against evictions (Kanokrat Lertchoosakul 2012: 192). According to one of its leaders (personal communication, 2013), even the Four Regions Slum Network had initially to associate itself with one of the most famous child-focused Thai charities, the Children's Foundation (*munithi dek*), as a strategy to garner funds under the banner of children's rights.

However, Suwit had broader political aspirations beyond support for the rights of children. In May 1992, he rallied hundreds of people associated with the Slum Organisation for Democracy (*ongkon salam pheua prachathipatai*), together with pro-democracy protesters, against military rule (Kanokrat Lertchoosakul 2012: 188). Meanwhile, his Four Regions Slum Network developed strong links with the Assembly of the Poor (AOP). This was an organisation of farmers and rural producers in crisis, coordinated by a group of NGOs, which organised a non-violent demonstration against the Thai parliament in 1996 that lasted 99 days. This new and heterogeneous political coalition aimed to act in the interests of the lower classes both in the city and in the countryside, by trying to publicly embarrass government officers and politicians (Baker 1999: 15–21). In the last decade, the organisation of slum inhabitants has developed a transnational dimension, flowing into the Leaders and Organisers of Community Organisations in Asia (LOCOA), which organised an International Housing and Land Rights Day in 2009 (Appayut Jantarapaa 2009).[14] From the 1990s onwards, slums came to be deeply entrenched

---

14 The inhabitants of the slum were also politically vocal during the recent protests that led to the *coup d'état* of May 2014. On 13 January 2014, the People's Democratic Reform Committee

as a central issue in Thai politics, playing an important role in wider structural tensions between society and state (Askew 2002: 151). Slum women played a major part throughout this process, especially in their roles as mothers. I would argue that this was facilitated by the rise of NGOs and their Western-based discourses, which imbued childhood in the slums with a new political meaning.

Thanks to her being locally and internationally recognised as an 'exemplary mother', Prateep was the first woman to raise political consciousness among the slum dwellers of Bangkok. This led to the success of Khlong Toei in avoiding evictions and the birth of the Four Regions Slum Network. In the eyes of the inhabitants of the slum, Prateep embodied *khunatham*, or 'moral goodness', a Buddhist concept associated with 'the pure love a mother has for her children' (Mulder 1992; Keyes 1984), but also with '[t]he home [...], the earth on which we depend for our living, the rice that feeds us, the water that sustains life, and the guardian angel that protects the young child' – which are all represented as female (Phya Anuman Rajhadon 1955: 55–61; cf. Ockey 1999: 35; cf. Mulder 1992).

In 2000, while Thaksin was in power, Prateep was elected to the Thai senate, representing Bangkok. In 2004, she received the World's Children Prize for the Rights of Children and the Global Friends' Award. Another woman from the slum, Prathin Wekhawakyanon, has twice been elected president of the Four Regions Slum Network, which is closely allied to the DPF. These are her words on the importance of a safe house: 'In a men's world, a house means only a place to rest or to live, but for women a house means a place to nurture the next generation of society' (Bangkok Post 2009).

These mothers' capacity to invest in the humanitarian value of their children as 'victims' is central to the processes through which slum dwellers have been construing themselves as a translocal 'imagined community' (Anderson 1983), politically able to integrate with other marginal groups at both national and transnational levels. Thanks to the strategic use of their relationships both with children and with NGOs, mothers have been able to push slum issues into the political spotlight, thereby making the urban poor more visible – a remarkable achievement in a country where political participation is traditionally considered a male prerogative (e.g. see Pasuk Phongpaichit and Baker 1996: 114; Iwanaga 2008; Darunee Tantwiramanond and Pandy 1991; Virada Somswasdi and Kobkun Rayanakorn

(PDRC), led by the former Democrat Party parliamentarian Suthep Thaugsuban, started the 'Shut Down Bangkok' movement, organising royalist and anti-government protests in order to obtain the resignation of prime minister Yingluck Shinawatra. This was followed a few months later by the coup led by current premier Prayut Chan-o-cha. Before the coup, the Four Regions Slum Network took part in the conflict, in collaboration with the Assembly for the Defense of Democracy (AFDD), an organisation of scholars who denounced Suthep's movement as an attack on democracy in Thailand (Prachatai 2013).

1994; Doneys 2002). Within the nation's cosmological, political and economic centre, Bangkok, slums communities constitute an 'other within' (Thongchai Winichakul 2000a), which the government struggles to govern.

A merciful mother

Pan is the woman who gave me shelter in Akhan Daeng. As already mentioned, she is the mother of five and has been the family's breadwinner since her ex-husband left her for a younger woman. As she explained to me, with some resentment: 'Men in the slum aren't responsible [*mai rap phit chop*]. They're lazy, constantly drunk and just interested in looking for minor wives [*mia noi*]. I myself decided to leave that bastard of an ex-husband when I discovered he had had a *mia noi* for years.[15] From that moment, I resolved to have nothing more to do with men. Now I'm the one who leads the family [*phu nam*]. I couldn't stand being a woman who is just a follower [*phu tam*] any longer'.

Pan was a seasonal migrant, squatting in Akhan Daeng, but her life changed when her children began receiving help from the Saint Jacob's Centre. Since then, Pan has become one of Father Nicola's most trusted collaborators and informal delegates within the slum. As part of this unofficial role, I found that it was usually Pan who guided NGO workers through the labyrinth of little lanes and cement paths in Akhan Daeng. Every morning she assisted the disabled of the community and catered to their primary needs. In the afternoon, when the children returned to the slum from school, she involved them in the social development programmes of the NGO, taking pictures and gathering information about the situations of their families on behalf of Saint Jacob's.

Over time, Pan has been able to make strategic use of her position: she is now at the centre of a number of aid networks focusing on the care of the community's children, and has been elected a member of the local committee in the slum. City district officials often contact her to organise celebrations for the neighbourhood at the Buddhist temple next to the slum. Together with other slum dwellers and parents, she also coordinates collective tactics to resist the systematic attempts at eviction that threaten the slum. Like Prateep, Pan is

---

15 The informal institution of male polygamy through the practice of taking minor wives has been widely documented in Thailand (Bao 2008; Cook 1998). Some authors (Manderson and Liamputtong Pranee 2002: 4) have described it as a strategy to manage male sexual desire without compromising those cultural normative and conservative values that protect the moral integrity of women and their pre-marital virginity. This only works when men are able to keep the two relationships separate, which is often impossible in a crowded slum.˙

described by the inhabitants of the slum as a virtuous and merciful mother who has Buddhist *khunatham*. All the children in Akhan Daeng call her 'mum' (*mae*).

Pan's children have shown that they also have the ability to lead, in the context of the recreational activities for *dek salam* that are organised by the various NGOs operating in the slum. Kaeo, Pan's eldest daughter, was a guest of Saint Jacob's. As well as receiving support from the Catholic organisation, she was also involved with a Buddhist NGO close to Akhan Daeng. She assisted university students when they volunteered to teach English to the slum youngsters. Kaeo moved regularly between the Saint Jacob's Centre, the slum, the Buddhist foundation and the Catholic private school that she was attending in the centre of the capital city. Driven by a 'capitalist desire for consumption' (Sopranzetti 2012), she seemed to have a strategy of changing her home regularly. One day, while we were busy preparing a papaya salad in her house, she explained: 'I decided to leave home in order to attend a famous high school. Also, my mum asked me to go and live at the charity [Saint Jacob's]. Besides, I can eat, sleep and have nice clothes over there'.

Thanks to what might be described as her children's 'humanitarian circulation', *mae* Pan has also developed a direct relationship with all the aid agencies involved and has become an important figure for the inhabitants of the slum. Through her mediation, single mothers in Akhan Daeng can, like her, access the networks and financial help available through child-focused NGOs. However, as it became clear during my stay in the slum, those running Saint Jacob's were unaware of Pan's and her children's wide-ranging connections. The Catholic missionaries did not know that there were other NGOs providing support to the same children whom Saint Jacob's was assisting. In fact, recipients of aid were careful to avoid contact between different NGOs: that way, they could simultaneously secure multiple sources of funding.

As sociologist Erving Goffman (1997 [1956], 2003a [1961]) has observed, social performances take place on a stage, the 'front region', so defined owing to the presence of an audience. If no audience is present, actors move into the 'back regions'. These are informal spaces in which the public behaviour of actors may be placed in question, and which thus have to be hidden from the audience (Goffman 1997 [1956]: 116). This is what *mae* Pan said to me about how she dealt with Western NGO workers, whom she aimed to convince that she embodied the 'good mother': '*Farang* are generous [*jai di*], they help us financially and advise us for free'. With regard to children, this was what she said: 'It's important to listen to children, to show interest in them, to ask questions, and to let them express themselves. It's the only way they will trust us'. This kind of statement fulfilled the moral expectations of NGOs with regard to 'proper parenting', giving the impression that she agreed with humanitarian formulations of children as full and capable social agents. However, such discourses are inconsistent with child-rearing practices in the slum, the private, ethnic backstage – or 'back region' – to use Goffman's term (ibid.), in which *mae* Pan lives.

When dealing with male slum dwellers, on the other hand, *mae* Pan could come across as someting very different from a model loving mother. If necessary, she could be aggressive and vulgar and could behave like a man (as defined by normative, gendered Thai codes). She knew very well how to persuade men to cooperate. If men wanted their children to have access to NGO networks, they had to prove to *mae* Pan that they deserved it, by becoming active community members and reliable partners for their wives.

The contrast between 'front region' and 'back regions' (ibid.) also came across in interactions that Pan and her family had with humanitarian workers. In such interactions, Kaeo, Pan's daughter, used to describe herself as a poor *dek salam*, fatherless and forced to grow up in an unsuitable environment. However, when she was in the company of friends, neighbours or peers, she was perceived as being fortunate and successful, a girl who attended a school for 'good people' (*phu di*) and had many *farang* friends. Both *mae* Pan and Kaeo actively managed their identity, constructing and deconstructing it according to social context, in order to survive and to promote the wellbeing of their group. Pan, in particular, was able to master the NGO-based 'moral economy of childhood' (Fassin 2013), thanks to her ability to display maternal *khunatham* on the right social stages.

How was I able to witness *mae* Pan's multiple performances? This was possible because although initially I only had access to the slum as a member of the 'audience' (being an NGO volunteer myself), once I settled in Akhan Daeng as a researcher and participant observer, over time I was able to redefine my position, becoming a sort of 'shill' or 'decoy' for Akhan Daeng residents, in Goffman's terms: 'Someone who acts as though he were an ordinary member of the audience but is in fact in league with the performers' (Goffman 1997 [1956]: 145–146). In other words, I chose not to undermine the credibility of slum dwellers' self-representations. Instead, I decided to play along with their 'front region' performances – for ethical reasons, but also in order to build mutual trust and familiarity. This allowed me to be gradually accepted, in the 'back regions' of the slum and of Pan's house, as a loyal friend and as a political ally in mediating with the various NGOs working in the slum.

MOTHERS AND CHILDREN: POLITICAL
WEAPONS OF URBAN POVERTY?

In his pioneering study of Trok Tai slum in 1970, Thai anthropologist Akin Rabibadhana (1976, 2010: 86–88) analysed the social organisation of the community as a vast network of patron–client relationships 'in which an individual of higher socioeconomic status (patron) uses his own influence and resources to provide protection or benefits, or both, for a person of lower status (client) who, for his part, reciprocates by offering general support and assistance, including personal services, to the patron' (Scott 1972: 91–92). Patrons were usually men with greater economic resources (e.g. money-lenders and landowners), and were often described as *nak leng*[16]: brave, manly leaders, ready to fight, and loyal to friends (Ockey 2004: 81–82). Since the 1970s, however, child-focused NGOs have been destabilising this male-centric power structure. The prominence and status of *khru* Prateep and *mae* Pan demonstrate how slum women have emerged as local leaders, capable of competing with male patrons for the community's moral and political leadership.

The first waves of Western feminism (e.g. see Firestone 1970; Ortner 1974) criticised the dominant gender representation of women as mothers because this was seen as depoliticising women and promoting their confinement to the domestic domain as the only appropriate space in which they could act. However, women living in the slums of Bangkok have shown that it is also possible for them to become political actors outside the domestic space precisely because of their roles as mothers. They can do this by drawing strategically on local gender perspectives that see womanhood and motherhood as equivalent. In fact, slum women's access to the moral economy deriving from their children's ability to manoeuvre among institutions of care is mostly based on their performance of good maternal behaviour. The spatial immobility of women (children bind them to their houses and neighbourhoods) is countered by their work at NGOs and the right to influence political decisions within the slum that they are able to claim through this work. Child-focused NGOs thus foster, even if somewhat involuntarily, women's 'economic and political aspirations' (Elinoff 2012) – specifically, those of young mothers.

---

16 According to James Ockey (2004: 81–82), *nak leng* emerged at the turn of the 19th century as a result of the increasing distance between the newly-established central state and rural villages. A *nak leng* would protect his village from theft, fighting against rival *nak leng* and would engage in raids at the expense of other communities. Respected and admired, he exercised a great deal of power, through both threats and rewards, sometimes to the point of being elected as village head (*phu yai ban*).

In order to win the trust of NGOs, these mothers have capitalised on the ethnicised outline of the slums as matrifocal and mother-centred humanitarian landscapes. They have drawn, in particular, on moral symbols that are prototypical of northern and northeastern rural contexts and that echo Thai Buddhist constructions of motherhood. They often become the main contacts for NGOs in coordinating aid activities addressing local children, who are cast as 'victims'. By contrast, slum men – often presented by women as unreliable and as alcoholics and gamblers – are usually excluded from economic and political links with NGOs.

Some mothers, such as *khru* Prateep, have mobilised humanitarian networks centred on childcare in order to create a national and transnational political voice capable of promoting housing rights. Others, such as *mae* Pan, have used the NGO networks to consolidate their own socioeconomic and political positions within the slum. With NGO social workers they act out the role of devoted mothers and vulnerable women abandoned by their mates; however, once they achieve leadership within the slums, they become fierce leaders, showing an ability to make effective use of traits that are supposedly male: they lead anti-eviction movements with determination, decide which families deserve access to the flow of money from NGOs, and increasingly contend with men for the leadership of the community. Prathin, the leader of the Four Regions Slum Network, has been described by the main Thai English-language newspaper, *Bangkok Post*, as 'a lion-hearted woman fighting for housing rights' (Bangkok Post 2009).

'Gender' and 'childhood' emerge here as inter-subjective political categories, socially constructed, open and fluid (Butler 1990). Slum women manipulate them as political instruments. Thanks to their activism, slum dwellers can now speak up within the public national political arena (Askew 2002: 151). These slum women are providing a voice for all poor migrants and their descendants in the big city.

To conclude, it is important to position the emerging leadership roles taken on by slum women in the context of contemporary scholarship on poor people's social movements in Thai society. In his analysis of slum dwellers' anti-eviction campaigns in Bangkok, Ockey (1996, 2004) highlighted certain key elements: the erosion of traditional client–patron links, the presence of different forms of leadership (often exercised by women), the emergence of a shared class feeling involving horizontal rather than vertical social relations, the newfound participation of subjects traditionally considered vulnerable (women, children, elderly), and the intervention of NGOs. Ockey's analysis attributes the changes in the traditional power structure in the slums to an interlocking set of factors, including class consciousness, horizontality, and the democratic contribution of NGOs. However, it is worth noting that all of these appear to be derived from Western political categories, which are ethnocentric and have the potential to generate a distorted understanding of the complex local socio-political phenomena at play here.

Prateep and Pan are examples of how women have been able to build their leadership through the political manipulation, rather than the mere appropriation, of definitions of childhood that derive from the matrifocal organisation of the slums, and that have moral import in the context of NGO concern for impoverished children and their needs. Cleverly moving between the multifaceted social levels and meanings activated by humanitarian aid in the slum, they have learnt to combine local and Western elements in order to produce configurations of power that are morally legitimated by their roles as mothers. These configurations are more horizontal than those in traditional relationships of patronage, but they can hardly be described as democratic, especially in the Western understanding of the term. While *khru* Prateep is clearly concerned about the plight of slum dwellers, *mae* Pan hardly seems to be interested in the political cause of the urban poor at all. Her leadership is based on patron–client ties within matrilineal networks and between matrifocal households. Her interest lies in protecting the group to which she herself belongs, and Akhan Daeng as a home for her own children, rather than in advocating for housing rights for all. NGOs, for their part, certainly do not always promote the socio-political and economic liberation of the poor. Indeed, because their focus is almost exclusively on childcare, they are often unaware of the anti-eviction manoeuvres orchestrated behind their back by those to whom they are giving humanitarian aid (Bolotta 2017b: 224–225).

It can be problematic to use the notion of class, along with the representation of slums as places of absolute poverty, to understand the social dynamics therein. In smaller, unregistered slums there are certainly poor people, often immigrants from neighbouring countries living in desperate conditions – not infrequently in crowded containers next to factories that feed on trafficked subjects, officially invisible to the rest of the world. However, in bigger slums (such as Khlong Toei or Akhan Daeng) the flow of 'moral money' provided by NGOs has made shanty towns increasingly palatable, and there is a new middle class in 'slums' like these, one that refuses, however, to represent itself as such to avoid losing its main source of support: the humanitarian economy aimed at poor children. *Mae* Pan herself never tires of reminding her children, who have now graduated and are well integrated into Bangkok's middle class: 'Don't even dare act as if you are a *phu di* ['upper-class person']! Remember that you were born here in Akhan Daeng, you were a *dek salam* and you still are' (ibid.).

Nevertheless, I agree with Ockey (2004: 124) when he suggests that the most vulnerable inhabitants of the slums (women, children, disabled people) are in possession of new 'weapons of the weak' (Scott 1985) – weapons that the urban poor can use to formulate effective resistance strategies. Slum children and women are often described by humanitarian discourses as vulnerable subjects, deviant or passive. However, the truth is that their conditions of marginality and urban poverty have led them to develop gendered and generational resistance as weapons in their battle for prosperity and wellbeing. These vulnerable subjects are drawing on the political value of their marginality to transform their exclusion into an instrument of socioeconomic integration. There is a specific example of this in slum mothers, who are showing how women can take on political roles by virtue of their very motherhood.

FINAL REMARKS

The side effects of economic and territorial policies that have favoured urban elites, slums are the result of historical, economic and political processes that reconfigured the Thai capital after World War II; and the products of structural violence that runs along numerous lines and creates inequities in the control of space. Just as *dek salam*, like other categories of 'non-Thai' subjects, are regarded and projected by the state as dangerous moral, social, aesthetic and political deviations compared to the standard model of the 'good Thai child', so the slums in which they live, which occupy a subordinate position in the wider urban context, are depicted by the government and the media as places full of danger, drug trafficking and moral degradation, and have been the target of aggressive eviction policies.

By insisting on a transnational discourse that focuses on the rights of children, NGOs and Western international agencies like the Saint Jacob's Centre have been precious allies for the inhabitants of the slums since the 1970s. They have been responsible for new forms of political organisation within the slum and for destabilising what was a hierarchical patron–client system. At the same time, this has led to a repositioning of childhood within the slum. Childhood has proved to be a symbolic resource with the potential to be cleverly manipulated by adults, and has been the basis for political negotiations centred on the use of urban space and access to financial support. The advent of Western aid agencies is thus redefining the structural position, everyday life and subjective experience of *dek salam* and is also, through the children themselves, redefining the hierarchical power relations between slum dwellers and the city.

Slum children, who are often hosted by charities or NGOs, are among the most mobile of the urban poor. While they are in the slum, intended as an ethnic 'back region' that is invisible to government or Western humanitarian eyes, they are considered *phu noi*, endowed with a good deal of autonomy, and cared for collectively by *phu yai,* echoing rural, 'non-Thai' sociality and popular culture. When they are at school, which is the central institution propagating 'Thainess', they are exposed to an ultra-regulated formal system grounded in Thai (royalist) ethno-nationalism and with a strong military character, one that conceives of them as dangerous deviations from the model of the 'good Thai child'. When they perform on the humanitarian stage provided by Western NGOs, they are cast as innocent victims needing protection.

The humanitarian politicisation of childhood has transformed poor children into what Bourdieu (1987, 2005) called 'symbolic capital', a term that refers to social properties that have a symbolic meaning, collectively recognised as able to confer authority and legitimacy. Bourdieu has emphasised the fact that 'the conversion of economic capital into symbolic capital produces relationships of dependence based on economy, but disguised under the veil of moral relationships' (Bourdieu 2005: 190). Nancy Scheper-Hughes (1987: 12, cited in Boyden 1997: 192) has taken this further, arguing that 'the instrumental value of children has been completely replaced by their expressive value'. While children's active contribution to the domestic economy of their household is becoming less and less relevant, *dek salam* are now incredibly useful for slum dwellers as symbolic capital, allowing them to gain access to political mediation and financial resources through NGOs.

As Part One of this book has shown, there are a number of different approaches to childhood (in which they are variously cast as *phu noi*; as citizens; as spiritually immature subjects; as God's beloved children; and/or as victims) confronting poor children in Bangkok. Each of these implies a different theory of family and of appropriate child–adult relationships, and these correspond to different political and moral ideals of hierarchy, society, ethnicity, and citizenship. A royalist military dictatorship and a democratic government are extremes in a continuum of political and moral social configurations, which are related to and refer to different ideologies of childhood. This is reflected in contemporary Thailand's political divide.

Subjected in their everyday lives to contradictory symbolic and political constructions that compete to define their nature, children act as mediators between irreconcilable perspectives, and are the litmus test of wider conflicts where continuity and change, local and global processes intertwine. The scene is now set to enable us to tackle this issue in depth and to examine 'childhood' through the children's own eyes and voices.

PART TWO

CHILDREN'S CULTURES
AND SELVES

CHAPTER 5

Children's Multiple Selves

In the first part of this book, I analysed the way in which 'childhood' is interpreted differently by adults in the various social and institutional contexts in which poor children move and live in Bangkok. Depending on whether they are at school, attending Buddhist temple, at the Catholic charity, or at home, these children are confronted by adults committed to saving, governing, re-educating, or re-moralising them in different ways. In fact, each of the constructions of childhood examined so far – children as *phu noi*; as *dek salam*; as social deviants; as victims; as sacred or as spiritually immature individuals – structures the social spaces in which the children live in specific, and normative, ways, by moulding the attitudes of the adults relating to them according to distinct, and sometimes conflicting, cultural politics of childcare. The children themselves are required to embody contradictory 'subject positions' (Davies and Harre 1990; Butler 1997; Foucault 1982) acting, for instance, as both Buddhist and Catholic, or as both vulnerable and independent, in relation to different social actors.

In the second part of this book I present the children's own perspectives and respond to questions such as: How do children understand the conflicting pedagogies and discourses held by priests, monks, teachers, parents, and humanitarian operators, about their specific state as *dek salam*? How do they experience living in a Bangkok slum, attending state schools, interacting with Western aid workers or with peers, while navigating through these kinds of ideological contradictions? It is often the case that children do not conform in a straightforward fashion to 'dominant discourses' (Foucault 1982) on (slum) childhood, and to the social and institutional structures set up around them by adults. In developing a sense of self, they often resist, appropriate, reinterpret or bend adults' discourses for their own ends.

In this chapter, I trace out the multiple sites and spaces in which these identities come together in the production of the children's senses of self. It is noteworthy that this process does not produce a coherent awareness of self; it tends, instead, to produce multiple selves that not only work with the identities prescribed by authority figures, but also challenge them. As I will show, this process of self-formation engages different cultural notions of personhood, 'Thainess', ethnicity and hierarchy, at various points in time and with different aims. Moreover, as my ethnography bears out, such processes of self-making are not unconscious; the children are acutely aware of engaging in them. I will show how this is the case by re-examining the environments in which the children live, this time through the prism of their own embodied experience, views, beliefs and practices.

As we have seen, the discursive category of *dek salam* implies the placing of these children in a wider ethnic and (im)moral category of 'non-Thai' Other, a category that carries a heavy stigma, especially in public contexts, where the state discourse of 'Thainess' is most strongly expressed institutionally. Consequently, children use different strategies in order to avoid being identified as *dek salam,* or to build self-worth despite their ethnic and class profile.

THE ANTI-SOCIETY OF CHILDREN IN THE SLUMS

As soon as I began my fieldwork in Akhan Daeng, it quickly became apparent that children's life in the slum was structured loosely, as compared with the institutionalised context of NGOs. It was also quite clear that social life in the slum was organised in anti-structural ways, in sharp contrast to the 'order and discipline' (*khwam riaproi*) ethos that reigned supreme in schools. As I have pointed out above, in Akhan Daeng children spent a lot of time among peers. They had many opportunities to organise their time independently, without having to adhere rigidly to any planned programme of activities designed by adults for them. Let us take a closer look at the children's peer-to-peer relationships in the slum.

Groups of children in the slum comprised individuals belonging to different generational cohorts, with no gender distinction. The groups were made up of *phi* ('older brothers and sisters') and *nong* ('younger brothers and sisters'). Adults often entrusted *phi* with the care of *nong*, whether they were biologically related or not. The care of *nong* by *phi*, in addition to lifting a burden from the mother's shoulders, reinforced and socialised hierarchies, transferring to children the ideas of status and hierarchical positioning which are the basis of life in the slum, as they are, in some sense, at the basis of social and political structures throughout Southeast Asia.

It is not only in Thailand that older children have a role in socialising their younger siblings. Scholars have described the relations between older and younger siblings as a key element of social structure in a number of Southeast Asian societies as well as in Austronesian societies outside Southeast Asia. In her work on language socialisation in Samoa, Elinor Ochs (1982, 1988), for example, emphasised that it is not so much that adults ask older children to look after younger siblings because this is convenient; they do this because they see it as a way to instil respect towards elders and to emphasise the social inferiority of those who are younger and junior, in the context of a highly stratified society.

In Akhan Daeng, too, adults encouraged the organisation of relationships into ones between *phi* and *nong* as soon as children learnt to speak. As I have shown, however, this differed from *phi–nong* interactions in public contexts and mainstream Thai society.

While at school it is Thai normative social hierarchies that are enforced, in the slums the relationship *phi–nong*, while also based on hierarchy, is intimate and informal, and is characterised by a greater degree of relational fluidity and reciprocity. In Akhan Daeng, the roles of *phi* and *nong* were not taken for granted nor were they formally established. It was not automatic that a younger individual recognised an older one as *phi*. Rarely would adults intervene in children's friendship choices, or in the internal social dynamics within a group, in order to impose the selection of certain children as *phi* rather than others. It was *nong* who chose their own *phi* and vice versa.

In 2012, a boy called Wat was *phi* to many children in Akhan Daeng. While I was a guest in his house, Wat, aware of my role as a researcher, was keen to share some of his reflections on friendship, which he had meticulously noted in his diary. One of these outlined the essential traits of *phi*:

> *Phi* [elder siblings] are *phu yai* [big people] who make us happy, make us laugh, take care of us day and night, often call us, comfort us when we're sad, stay by our side through hard times, don't love us only for our physical appearance, worry about us, keep us from danger when we make mistakes, teach us how to live. [...] Their heart always turns to us spontaneously. When we meet our *phi*, we meet them for life. *Nong* must listen to *phi* and be grateful to them, they must show them their gratitude [*khwam katanyu*]. (Wat, July 2012)

Wat's description reveals moral elements that reflect a normative interpretation of *phi–nong* relationships as conveyed by the Buddhist rhetoric of 'Thainess'. On the other hand, the formal, reverential, almost mystical flavour that *must* imbue interactions between *phu noi* and *phu yai* in public contexts did not apply to children's social universe in the slum. *Nong* did not greet *phi* with *wai* every time they met them. On the contrary, they often, in a rather endearing way, addressed their *phi* – who were nonetheless recognised as the leader – using insults and derogatory remarks. Also, the decision of *nong* to assign the role of *phi* to certain individuals was reversible, should those individuals not come up to scratch morally. For these children, the emotional and moral dimension of friendship between *phi* and *nong* is central. An older friend who can 'make [us] happy, comfort [us], take care [of us]', who is prepared to give advice, protection and shelter, demonstrates the legitimacy of his role as *phi* – a legitimacy that he or she will nevertheless have to constantly prove in everyday life.

As I have shown, the 'non-Thai Tainess' of the slum frees the hierarchical verticality of social relationships from the institutionalised, coercive and martial elements that are present in the school context. The recognition that children from Akhan Daeng accorded to teachers as *phi* or *phu yai* was only formal (despite the institutional injunction to consider them to be such). In the slum, by contrast, relationships between *phi* and *yong* came into being more spontaneously, out of intentional choices, and constituted both a central organising principle of children's socialising and friendships and a fundamental source of emotional support in situations of recurring intrafamilial distress.

'Akhan Daeng is our home!'

The disciplining of bodies and minds imposed through the school by the militarised state code of 'Thainess' was strikingly in contrast with children's everyday lives in the slum. This was their native, domestic environment. At the time that was described as *pit toem* (the period at the end of the school term and the beginning of the holidays), this became quite apparent.

Many children grew and dyed their hair (the more reserved bleached it, others chose more eccentric dyes), romped about shirtless, unconcerned with *marayat* (a term used to describe Thai 'good' manners), rode the same moped in groups of four or five, smoked Krong Thip cigarettes – as Ciord, 13, explained, 'the strongest' and therefore the 'manliest' cigarettes that were on sale. Many girls, even the very young, strutted down the lanes of the slum wearing revealing clothes and heavy makeup, indulged in romantic and sentimental tête-à-têtes by the railway track, or spent hours on the phone with a boyfriend they had met on the internet but never in real life. All children and youngsters, not just *dek salam*, welcomed school holidays as a time of greater freedom. In the slum, however, the contrast between institutionalised and informal expressions of childhood was particularly obvious.

Because the houses in the slums are so tightly packed together, the only place to play in Akhan Daeng was the railway tracks (Figure 7). Despite the fact that *farang* and NGO workers regarded the railway tracks as an extremely dangerous site and warned the children against playing there, this was the main place where the *dek salam* gathered.

During the summer, when I was living there, the *dek salam* spent their days running barefoot along the railway tracks. These led to the railway terminal, where train carriages in an apparent state of abandonment were parked, blackened by grease and tar. The children clambered over these, lay down on top of the carriages, made hiding places and hid objects. Jumping from the roof of one

Figure 7. Children sitting and chatting along the railway tracks. Bangkok slums, April 2013. Colour version, p. 231

carriage to another, exploring their nooks and crannies, trying out acrobatic moves that would make any average Western observer panic, children seemed to unleash motor and imaginative energy that was normally kept in check in the institutional folds and ritual rigour of 'Thainess'.

I generally sat on a patch of grass beside the carriages waiting for the children. They would join me, exhausted, bringing treasures they had collected or that they had hidden around the terminal: potato chips, sweets, drinks. The children would often start telling stories about a ghost who was said to haunt the station. This was usually said to be the spirit of a child killed by a train while on the tracks. Drawing on a popular ethno-cultural set of beliefs, children thought that violent deaths released merciless spirits who sought revenge among the living. Dramatic events such as the death of one of their peers were thus made intelligible through a ghostly imaginary that represented a warning to the youngest children – that crossing the railway tracks did require caution.

Building *ban dek akhan daeng* ('Akhan Daeng children's houses') was another of the children's favourite pastimes. Using the waste material abundant in the slum, they built tiny makeshift houses in the no man's land separating the railway terminal from the edge of the settlement of Akhan Daeng. They proclaimed proudly: 'These are our houses, *ban dek akhan daeng*. There's no one here that can throw us out'. The analysis of children's peer cultures made by sociologist of childhood William Corsaro (2011) is pertinent here. Children do not passively embody societal norms, for they contribute themselves to cultural innovation and social change. By interpreting and reproducing adult worlds, they creatively re-configure their society's cultural models in new ways. This 'interpretive reproduction', Corsaro argues, occurs especially within the context of a 'peer culture: a set of routines, artefacts, values, and concerns that children engage in with their peers' (Corsaro 2011: 120). Building small makeshift houses in a space perceived to be safe from eviction appears to be a good example of children's interpretive reproduction. The possibility of eviction is, in fact, constantly present in the slum. Many children had already moved home a number of times. Erecting their own houses using scrap materials, Akhan Daeng children were not merely imitating adults; they were creating a space of their own that could not be trespassed upon, and that both denounced and symbolically responded to the main worry of the adults: the possibility of being evicted.

In the late afternoon the children would usually return to the slum. They would pile onto the old mattresses that they had laid between one track and the next, unconcerned by the regular arrival of trains. The group's *phi* would strap on a guitar while other children started to sing songs, drawing on a diverse range of influences from church songs and English pop music to what are described as 'songs for life' – *phleng pheua chiwit*.[1] Around 6 pm every day, they would have a soccer match. This generated a temporary gender-based separation. Boys put on cleats and jerseys and took their positions on a field carved out between the tracks. Girls seized the opportunity for some playful gossip behind the backs of the boys.

After sunset, the youngsters returned to their respective homes, where they were entrusted with the preparation of meals, washing dishes and pots, and bringing in the laundry. Anyone who arrived late risked being soundly scolded by the *phu yai* of the house. They ate supper with their family, including any neighbours who happened to be passing by and dropped in.

When missionaries, *farang*, and government officials were not around, *dek salam* saw Akhan Daeng as 'home', despite the slum was publicly described as being a dirty

---

1   This term is a combination of two expressions: *sinlapa pheua chiwit* ('art of life') and *wannakam pheua chiwit* ('literature about life'). It refers to musical motifs that explore the difficulties of rural life in the fields and, more generally, the struggles of those belonging to the poorest social classes. The *phleng pheua chiwit* genre gained popularity in the years following the events of 14 October 1976 – the massacre of students at Bangkok's Thammasat University at the hands of the army – and is associated with the people's demands for democracy. It has been linked to the influence of American rock artists such as Bob Marley, Bob Dylan and Neil Percival Young (Clewley 2000: 244).

and dangerous place, and notwithstanding the fact that the children themselves, when asked by NGO workers about the slum, were quite capable of reproducing the same rhetoric. As Pepsi, a 12-year-old boy, said: 'Here I have a lot of friends. We have fun because we see each other every day. Akhan Daeng is our home!'

Drugs and video games

Besides the railway tracks, another meeting place for children in Akhan Daeng was a *ran kem* (a video game shop) with a dozen computer stations. The owner of the shop was a 50-year-old man who had been living in the slum for a long time and who was described by some of my informants as a crook (*khon mafia*). He had started this illegal business in 2011. A number of the children spent hours here, on Facebook, challenging each other to video games, and gambling. Many, in spite of their family's disapproval, skipped school or committed petty larceny in order to be able to enjoy *ran kem* regularly. Like the *ban dek akhan daeng*, the *ran kem* was the realm of children. Almost as if to delineate an uncrossable threshold, some of the children had drawn graffiti on the concrete path leading to the shop. The red spray paint declared *Rawang dek kat* ('Warning! Children bite'), explicitly advising strangers against venturing into a space that the children felt that they owned (Figure 8).

It is well known that competitive games are social laboratories that are important in formalising key interactional dynamics: they allocate roles (bettor, referee, supporter, etc.), establish alliances, calm conflicts or feed power struggles among rivals (e.g. Goldman 1998; Singer and Singer 2012). In Akhan Daeng, video games (generally soccer games and war games) served several social purposes: building friendships, solidarity, articulating hierarchies and roles, and promoting camaraderie among children. Video games, more importantly, offered newcomers (who are regarded as *nong*, 'younger siblings') the possibility of progressively (learning and) embodying group's rules, values and roles. Playful gambling also helped refine financial skills that were essential in the everyday lives of *dek salam*, such as mathematical reasoning and mental calculations. Children would bet small amounts of money, and usually used the winnings to benefit the group (buying, for example, food or sweets for everybody), thus generating a resource (re)distribution that mitigated against any bad feeling among the losers.

As well as playing video games, some of the children spent a lot of their free time taking drugs, contributing to the public representation of *dek salam* as a social danger. At night, those children who took amphetamine pills (*ya ba*) would gather in the unattended house of a *phi*. These were often parentless *dek salam*

Photo: Giuseppe Bolotta.

Figure 8. *Rawang dek kat* ('Warning! Children bite'). Akhan Daeng, May 2013. Colour version, p. 232

who organised into families made up of children, for survival. When they did not have enough money to buy *ya ba*, they usually got high by sniffing glue (*dom kao*).

The issue of substance abuse blocks proper discussion and shapes both state and humanitarian representations of the slum and its inhabitants in monolithic terms. However, in Akhan Daeng the phenomenon was irrelevant in terms of numbers, especially among the children who came within Saint Jacob's sphere of influence, which made up about 60% of children living in the slum. It is likely that those who habitually used *ya ba* were more difficult to reach. I managed to interact with only one of these children. His name was Phud. He was a 10-year-old orphan who had stubbornly refused the support of NGOs, and lived with another four orphans. When I asked him why he kept taking drugs, he answered: 'When I smoke *ya ba* it feels like I'm in heaven [*kheun sawan*]; I don't think about anything! My worries disappear, even though then I can't do without it anymore'. Phud had left school: 'At school there are too many rules, we're not free and then poor children [*dek jon*] like me are always humiliated [*du thuk*]'. He supported himself by working as a *ya ba* smuggler for drug dealers (including policemen) who, according to him, 'are good *phi*, they pay and protect me'. Not all *phi* operate within the realm of law.

All of the children whom I asked about substance abuse condemned it strongly, and many confirmed that it was a problem in the slum. They echoed the moralising narratives to which they were exposed in Akhan Daeng as well as at the various NGOs, foundations and institutions that were involved in promoting social development in the slum. The use of drugs was regulated by peer groups. Those who showed signs of intoxication were severely admonished by other children. In this way, groups of children tried to exercise some control over the behaviour of their members and to reduce the risk of some individuals going too far in their challenge to the dominant society's moral standards.

Challenging 'Thainess'

In the slum, the children's anti-structural and cathartic behaviour played out a symbolic overturning of the normative social order: the audacious explosion of a removed, denied and hidden self that in some cases ended up causing them to engage in the illegal practices that are publicly assumed to express the 'natural' tendencies of *dek salam*. However, these youngsters' anti-social behaviours should not be regarded as expressions of congenital personality traits; they are, rather, a defensive response on the part of the frailest subjects to the structural violence wrought by the state. This violence leads to those very outcomes that are presented by public authorities as requiring control over the poor. This same dynamic has, after all, been described by many social scientists in many peripheral areas in the Global South (e.g. M. Davies 2008; Mickelson 1999; Panter-Brick 2002; Young 2003; Burr 2006).

Anthropologist Matthew Davies (M. Davies 2008), for example, has highlighted the way in which 'street children' in Makutano (Kenya) organise themselves in social groupings whose stability is based on criminal behaviour. Referring to Halliday's reflections (1976: 570) on 'anti-languages', Davies has described the (individual and collective) self-expression of Kenyan children as an 'anti-society' (ibid.) organised in opposition to dominant social rules. Davies argues that the children's anti-society 'can be seen as counter-hegemonic in that it formulates an alternative view of the world in response to an elite's implicit domination of discourse' (M. Davies 2008: 325). Within this counter-reality, the re-development and re-interpretation of normative social values is an act of agency. The children's anti-society is effective because it plays on the fears of the dominant society: that 'street children', in sharp contrast to 'normal' children, are dirty, dangerous and wild (Ennew and Swart-Kruger 2003). It is precisely these attributes that children deliberately take on in order to delineate the external boundaries of their group identity, as a practice of collective agency.

In a rather similar fashion, *dek salam* in Bangkok sometimes appear to invest, symbolically, in the label of 'different and deviant children' that the upper-middle class world of Bangkok uses to marginalise them. *Dek salam* do this in order to create a boundary between them and that external, wider Thai society, thereby increasing the internal cohesion of the group. In Akhan Daeng, some children have constructed their selves in open opposition to the categories of childhood to which they are exposed in the context of institutions that are variously devoted to their rehabilitation, correction, or protection.

CHILDREN'S RESISTANCE TO STIGMA AT SCHOOL

In the context of school, as previously discussed, poor children from the slums of the capital are confronted with stigma and with discrimination that points to and decries the discrepancy between *dek salam* and the aesthetic, moral, and ethno-linguistic model of the 'good Thai child'. Goffman has described the processes of social classification that lead to the categorisation of an individual as liable to stigma:

> Society establishes the means of categorising persons and the complement of attributes felt to be ordinary and natural for members of each of these categories. [...] When a stranger comes into our presence, then, first appearances are likely to enable us to anticipate his category and attributes, his `social identity' [...] While the stranger is present before us, evidence can arise of his possessing an attribute that makes him different from others in the category of persons available for him to be, and of a less desirable kind – in the extreme, a person who is quite thoroughly bad, or dangerous, or weak. [...] By definition, of course, we believe the person with a stigma is not quite human. On this assumption we exercise varieties of discrimination, through which we effectively, if often un-thinkingly, reduce his life chances'.   (Goffman 2003b [1963]: 13–15)

The signs and symbols that stigmatised individuals bear are described by Goffman as 'stigma symbols' or 'disidentifiers', and he places them in opposition to what he calls 'prestige symbols' (ibid.: 60–61). In the case of slum children, 'stigma symbols' (ethno-linguistic, aesthetic, socio-economic, etc.) of this kind are formulated with reference to and in contrast with an ideal and hierarchically superior model of childhood, corresponding to the 'good Thai child'. *Dek salam* employ various strategies to protect themselves from this Thai ethno-nationalistic discrimination. These entail trying to control the flow of social information, adopting – to use Goffman's terminology – 'identity covering' (ibid.). At school, in particular, they may deny or conceal their identity as *dek salam* and institutionalised children. In this context, however, it is important to distinguish between private and public schools.

The problem of stigma is more relevant in (Catholic) private schools, as these are mainly attended by Thai or Sino-Thai upper-middle class students. In these contexts, therefore, the lower socio-economic status of *dek salam* is extremely apparent: they are, here, identified with a specific sub-group not only by teachers but also by other students. To avoid being recognised as *dek salam*, some of the children strive, therefore, to prevent their classmates from discovering where they live. When NGO workers drove the guests of Saint Jacob's to school in the Catholic charity's pick-ups, many requested a drop-off far away from the entrance, so as to disguise themselves among 'normal' students. At the end of lessons, for the same reason, they asked to return to the Centre on foot.

Luis, a 10-year-old *dek salam* who was enrolled at a prestigious Catholic private school, admitted: 'I'm ashamed to arrive at school in the NGO pick-up. I don't want my classmates to realise that I'm coming from Saint Jacob's'. However, little consideration was given to the reasons for the children's efforts to negate or re-invent their selves. As one of Luis's teachers explained: 'The children try to deny their origins, and are embarrassed to say they live at Saint Jacob's, but the problem is that after a while they come to school dressed badly: their shorts aren't ironed and their shirts are creased. So the other children see them as different. We try and treat them like normal students but we cannot expect them to live in complete peace with the others'.

The situation is different in small suburban state schools. The students at these schools tend to come from similar socioeconomic and ethno-linguistic backgrounds, so the *dek salam* do not stand out so sharply. Many of the students who attend these schools live in the capital's slums. Others are the children of peasants, who work in Bangkok during quiet periods of the farming year. In this type of school, the guests of Saint Jacob's integrate more easily with their peers. They tend to be quite open about their identity as *dek salam*, rather than denying their origins. Some even choose to proudly assert the fact that they live in an institution, presenting themselves as '*dek salam* from Saint Jacob's'. Compared to many of their schoolmates, in fact, Saint Jacob's children are often better off, as they benefit from financial support from a Western institution. They can count on daily pocket money and school materials; they do not have to walk kilometres to reach school; and they know many *farang* (volunteers at Saint Jacob's, who often pick them up from school). As Wat put it: 'Unlike other poor children, *dek salam* from Saint Jacob's have everything: food, a place to sleep, clothes, money. Also, they're not a burden on their parents. Once they are at Saint Jacob's, the children's mums do not have to pay for school fees, uniforms, books, other things they need for school, bus tickets or food. Once they are at Saint Jacob's, the children's lives change completely'. In small state schools, being a *dek salam*, which is associated with stigma in private schools, is something that can be successfully used as a source of secondary advantages. In these schools, a category like that of *dek salam* does not necessarily imply material poverty. On the contrary, it marks a child as being in a privileged situation, and thus it passes from being – in Goffman's words – a 'stigma symbol' to being a 'prestige symbol' (ibid.).

There are other reasons why *dek salam* are likely to feel more comfortable in small suburban state schools. Here, poor infrastructure, precarious employment and overcrowded classes affect education and make controlling students more difficult, as I have discussed above (see Chapter 1). Because of this, the order, martial discipline, and Buddhist morality associated with 'Thainess' in bigger schools is here fully visible only during ministerial inspections. Teachers in smaller schools, who are poorly paid, often skip classes, to the delight of the children. School principals, short of funds to pay for such things, involve students in extra-curricular jobs, such as painting the walls of the school buildings, cutting the grass, picking fruit or playing instruments.

Many *dek salam* greatly enjoyed these activities. Khwan, 13 years old, was one of these children. As a Saint Jacob's child, he was initially enrolled at a Catholic private school, but he was quickly expelled because he kept getting into confrontations with the teachers. Father Nicola then accepted the boy's request to be moved to a less 'ambitious' state school. Khwan was delighted with his new environment, as he saw it as a more inclusive social space where he would not suffer discrimination. As he explained: 'I feel very good in this school. I have a lot of free time and I don't have to study too much. My friends here are poor so they don't look down on me. I play the guitar and sometimes I can also sleep in class. The teachers often let us play. Sometimes the school principal makes us work, but it's a lot more fun than studying with the nuns [at the private Catholic school]'.

Girls, in comparison to boys, appeared more capable of tolerating the hyper-normative and stigmatising environment of private schools. Many were aware that a private school diploma could significantly facilitate their access to higher education, and thus increase their (limited) chances, as poor girls, for socio-economic mobility. They saw their future in perspective, thinking of stigma as an unavoidable price to be paid. Cioi, a 14-year-old girl who was born in Akhan Daeng and was a guest at Saint Jacob's, claimed, for example: 'Even if they see us as *dek salam*, in the end, with a diploma in our hands, we will be just like them! A diploma from a private school is prestigious and allows us to get into the best universities!'

SOCIAL DEVIANCY AS AGENCY

In many cases slum children's social identity as *dek salam* is known because it is verbalised or publicly signalled by teachers. When this happens, and the children are unable to conceal their ethno-linguistic, social and class origin, they sometimes unite and leverage those very same identity attributes that they previously tried to deny – a process that Goffman describes as 'in-group alignments: the aggregate formed by the individual's fellow-sufferers' (Goffman 2003b [1963]: 140). As one private school teacher lamented: 'When they come here, *dek salam* always stay together, they do not integrate with others. The missionaries at Saint Jacob's tell me that I must teach the other students not to discriminate against them, but kids will be kids. I cannot prevent them from being kids'.

Sometimes *dek salam* attempt to break free from the drip-feed of stigma by competing for prestigious roles within the school. Given the obsessive way in which Thai schools aim to establish rankings between what are known as 'morality champions' (with blown-up pictures of the winning students pasted up all over the school), it is not surprising that, for most schoolchildren, visibility and popularity constitute major aspirations – even for *dek salam*. Thanks to their keenness to spend time practising in the music room at Saint Jacob's, a few of the children from the Catholic NGO have succeeded in becoming members of their school bands, as singers and guitarists – who are very influential among students. Others have been successful in school sports, especially football and *muay thai* (Thai boxing). Far more often, however, poor children are not considered 'Thai enough' to represent the school, and they end up achieving popularity by breaking rules (e.g. growing their hair longer than is allowed, wearing their uniform shorts above the knee, smoking in the toilets, etc.), using bad language, and challenging *phu yai*.

Infringements of the 'good Thai child' protocol could take a number of different forms. During the nationalistic rituals that precede lessons, for example, I often saw students stealthily taking out ear-buds and phones from below their shirt collars, already tuned in to their favourite song, using a schoolmate's back as a protective screen so that the teacher would not see what they were doing. Sometimes they broke the rules even more obviously. During a computer lesson I attended, the teacher had asked the children, each of whom was provided with a PC station, to research *sethakit pho phiang* (King Bhumibol's 'sufficiency economy'). While the teacher sat at her desk, I walked among the stations. I was astonished by the ability of the *dek salam* to rapidly switch from page to page on the computer, alternating between their Facebook profile, video games, and chat windows with friends at other stations. At *ran kem*, children had had the opportunity of quickly learning how to use information technology, and they used it not only to impress their classmates but also to create virtual expressions of their irreverent selves. Mocking the teacher, downloading pornographic images, arranging secret meetings, they fully embodied the 'good Thai child's' nemesis. This nemesis sometimes took on gendered forms that reflected and challenged normative ideas of masculinity and femininity in Thai society. An examination of these gendered ways of being provides another lens through which to understand the selves that these children project in public contexts.

Boys as anti-leaders

Against the backdrop of Thai society's prevailing military ethos, many boys built up roles as male leaders that were tinged with machismo, which emphasises gendered qualities such as physical strength, courage, and emotional control. This drew on an image of a proper leader as a noble warrior ready to sacrifice himself for the sake of his *nong* (his younger brothers and sisters) and his followers.

A few Akhan Daeng boys became the informal *phu nam* ('leader') of their classes through acting out (or aggressively imposing) this leadership model, built on the traditional role of the *nak leng*. They established patron–client relationships, which they sought to stabilise in their roles as patrons and guarantors of the group's internal hierarchy. To confirm themselves in the position of *phu nam*, they had to confront *phu nam* of opposing groups, or anyone who went against the interests of, mocked or disrespected the *nong* affiliated to the group. They had to always be ready to demonstrate their moral superiority as leaders able to defy the system and protect their group members. They had, of course, adopted these social and power relationships because these were the relational models to which they had been exposed in their lives, not only in public contexts but also – to a different extent – in the context of the informal sociality of the slums (see e.g. Kemp 1982: 142–161; Akin Rabibhadana 2010: 86–88).

One such leader was Ton, a 15-year-old slum boy hosted at Saint Jacob's and enrolled at a Catholic private school. He was the source of many headaches for those running the NGO. He was said to be violent, aggressive and inclined to break rules, and he was often involved in physical fights that hurt other students. While I was at the Catholic organisation, I asked him why he was always in trouble. With the utmost seriousness, he replied: 'I'm the *phu nam* of the third-year class. A boy from another school came and belittled one of our *nong*. I asked him to stop, but his group started to pester some of our girls. I had to defend my friends. I couldn't not do it because I'm the *phu nam*! It's my responsibility, otherwise I would lose face [*sia na*]!'. In relation to the disrespectful attitude that

134

he was said to have towards teachers, the boy added: 'The vice-principal [the teacher in charge of discipline] insults me, calls me *dek tang dao* ['child without citizenship'] or *khwai* ['water buffalo'; in other words, 'stupid'], even when I behave well and don't do anything. I can't accept it [*rap mai dai*]'.

Ton's informal leadership was a challenge to the formal leadership of the class representative (*huana hong*). One child is chosen by the teacher in each class for the role of *huana hong* – a child who is the most convincing example of the 'good Thai child'. *Huana hong* is generally a student with fair skin, from a family considered 'good', respectful of *phu yai*, who does not smoke or drink alcohol, and who has excellent marks at school. His role is to provide classmates with moral guidance, holding high the torch of 'Thainess'. Compared to *huana hong*, Ton's anti-leadership, like that of many other *dek salam*, established a counter-morale in the school, with the potential to disarticulate the state's national identity mantra.

There were benefits, both social and economic, for a slum child in holding the position of *phu nam* in a private school. In a school like this, the *nong* affiliated to his group will be students of a relatively high socioeconomic status. In their position as *nong*, nonetheless, they are interested in earning the respect of their *phu nam*, in order to gain his protection and undermine the ambitions of other *nong* within the group's internal hierarchy of authority. Ton, as *phu nam* of his group, was often invited by the wealthiest students in the school, who were his *nong*, to go on trips, shopping sprees, etc. Through them, the boy had access to the exclusive lifestyle of Bangkok's middle classes, moving between a slum, a mega-mall of the capital, an institution for poor children, and a three-storey house with air conditioning in the city centre, thus enjoying – if only by association – the glittering world of global consumerism.

Girls' 'non-Thai' sexuality

Girls living in the slums of the capital are usually excluded from school plays involving cultural exhibitions of Thai femininity (e.g. Thai traditional dance shows). Or, if they are allowed to perform, they are usually relegated to the back of the stage so that they are not visible in the front stage, where only modest, gracious girls from 'good families' are allowed to stand. When they are not able to disguise themselves as normal students or, to paraphrase Goffman (2003b [1963]: 142), to 'align themselves' with the 'good' Thai girls and mix with them, they try to become popular by explicitly subverting the usual Thai models of feminity, making 'improper' use of their sexuality (Lees 1993; Manderson and Pranee, 2002) and using peers, rather than hostile teachers, as their social points of reference.

The greater emphasis that youngsters at school place on relationships be-tween themselves, and on friendships with peers, than on keeping school rules has been widely documented, both in the West and elsewhere. Dorothy Holland and Margaret Eisenhart's ethnography (Holland and Eisenhart 1990) of the importance of female friendship in two North American campuses is a good example. In their study, the teachers played a marginal role in shaping the values held by students, compared to the role of peers, whose views were central to the girls' collective definition of themselves and to the ways in which their norms, dominant social values and individual choices were shaped. Prestige derived not from academic results but was related to notions of charm, attractiveness and sexuality that were rooted in culture. Status among the girls was specifically linked to their ability to construct themselves as sexually desirable subjects.

A similar dynamic is at play among poor female students in Bangkok, although for very different reasons. These students are marginalised in school because they are regarded as personifications of the 'non-Thai' Other. Some secretly put make-up on in the bathrooms and smoked cigarettes (smoking is traditionally considered male behaviour, and females who smoke are regarded as particularly immoral). They had no trouble overcoming gender barriers and integrating into male groups. They engaged earlier and more easily than other girls in sex, competing for popular partners who could elevate their status, and attacking rivals if they were courting a potential boyfriend.[2]

Noei was a 14-year-old girl who lived in Akhan Daeng with her mother, ma-ternal grandmother and six siblings. She had been a guest at Saint Jacob's since she was 9, and she attended a Catholic private school thanks to the Catholic or-ganisation's financial support. The girl identified sexual competition as the main reason for conflict between her friends in the slum and other female students: 'They fight for the boys. I'm good and I study hard, but many of my friends are crazy about popular boys [phuchai dang]. The other day a group of friends of mine waited at the back of the school for a girl who was courting a boy who was in demand. They slapped her and called her a slut'.

Girls can thus openly challenge the normative gender roles that identify women with a passive position in courting and that associate pre-marital

2   Rivalry amongst women competing for a man is often portrayed in Thai soap operas. The script generally involves a happy couple threatened by the aggression of a third person (the anti-heroine): an exuberant woman, cunning and evil, who plots against her rival. While the heroine, the official girlfriend, represents the normative gender construction of Thai feminin-ity (modest, sweet and entirely devoted to the care of the house and the family), the anti-her-oine is often portrayed as an indigenous woman characterised as 'non-Thai'; or, conversely, as an upper-class or middle-class woman with male interests, who has been corrupted by taking on a Western, consumerist and individualist value system.

chastity and postponement of sexual activity with positive moral values that safeguard family honour. At school, when they are not monitored by adults, slum girls may do things that are supposedly the prerogative of the male, such as making the first move in courting and aggressively competing for the most popular partner with the aim of engaging in sexual intercourse. This has more to do with raising their status than with any romantic desire for a long-term relationship. In this way, they attempt to defy the normative model of Thai femininity, from which they are excluded *a priori* because of their categorisation as *dek salam*.

THE PEER GROUP: DOHD DIAO GANG

As discussed above, the interaction between *phi* and *nong* is the main basis upon which children's social relationships are built. However, these relationships can take different forms depending on individual circumstances and social environment. In the context of Western NGOs, the hierarchical gap between *phi* and *nong* is challenged by an individualistic, Euro-American concept of identity that considers a child to be a separate individual, with his or her own inner reality, identical to other individuals in terms of rights and duties. In state institutions (such as schools), *phi–nong* interactions are governed by the metaphysical, Indo-Buddhist and military logic of the Thai centre. In the slum, and generally in domestic and informal spaces, the moral and generational principle of social hierarchy is dominant, although it has some distinctive vernacular characteristics. I will now focus on slum children's peer culture, as this is significantly different from the dominant Thai social structure.

Anthropologists and sociologists have carried out a number of in-depth studies of children's socialisation through the prism of peer group, friendship and 'child cultures' in (but not limited to) non-Western cultural contexts (see e.g. James 1993, 1995; Adler and Adler, 1998; Hirschfeld, 2002). These studies have demonstrated a great deal of transcultural variability in peer-to-peer relationships, providing a powerful challenge to the essentialist and individualistic definitions, within Western psychology, of adolescence and the peer group as 'natural' stages of identity development.

When it is analysed within the peer-group, the relationship between *phi* and *nong* tends to fade into those social formations that are, in a derogatory way, described as 'gangs' in public discourse: children belonging to different generational cohorts, of both genders, strongly connected to a specific territory, and sharing their own slang, system of values, symbols and collective identity. In the slums, gangs provide a fundamental source of socialisation, emotional sharing and cultural development, overriding crumbling, fluid and mobile family structures. Parentless children (especially if they are motherless), institutionalised for most of the time together with their friends, find in the gang an essential social and emotional point of reference and source of identity. For this very reason, gangs are also targetted by the state.

As an alternative form of family, gangs are regarded as threatening the moral foundations of the Thai social pyramid, together with the imperatives of respect, devotion and unconditional service that *phu noi* are expected to express towards *phu yai*, first and foremost to parents. The media, public and moral description of gangs is grounded in an indignant condemnation of children's privileged attachment to friends. The possibility of children being primarily influenced by friends rather than by their parents is construed as the core moral violation from which all other deviations (drugs, aggressiveness, delinquency, etc.) derive, feeding into the construction of the dangerous nature of *dek salam* from a socio-political perspective.

During my research, I realised that many *dek salam* were members of gangs. Gangs are, in fact, simply a form of children's sub-culture organised in opposition to the Thai social body and conceived of by children themselves as a secret social dominion, invisible to 'big people's' institutional surveillance at school, at the temple or at an NGO like Saint Jacob's. My discovery that there was a gang at Saint Jacob's was made by chance. One day, while I was smoking a cigarette outside the NGO, I noticed something written in marker on the pick-up that took the children to school: *kaeng dohd diao* ('gang of loners' – i.e. those who feel lonely). At first, I did not pay too much attention, but when I began my fieldwork at school, I happened to notice the same sentence scribbled on the outside wall of the school building and also in the student toilets. So one afternoon, after class, I decided to ask Ton what he knew about the tag. The boy, visibly worried, instantly replied: 'How do you know about us?', which made me realise that I had hit the jackpot. I said I had seen the phrase *kaeng dohd diao* written in several places and thought it must be something important. Ton, scowling and increasingly concerned, asked me whether I had told the schoolteachers about this. I reassured him that I had absolutely no intention of doing so and that their secret was safe with me. I jokingly added that I would rather like to become part of the group. Ton relaxed, smiled, and gradually allowed me to tap into the social universe of the gang he belonged to.

'We're all the same'

Ton was one of the key members of *kaeng dohd diao*. The group comprised about 50 members, boys and girls, aged roughly nine to 17. They had similar socioeconomic and ethnolinguistic backgrounds: most of them lived in poverty in the capital's slums and some were being helped by child-focused NGOs (including Saint Jacob's and the Suan Kaeo Foundation), were parentless or came from broken homes. However different their paths through life, all of them found in the term *dohd diao* an emotional and conceptual signifier for a group identity in the making. The feeling of being different, the discrimination and the social isolation to which Bangkok's *dek salam* are regularly exposed was, for *kaeng dohd diao* members, the very foundation of their sense of belonging to the gang, as well as the criteria that regulated the inclusion of new members into the group.

Over time, the gang has equipped itself with identifying symbols, known exclusively by the group members and off limits to outsiders, especially *phu yai*: a specific greeting,[3] distinctive insignia (bands and cuffs with the name of the gang in gold on a red background), a colour (red), and a song. This was a Thai rock and metal song entitled *Su: hin lek fai* ('Fight: stone metal fire'), which described the harsh feelings that arise as dreamers crash down to reality and the need to fight for social change – an alluring message for young boys and girls unable to live up to Thai society's normative expectations. Membership of the gang was marked by special phrases, body language and symbols, which defined the group and created internal cohesion within it. Through their gang, children both embodied and emphasised their publicly-ascribed role as untidy and disobedient *dek salam*, while reformulating their otherness as poor children among their peers. This otherness was, at the same time, both produced and enacted by excluding outsiders from the social universe of the 'loners'.

Kaeng dohd diao has created a Facebook profile, which serves as a platform for coordinating group activities and for the digital expression of members' hidden, anti-structural selves. On the gang's Facebook page, the children have the opportunity to craft their own group culture, very often in the form of counter-positions towards and attacks on school-enforced *marayat* – rules of good manners and proper etiquette as defined by the official moral system of the state. Posts and topics of conversation on the page were, I found, very varied, ranging from sexuality to the consumption of alcohol. The most frequent theme, though, was denigration and mockery of *phu yai* at school.

An analysis of the jargon used by gang members, by contrast with formal Thai as prescribed in public spaces, provides an insight into the (anti-social) values of *kaeng dohd diao*. Compared to other gangs, *kaeng dohd diao* stands out

---

3   The official greeting of the gang, substituting the Thai *wai*, is made joining the index and little fingers in order to create a pentagonal shape.

as not being linked to any particular territory (for example, a specific slum, block or school). It is a specific feeling, instead (the loneliness experienced by children who suffer from the isolation, discrimination and alterity imposed on them), that serves as the cornerstone of the group's collective identity.

Group members constantly insulted each other by using bad words (e.g. *khwai*: water buffalo – in street slang, 'idiot' or 'fool'; and *hia*: monitor lizard – in street slang, 'asshole', 'fuck', or 'shit') rather than first names, nicknames, or kin terms, as is usual in formal Thai speech. In place of kin labels or standard Thai subject pronouns (*phom*: 'I' for male speakers; *dichan*: 'I' for female speakers, and *khun*: 'you' for both male and female speakers), the boys and girls of the gang used *ku* (I) and *meung* (you) to refer to each other. These are impolite pronouns, derived from the Tai language family, which are banned in school and all formal conversational spaces as 'hate speech'. The use of *ku* and *meung* is, however, a mark of intimate relationships in informal and private contexts, not just within gangs. As Nen, a 15-year-old female member of *kaeng dohd diao*, explained: 'If we don't insult each other it means we're not friends, we're not intimate [*sanit jai* – emotionally close]!'. While this speech pattern is widespread in informal discourse (and, increasingly, in Thai songs, comedies, TV shows, and social media) across class and generational lines in Thailand, for *kaeng dohd diao* members obscenities and insults were not just a simple linguistic choice; their use was a distinctive characteristic of communication among gang-affiliated individuals. For them, transgressing the rules of normative Thai language was an essential prerequisite for authentic self-expression as well as for social and emotional intimacy.

An additional point to consider in relation to these subject pronouns is fundamentally structural, and relates to the broader political implications (egalitarian vs authoritarian) of address terms and kinship labels in Southeast Asian (especially Thai) political language. As recent studies have made clear, the use of specific terms of address is, in fact, a fundamental component of Thai political speech (e.g. Nusartlert 2015, 2017; Carreon and Svetanant 2017). Politicians commonly address their followers as *nong*, casting themselves as *phi*, to establish emotional closeness as well as the illusion of family-like relationships with voters (Sanit Samakkarn 1994: 160–170). Crucially, in this context, *ku* and *meung*, unlike *phi*, *nong* and other kin terms (e.g. *pho*: father, or *mae*: mother), do not mark the speaker's hierarchical position in relation to interlocutors.

While the term *nong* verbally marks or – to use Althusser's (1970) term – 'interpellates' someone as a younger (and therefore hierarchically subordinated) 'sister' or 'brother', *ku* identifies, in *meung*, a subject of equal status. The use of *ku* and *meung* is thus strictly sanctioned in formal and institutional spaces (especially in Bangkok's Central Thai society) for it implies an attack on the stratified structure of the Thai social body. An attack of this kind is articulated quite clearly in the declaration of intent or manifesto of the *dohd diao*, proclaimed on their Facebook page: *Kaeng dohd diao: mai mi kham wa phi, mai mi kham wa nong, mi khae kham wa pheuan* ('Gang of loners: the words younger and older siblings don't exist. There's only room for the word friend').

Those who created the slogan of the gang are slum children who, like Ton, have partly grown up in environments like Saint Jacob's, and whose social experience and experience of self have been variably co-shaped by alternative religiopolitical constructions of childhood, poverty, hierarchy, ethnicity and rights. When I asked children what their slogan meant, they told me, earnestly: 'In the gang we're all the same. There are no *phu nam*, *phi* or people in a higher position than others. We're just friends [*pheuan*]!'.

Gang violence: The price of military hyper-nationalism

It is not only *dek salam* who have a tendency to band together in gangs. Disputes between gangs of students in the city are often reported by the media.[4] In 2010, to give an example, a 10-year-old child was killed in Bangkok by several rounds of gunfire while on his way to school in a public bus. All the perpetrators were teenagers, members of a local gang. The majority of assaults of this kind are premeditated, involve armed minors and occur in public places (Asian Correspondent 2011).

Scholars have discussed group violence as a by-product of impenetrable, essentialised and conflicting collective identities. There has been persuasive research on this topic in the field of social psychology. In 1971, in a controversial study conducted in the basement of Stanford University, Philip Zimbardo (2007) asked 75 students to split into two groups: 'prison guards' and 'inmates', each provided with appropriate uniforms and identity markers, and with the task of simulating everyday life in prison. The social experiment was suspended soon after, because of the sadistic behaviour of the 'prison guards' towards the 'inmates'. Zimbardo explained the guards' violence with reference to certain mutually interrelated sociopsychological processes: group-based diffusion of individual responsibility, dehumanisation of those external to the group and, especially, an ideological legitimisation of their humiliation. Somewhat along the same lines, Tajfel (1981) has described 'inter-group discrimination' as the ultimate result of

---

4   According to the United Nations Asia and Far East Institute for the Prevention of Crime and the Treatment of Offenders (UNAFEI), juvenile delinquency (without distinguishing by gender) in Thailand increased by 70% between 2003 to 2007 (Korakod Narkvichetr 2009). A significant number of recorded offenses committed by minors relate to violence between gangs of students.

a dichotomous social distinction between the ingroup (the group one belongs to) and the outgroup (outsiders to the group), which – in some circumstances – can lead to a fundamental devaluation of outgroup members. The existence of an inextricable link between group violence and identity politics has also been pointed out by other social scientists (see e.g. Bauman 1989, Scheper-Hughes & Bourgois 2004). A violent attack against the alien Other, external to the group, is the probable outcome – 'normal' or 'banal' as Hannah Arendt would put it (1963) – based on certain assumptions. These are that the Other, because it is external to the collective self, is not like Us: those who are Other are inferior, immoral, and therefore less human. The Other, moreover, precisely by virtue of their difference, represents a threat to the core of the collective self, and can, as such, be eliminated without a shred of remorse.

In developing the concept of 'Thainess', military regimes and royalist elites have historically exacerbated the binary logic of ethno-linguistic distinction between Self (Thai) and Other ('non-Thai') (e.g. see Thongchai Winichakul 1994; Pavin Chachavalpongpun 2011; Siwach Sripokangkul and Cogan 2019). The rhetoric of national identity serves, therefore, as a discursive matrix for the cultural fabrication of closed and essentialised group configurations. The socio-political, religious and ritual aspects of the state emphasis on 'Thainess' come together organically to create a sense of the nation's people as a collective, hierarchically organised, and authentically Thai 'social body' (Aulino 2014), outside of which the individual would cease to exist. This implies that the 'Thai self' is carved out by way of contrast with an immoral, inferior, and dangerous 'non-Thai' Other. It follows that an individual's social value depends on their contribution to the collective self: if they are ready to sacrifice for the sake of the nation (and its tutelary deities: kingship, Buddhism, and the military), they are worthy of respect and admiration.

In 2012 I visited Ban Meta ('House of Compassion'), the juvenile detention centre in Bangkok, where *dek salam* represent a remarkable portion of inmates. Here I was allowed to interview Kim, 13 years old, born in the slum of Khlong Toei, who was accused of having killed a boy his own age, a member of a rival gang, with a gun. I was already quite tense at the idea of meeting a child murderer but what struck me the most was Kim's appearance. I had expected the perpetrator of such a serious crime to embody, physically, his supposed 'deviancy'. However, Kim was a frail boy, shy, good-mannered and respectful towards *phu yai*. I was baffled by a child who seemed, to me, to bring together two images that were diametrically opposed: that of murderer and that of victim. We started to talk in the courtyard of the facility. I tried to be as tactful as possible in addressing the topic, and after some neutral questions, I finally asked him why he was at Ban Meta. Here is an extract of our conversation:

Giuseppe: Why are you here?

Kim: I killed a child [lowers his eyes].

G.: What happened?

K.: I didn't want to and I was very scared. But I had to show my friends I deserved to be part of the gang.

G: Did your friends ask you to do it?

K: They gave me the gun, and they asked me to hurt him, because he had disrespected our *phi* [older brother]. I was a newcomer, it had to be me. I couldn't say no, I had no choice. If you refuse, people from your school exclude you and beat you. If you accept, people from the rival school will beat you. There's no way out.

(Interview with Kim, Ban Meta, July 2012)

Through national celebrations connecting public and domestic notions of parenthood and childhood (such as Father's Day and Mother's Day), the ritualised enforcement of 'Thainess' mediates the top-down penetration of the national identity ideology into family and into the social micro-cosmos. However, there is still room for the expression of alternative or additional sub-identities. In schools, for example, standard rituals of national loyalty are often accompanied by activities specific to the identity of that school: besides the national anthem, the royal anthem, and a Buddhist chant, schools often have a school song to sing as well. Alongside national identity, each school thus sacralises their own identity symbols (the school uniform, colour, and culture), with which all students are expected to identify. These sub-identities confront each other in the context of inter-school national competitions aiming to establish which school is the most 'Thai', generating inter-group conflicts within the wider framework of the national 'Thai self'. Identity tensions of this type can develop in various directions and ways. Inter-group violence does not only affect child gangs but is intrinsic to the country's socio-political dynamics, as shown by the disputes that have occurred historically between centres and peripheries, between Thai and 'non-Thai', between the urbanised middle classes and rural classes with minority ethnic identities, between 'yellow' and 'red'.

'Thainess' has the official goal of promoting a cohesive collective self. Sometimes, however, it ends up fragmenting the citizens of Thailand into conflicting collective micro-selves organised around local (as opposed to national) ethno-linguistic affiliations and solidarities. This is especially the case for marginalised groups, who experience a growing frustration with their subaltern position within the Thai social body. This can lead them to create collective identities pivoting around subversive parameters (in relation, for example, to generation, ethnicity or class) with respect to those prescribed by the state.

VICTIMISED CHILDREN, RESPONSIVE FARANG

Although while in the slum and at school children are likely to construct themselves in open contrast to the 'good Thai child' model, when they relate to *farang* and to NGO workers they quickly come to realise the socioeconomic benefits of victimhood.[5]

In 2011, while I was volunteering at Saint Jacob's, I came to know Bon, an 8-year-old boy, sweet and always smiling. He was addressed by all as Bon *lek* ('little Bon') because he was frail and quite short compared to his peers. When I first met him, he was walking alone on a dirt road leading to the main site of the NGO. Returning from school, he was carrying a backpack that looked bigger than himself. Father Nicola told me that Bon had been accepted by his organisation only a few months before, after his mother tragically died from an AIDS-related illness. The priest told me that Bon had always lived with his mother in Akhan Daeng.

I quickly grew fond of the child. I was not alone in feeling compassion towards Bon; other Western volunteers at Saint Jacob's felt the same. Initially, I tended to interpret Bon's life story by using moral and psychological yardsticks that defined him as the quintessential victim, the innocent traumatised child whose parents have died, whose seemingly serene and joyful appearance conceals a secret suffering. Bon was quick to notice my cultural prejudices.

During dinner, he always sat next to me, poured my drink, and waited until I had swallowed the last bite of food, ready to pounce on my empty plate so as to relieve me of the task of washing it myself. After dinner, when all the children usually gathered around the communal TV, Bon went to clean my room and did my laundry. Before I went to bed, he insisted that I let him massage my back, an art that all Thais are generally trained in from childhood. His subservient behaviour made me feel uncomfortable and embarrassed. I was supposed to be taking care of him; he was not supposed to be caring for me. At the time, I did not completely understand that Bon was behaving as does a proper *phu noi*.

---

5   Elsewhere (see Bolotta 2019), I have developed some of what I argue in this section to scrutinise the epistemic value of the researcher's 'humanitarian emotions' in ethnographic work with vulnerable children.

During the first weeks of my stay at Saint Jacob's, Bon related to me in a way that reflected local dynamics between *phu noi* and *phu yai*, especially in the presence of the NGO staff. However, my response to his efforts was quite different from that normally provided by Thai *phu yai*. Convinced that Bon was particularly in need of affection due to his mother's early death, and moved by Father Nicola's dramatic description of the child, I told Bon that I loved him even if he did not wash my clothes every day, and that the role of caregiver should have been mine. Bon replied to my statement with a chuckle. Only later did I realise that with his chuckle the child had placed me – together with most Western NGO workers who were dealing with *dek salam* in Bangkok – in the category of *farang*. Bon had witnessed the emotional discrepancy between this strange adult I was in his eyes and local *phu yai*, and was playing with it.

One evening, while we were sitting at the side of the large courtyard of the NGO, Bon told me about his mother. '*Phi* [elder brother], did you know that my mother died?' he asked. According to Father Nicola, Bon had never talked before about his mother's death with any adult. When I asked why he was reluctant to address the subject with the Thai staff at the NGO, or to talk about how he was working through his loss, he replied: 'I talk about these things with friends. Mum left me with Father Nicola. Then she promised she would come back to get me. But instead, she died'. Why had he chosen to share this with me? Did he now see me as one of his friends? I sensed some anger in his words, but I was still troubled by Bon's apparent emotional detachment.

The death of a child's family member was not uncommon at Saint Jacob's. Right after his mother's death, Bon had shaved his head and put on the orange robe of a novice (*samanen*). In Thai Buddhism, sons temporarily ordain as *samanen* at the Buddhist temple where the cremation ritual has taken place in order to pay off their karmic debt to their parents (Tambiah 1976). At the temple, *samanen* have the opportunity to understand the natural character of death as well as the fact that life comes to an end and is transient and ultimately an illusion. They are also trained to take up a serene and emotionally detached spiritual position, which enables them to accept the unavoidable. Feelings like despair signal attachment and weakness and must be neutralised through Buddhist meditation.

The caregiving model drawn on by most Western volunteers derives from culturally-shaped notions of 'childhood' and 'children's suffering' that are very different from local ones. The humanitarian portrayal of children as victims – grounded in a Western, middle-class concept (thought of as universal) of children as vulnerable, not yet fully-formed individuals – generates emotional pathos and a disproportionate emotional response among *farang*, a response that contrasts with the usual interactions that children like Bon experience with Thai adults. In fact, the inter-affective dynamic between *farang* and *dek salam* in NGO contexts could be regarded as opposite, even antithetical, to the relationship that is considered appropriate between adults and children in Thai Buddhism. In describing his mother's death, Bon seemed anchored to a culturally normative, Buddhist-informed, description of his emotional experience. At the same time, he seemed to understand the emotional potential of the drama, if this was played out with *farang*.

After he had confided in me the details of his mother's tragic death and had gained my sympathy and attention during what I thought would be a challenging emotional transition for him, Bon began to make demands of me. Every evening, after curfew, he sneaked out of the children's dormitory and crept into my room to request the key to the pantry, for which I was responsible. He would come in with a smile – I could not tell if this was mocking or tender – and would timidly say: 'I would like to drink a glass of Ovaltine with you before I go to bed. May I?' I could never say no. In the deserted and unusually quiet courtyard of Saint Jacob's, the secret night rendezvous with Bon became a sort of ritual. During those nights, while we broke the curfew together, Bon told me in even greater detail how difficult his life had been. Without realising it, I soon began to favour Bon among the children. He began to ask me for small amounts of money, or to accompany him to the market, confident that I would pay for him. A frequent request was that I call his aunt from my cell phone. When I finally had the chance to talk directly to his aunt, I discovered that Bon – contrary to what I had been told by Father Nicola – had always lived with her and that he had never really known his mother. This made me feel that it was I who was the small child, not Bon! Over time I understood that, because of our special relationship, the child had sidestepped a number of the rules that were meant to be observed by *dek salam* at Saint Jacob's. I also realised that other children recognised this and that, as a result, Bon's reputation and social position within his peer group had increased.

The parents of *dek salam* like Bon come from rural areas in the ethnic minority regions of northern or northeastern Thailand, and such children are not commonly brought up in a nuclear family environment. Bon was raised by his maternal uncle's extended family, after his mother entrusted him to his grandmother because of her illness. For Bon, the attachment relationship be-tween mother and child, which Western psychology regards as the cornerstone of child development, was not the main emotional framework in which he developed (Bolotta 2017a).

The effectiveness of 'suffering' among dek salam

My readiness to react to children's expressions of apparent emotional distress put me in a complicated and emotionally challenging situation. Other guests of the NGO besides Bon began to ask me to mediate on their behalf in attempts to circumvent some of the rules at St. Jacob's. They sought my intercession to allow them an extra hour to play football on Sundays, to watch more movies, to return to the slums more often, and so on. Rather than putting their requests to the Thai staff – the *phu yai* – directly, the children put them to me, having identified me as a *farang* who was sensitive to their needs, emotionally manoeuvrable, and had the ability to influence the NGO staff. Eventually, the children began competing for an exclusive relationship with me, which they could use to achieve various social, economic and affective objectives.

One afternoon, while playing football in the yard, Bon fell spectacularly to the ground, scraping his knee. Except in real emergencies, boys aged over eight were encouraged to be independent, including dealing with their own medical needs. The infirmary was open and accessible to them all. Instinctively, however, I rushed to his aid. I picked him up and went to get gauze, ice and disinfectant to dress the wound. The other children – who, in the meantime, had followed us to the infirmary – stood gazing at us, incredulous that a (male) *phu yai* would take care of one of their number in that way. Over the next few days, on their way back from school, the children began to show me the wounds – sometimes very minor ones – they got during their reckless, daring and fun-filled adventures, saying: 'Look, *phi*, I've been hurt!'. They knew that I would immediately go to the infirmary and devote myself to them. Taking advantage of my willingness to help, they quickly turned me into a kind of nurse, and they began not only to ridicule my clumsy actions but also to manipulate my emotional responsiveness, using this as 'symbolic capital' (Bourdieu 2005). The children progressively began to apply this approach to other types of behaviour that they realised would elicit an emotional response from me. For example, while I was present and the Thai staff were not some of the children began to simulate fights. The Thai staff normally left the children to resolve conflicts on their own. Not me! I was still affected by a tendency to intervene. Once, Ton staged a drama. He called out to me, laughing, and then pounced on a younger child with kicks and punches. Both children knew that I would get upset and stop them. As soon as this happened, the boy and his alleged victim cracked up, seeing how their manoeuvre had succeeded in dragging the stupid *farang* into their field of action.

As I have discussed above, the expression of negative emotions while relating to Thai *phu yai* is normally considered unbecoming. In today's militarised

Thailand, demonstrations of emotional vulnerability are also discouraged by a dominant construction of male identity that promotes the assumption of warrior and soldierly characteristics in boys. In spite of this, I was still convinced that it was essential to enable 'traumatised children' to express negative emotions in the context of a positive relationship with an adult, so I treated every sign of discomfort with the utmost seriousness. Especially at the beginning of my fieldwork, I used to call aside children who appeared to be sad, trying to convince them to talk. In response to this, the children often pretended to cry, reminding me of their status as poor *dek salam* in need of help.

The fact that expression of emotion is considered inappropriate is also expressed in attitudes to bodily contact. In the relationship between children and the Thai adults, respect and mutual affection were expressed through relational emotional codes that did not involve physical contact. Western missionaries, by contrast, would touch and hug *dek salam* fondly, even if the 'child' was 17 years old. Bon and the others seemed then to understand how effective it was to accompany requests they made to me or to other *farang* with physical contact.

Aware of my influence over those who ran Saint Jacob's, the children thus turned me into their mediator, the spokesperson of their concerns and desires. Although in the slums – in the absence of an audience of humanitarian workers – the children appeared anything but children or victims, in their relationships with the representatives of 'humanitarian reason' (Fassin 2012; Barnett 2011) *dek salam* articulated their agency through adhering, strategically, to a projection of themselves as 'vulnerable children' or 'victims'.[6] They projected themselves in this way through deploying what might be described as a 'language of suffering', which was made up of emotional performances – both narrative and bodily – that were aimed at manipulating *farang* humanitarian workers.

The emotional economy of victimhood

As Andrew Beatty (2013: 25) has observed, emotional narratives do not only project an alleged sentiment; they also have a pragmatic effect, in that they produce a reaction.[7] This is precisely what happened during my encounters with *dek salam*. A few important points must be considered in this regard.

6   The political value of Western discourses on 'victimised children' has also been documented in other contexts recently: see for example the studies carried out by Vignato in Indonesia (Vignato 2017), and by Cheney in Uganda (Cheney 2004, 2013). These demonstrate how the image of children as 'victims' can be used and appropriated, strategically, by those in receipt of humanitarian assistance.

7   Anthropological reflection has largely deconstructed the notion of emotions as universal and individual biological events that are outside the culture of those who feel those emotions

In order to produce specific emotional responses in humanitarian workers, Bon *lek* ('little Bon') and Ton must have identified, beforehand, a number of things: firstly, the meaning of the emotions experienced by *farang* at the NGO (which are grounded in different cultural norms to their own); secondly, the inter-subjective, situational and pragmatic character of these emotions (they must, for example, have realised that if an Italian encounters a crying child, he will usually be sympathetic and helpful); and thirdly, the fact that *farang* have a model of caregiving that is grounded in humanitarian notions of *dek salam* as victims. The children have clearly gone through an emotional and cultural learning process, in the context of constant interaction with the many missionaries, NGO workers and Western volunteers who frequent the slums as actors on the cosmopolitan humanitarian stage. The complexity of the emotional understanding that these children display clearly destabilises NGOs workers' normative representation of 'the child' as a vulnerable, passive and low-skilled subject.

Children must also have come to understand the nature of these culturally-shaped inter-affective schemas in order to be able to reproduce – not in a reiterative fashion but 'performatively' (Butler 1990) – a certain emotional experience, for instance sadness, in a culturally convincing way. In other words, if they want to elicit the empathetic response that a child who comes across as desperate is able to stimulate in *farang*, they must be able to mimic the bodily and verbal expression of desperation to which *farang* are accustomed in their own cultural contexts. It is often quite clear that the children's performance is intentional and that it is designed to produce a certain desired emotional response from missionaries and from social workers at a Western NGO like Saint Jacob's: compassion and a willingness to intercede on their behalf in relation to specific requests.

Thomas Stodulka (2014, 2015) has analysed similar affective interactions between researchers and marginalised children in Java, Indonesia. In relationships with the actors of Java's humanitarian landscape (activists, researchers, NGOs workers, etc.), 'street children' would tell dramatic stories that were loaded with moral and emotional implications – stories that were similar to those described by the *dek salam* in Bangkok, related, for example, to the death or serious illness of a parent. Making strategic use of these accounts, children

---

(Beatty 2013). With the emergence of discursive and constructionist paradigms, emotions have, in fact, come to be described using terms such as 'cultural artifacts' (Geertz 1973), 'social constructions', 'embodied thoughts' (Rosaldo 1984) or 'bodily cognitions' (Lutz and White 1986). These approaches fail, however, to take proper account of the subjective and experiential sphere of emotions, focusing exclusively on their social determinants (Davies and Spencer [eds] 2010). Here, avoiding any essentialist theoretical formulation, I look at emotions as a polythetic class of bio–cultural inter-subjective events, which vary according to social context and are co-produced by the ethnographer and local social actors.

would present an appearance of hopelessness and would beg for money, only for it to later become apparent that they were anything but desperate in more everyday social contexts. Stodulka describes these children's ability to turn their marginality into emotional and economic ties with humanitarian workers as 'emotional economy' (ibid.). By linking their emotional expressions to the ideological context of their encounter with a (Western) humanitarian worker, the children were able to expand their social networks and to generate 'social capital' (Bourdieu 2005).

This is similar to what I observed in the slums of Bangkok, where *dek salam* were often able to access the resources of NGOs thanks to their ability to produce emotionally well-orchestrated performances. As Stodulka has pointed out, such performances are grounded in a survival strategy that is learnt collectively. The children's self-presentation as victims, and their focus on the expression of emotions related to suffering, is not the outcome of individual subjective choices. On the contrary, the fact that many *dek salam* selectively exhibited certain emotional patterns in their interactions with *farang* shows that these are grounded in collective knowledge.

At the same time, it should be borne in mind that while *farang* working in aid organisations constitute an affective and relational reservoir for the children, one that can be turned into social and economic capital, *dek salam* also constitute humanitarian capital for *farang* (e.g. see Bornstein 2001). In this regard, it seems important to complement Stodulka's investigation of the interrelated 'emotional economies' of marginalised children and of NGOs workers by making it clear that these are both connected and informed by a political transnational superstructure, namely the humanitarian 'moral economy of childhood' (Fassin 2013).

Humanitarian perspectives and practices provide a useful framework within which to examine how transnational 'industrial chains of charity' use categories of 'disadvantaged children' to direct global resource flows (e.g. Cole and Durham [eds] 2008; Wells 2009; Rudnyckyj and Osella [eds] 2017). NGOs, in particular, continue to reify and commodify images of 'children in need' in order to stage 'a spectacle of suffering' (Boltansky 1993; Mesnard 2004) that is essential to raise funds and bring in donations. The depiction of children as victims to be saved is thus at the centre of a moral economy that is one of the main channels through which post-colonial compassionate governmentalities are able to penetrate the cracks of the world's internal and external peripheries. By drawing on and utilising the humanitarian categories to which they are exposed, 'victimised' children, for their part, unconsciously perpetuate the need for humanitarian interventions, thus revealing the complementary nature of the relationship between local emotional economies and transnational moral economies of childhood.

CONCLUDING REMARKS

In this chapter I have shown how the range of cultural politics to which Bangkok's poor children are exposed shapes the children's own experience, generating a plurality of childhoods. In an effort to craft a sense of self, children do not passively follow scripts presented to them by adults but creatively reinterpret social structures through what are sometimes riotous acts of agency.

In the slums, in the absence of *phu yai*, children are far from appearing as 'victims'; and they construct themselves in antithesis to the identity model prescribed by 'Thainess'. The relationship between *phi* and *nong*, clothing, language, games and group activities all create a space for children that is intimate and everyday – one to which *phu yai* do not normally have access. At school, *dek salam* also seem to overturn the ethnicised and stigmatising logic of the state through a number of different strategies: boys can exaggerate their social 'deviancy', define a form of leadership that is 'non-Thai', and openly defy the axiom of the 'good Thai child'; girls can re-articulate their sexuality in anti-normative directions, and establish female alliances based on taking on traits that are supposedly male.

The 'gang of loners' (*kaeng dohd diao*) is a reference point for many *dek salam*. It demonstrates the children's ability to co-construct themselves – not only in their relationships with adults, but also among peers. Through a shared creation of symbols, languages, practices and unique gestures, signatures of the gang, children have brought into being an axis of collective resistance out of their own condition of difference, the exemplary expression of which is an emotional past constituted of loneliness. The social reality they construct in the *kaeng dohd diao* projects an alternative organisation of the social world, one in which *phi* and *nong* statuses are levelled out and that refuses the principle of hierarchy. In doing this, it desecrates the cosmological heart of the Thai socio-political order. However, although the ideological heterogeneity in which they are socialised allows them to define social and cultural worlds that appear to oppose the paradigm of 'Thainess', even *dek salam* become bearers of the Thai social world. The frequent violence between gangs is a sad example of this, expressing the binary logic that demonises the Other as different from Us.

On the other hand, in the context of humanitarian organisations and NGOs, *dek salam* learn to embody the position of 'victim': through a physical and verbal language of suffering, children are able to manipulate humanitarian workers (especially *farang*) to their own advantage. The compassionate discourse of NGOs feeds into transnational moral economies of childhood. At the same time, it creates 'victimised' subjects who display their vulnerability as an act of agency.

At the Suan Kaeo Foundation and at the Saint Jacob's Centre, however, *dek salam* are not only exposed to narratives related to children's rights. Here, they also encounter specific religious theories around the suffering of children, ones that conflict with local political and moral notions of family, the education of children, ethnicity and urban poverty. Father Nicola and Sister Serafina's political theology of childhood, in particular, plays an important part in the children's self-formation and in their agency-related practices. As I will show in the next chapter, the strong emotional bond with these missionaries has offered some children a religious space where their ethnic, class, and generational identities can be revalued and potentially transformed into a subversive political self.

CHAPTER 6

Beyond the 'Thai Self'

> One may regard the relational matrix within which each of us lives as a tapestry woven on Penelope's loom, a tapestry whose design is rich with interacting figures. Some represent images and metaphors around which one's self is experienced; some represent images and phantoms of others, whom one endlessly pursues, or escapes, in a complex choreography of movements, gestures, and arrangements woven together from fragments of experience and the cast of characters on one's early interpersonal world. Like Penelope, each of us weaves and unravels, constructing our relational world to maintain the same dramatic tensions, perpetuating [...] the same longings, suspense, revenge, surprises, and struggles. (S.A. Mitchell 1988: 272–273)

This chapter focuses on the life trajectories of children, examined longitudinally over a 10-year period. Over this period, I saw these children grow up and go through radical transformations, creatively crafting and re-crafting their plural selves out of the multiple norms, social identities, and knowledge systems that had been imposed upon them – and presented to them as opportunities – by a wide range of competing caregivers, cultural institutions, and socio-political actors. Teachers, monks, missionaries, NGOs, families, soldiers, and friends all play a role in fixing the fluid and ever-changing subjectivities of these children into contradictory 'subject positions' (Laclau and Mouffe 1985: 111, Foucault 1994); 'symbolic anchors' (Phillips 2006: 310); or affective 'points of identification' (Hall 1996: 5). These make *dek salam* socially intelligible in the context of broader debates and discussions in which they, as poor slum children, are implicitly embedded. Children's agency is both constrained and enabled by this type of identity politics (Butler 1993: 15), with each child endlessly weaving and unravelling a range of strategic threads in order to negotiate their way, and construct their self, through a complex social and political landscape. Although each child negotiates a slightly different path, certain recurring socio-cultural and psycho-political dynamics can be clearly discerned that demonstrate the entanglement between the cultural politics of marginal childhoods and the complex and conflicted way in which the underprivileged form their selves in today's militarised Thai society.

THE (UN)MAKING OF CHILDREN'S SENSE OF SELF

'Poor children are the sons of God!'

I met Kla in 2008 at Saint Jacob's, when he was 12 years old. Despite his youth, he was already a real chatterbox. Before moving to the Catholic NGO six years earlier, he had lived in Akhan Daeng with his father, who was 30, and with his paternal grandmother, who was 65, both from the (Thai-Lao) northeast of Thailand. His mother, pregnant by another man, had left his family when he was five. When Father Nicola began visiting the slum, Kla was always home alone: his father was serving a six-year sentence for drug dealing and his grandmother returned home late every evening after collecting plastic bottles and cans all day at the nearby Mo Chit bus station. Kla vividly remembered his first encounter with the missionary:

> When I was a child, I was always alone. I had many friends but grandma and dad were never at home. One day I saw *pho* [father] Nicola coming to Akhan Daeng with a bag full of chips and candies. He put me up on his shoulders and we visited the whole community together. He was very good to us children; he treated us all as his sons. *Pho* has saved me; he brought me to Saint Jacob's to live in a big house. Now I have lots of clothes and I go to a private school. It's as though *Pho* Nicola were my real father. (Kla, August 2008)

After that, Kla followed the missionary about like a shadow. However, while he regarded the missionary as his 'new father' (*pho mai*), Thai *phu yai* never earned the child's respect. Prasit, the head of staff at St. Jacob's, considered Kla hard to handle: 'He doesn't follow the rules, he lacks respect for *phu yai*, and he only behaves like a 'good child' [*dek di*] in Father Nicola's presence'.

In 2011, while I was at Saint Jacob's, I noticed that Kla had some influence over other children. The intimate relationship that he had with Father Nicola gave him authority. For many children at Saint Jacob's, Kla was *phi* ('elder sibling'). However, the form that his leadership took was very different from that of Thai *phu yai*. Kla emulated his hero, Father Nicola: he taught catechism to *dek salam*, gave them advice on the most disparate matters, and reprimanded those who made mistakes. While teaching good manners and Thai cultural etiquette to the youngest children, he was also careful to stress the beauty of Thailand's ethno-linguistic diversity. I heard him expressing, at the same time, scathing criticism of 'Thainess', which he regarded as an identity grounded in unfairness because it was premised on the urban poor's social inferiority – quite a bold and unusual position to take on the part of a slum child.

Kla was particularly critical of Thai teachers channelling negative moral models in their teaching: 'Father Nicola taught me that children must be listened to. But the teachers only know how to give orders and impose rules. They think that *khon isan* [people from Thailand's Thai-Lao northeast] are stupid, dirty and dangerous'. His judgment was based on a systematic comparison between Thai *phu yai* and the missionary: a comparison in which all *phu yai* came across in a bad light and one that painted Father Nicola as an ideal model with whom to identify, one of unattainable perfection. For the Thai teachers, Kla's attitude meant that it became difficult to manage the child, as he not only questioned their authority but also self-identified as a perfect replica of the missionary. Kla felt that he could educate *nong* better than any Thai *phu yai* could. Between 2011 and 2013, he was expelled from two Catholic private schools for accusing some of the teachers there of abusing their positions of power, and of discriminating against *dek salam*. Even the Thai staff at Saint Jacob's often complained about Kla's irreverent behaviour; but *pho* Nicola's affectionate acceptance of the boy implicitly legitimised his anti-leadership.

When *pho* Nicola was transferred to another parish by Bangkok clerical authorities in 2013, things changed for Kla. Just three months later, he left the NGO to go back to Akhan Daeng. By then he was a young man of 17, and he found a job at Mo Chit bus station with the help of his grandmother. However, he continued to dream about working for Father Nicola. He was still in touch with the guests (past and current) at Saint Jacob's through Facebook, monitoring their development and regularly providing them with different advice from that given by Thai teachers. In the slum, he began to take care of a number of *nong*, distributing small sums of money and buying meals for the children of Akhan Daeng – quickly squandering his meagre salary as a result. I often had to lend him money, or intervene in quarrels with *phu yai* who were unwilling to tolerate what they regarded as the boy's disrespectful behaviour – a sort of 'desecrating resourcefulness', indeed. However, his position as one of Father Nicola's most beloved sons always served to protect him. Kla was not only aware of this, but actively used this knowledge to reinforce his own leadership within the slum.

On his return to Akhan Daeng, Kla began writing his reflections on the struggles of *dek salam* in a diary every day. One afternoon in 2012, he was keen to share with me one particular entry, entitled 'Jesus in my everyday life' (*phra yesu jao nai chiwit prajam wan khong phom*):

> We can find Jesus with the poor, the sick, the orphans, the disadvantaged children [*dek doi ohkat*]. God wants us to understand the importance of such people, because they are the sons of God. Jesus said: 'The kingdom

of heaven belongs to children'. With these words, Jesus wanted to suggest to all of us that we should be like children, that we should, with faith, serve people 'lower' than us. God has seen the purity of children and has stated that: 'If you do not become as these little children, you will not gain access to the kingdom of heaven.'   (Kla, August 2012)

I asked Kla what he meant by 'the purity of children', and he answered: 'Children don't know what poverty is, what illness or disadvantage mean. Children are pure because to them all people are equal. There is no one above or below. Just people.'

Kla has never really lived with his biological parents. He has mixed feelings towards them: when he speaks of them harshly, he suddenly feels guilty, like someone who realises that he has said something that should never be said. He has often described them as irresponsible, but regrets not being able to support them. He says that even though his parents abandoned him, they nevertheless gave him the gift of life. He told me more than once that Mum and Dad are 'the *phra* [monks] of the house', recalling the Buddhist state mantra of gratitude (*khwam katanyu*), and tormenting himself over not being a sufficiently deserving son. While his feelings for his parents confused him, his paternal grandmother was the key figure he could rely on. He usually went to the Buddhist temple with her. The last time I met him, in 2014, I asked him for his thoughts on state religion. I took for granted that he must have become a fervent Christian, but his answer took me by surprise: 'Buddhism is a good religion, like all religions. It helps to calm your heart, it teaches *dharma* and compassion. I have not chosen my religion yet. When I was at Saint Jacob's, I was a Christian. Now that I am with grandma, I am a Buddhist. My *pho* [i.e. Father Nicola] is Christian and my grandma is a Buddhist, so I don't know which religion is mine yet'.

Trajectories of status

Today Wat is a 23-year-old young man, well-built, dark-skinned, covered in tattoos. Despite the intimidating, thug-like impression that he gives, he is a very sensitive guy to those who know him, a tender heart trapped in a giant's body. As a child, he spent some years at Saint Jacob's because his mother, who lived in Akhan Daeng, could not afford to send him to school.

I first met him in 2009 at the Catholic NGO. Wat was then a 12-year-old boy, small and funny and totally in love with football, like many of the other guests at Saint Jacob's. We spent entire afternoons playing together in the courtyard of the NGO. He was very sociable, extremely caring with younger children, but also brash and demanding with peers. During my stay at Saint Jacob's, Wat went through radical transformations. He was older than most of the other *dek salam*, and the stage was set for him to take over the role of *phi*. However, the formation of social hierarchies in the peer group was hampered by the NGO's rules, which were influenced by Western notions of childhood that required adults to deal with all underage *dek salam* as 'children' of equal status (and with equal rights). In 2011, Wat decided to escape from the Catholic charity and return to the slum, where he has lived since then with his mother and younger sisters. In 2012, while we were having dinner in his family's house, he explained his choice to leave the NGO as part of his childhood-to-adulthood transition: 'If I had stayed there, I would have remained a child and I wouldn't have known how to face problems in life. Outside, real life is different'.

Although it operates within a distinct religious framework, Saint Jacob's shares a globalised, Eurocentric construction of childhood with other secular NGOs, one that is laid out in the UN Convention on the Rights of the Child. This predominantly Western, middle-class ideology (see e.g. Burman 2017; Jenks 1996; Boyden 1997) sets out a system that establishes equality between all, which tends to level differences in status, thus hindering social differentiation between children as *phi* and *nong*. All underage children must have the same rights (and duties).

Slum children only adhere to these egalitarian norms on the surface. In the context of Thai society all relationships must be seen through a hierarchical filter. This means that all children are not the same and there can be no simple polar opposition between 'children' and 'adults'. From the age of 12 or 13, Saint Jacob's guests sometimes became impatient with this form of imposed equality. They may, for example, feel humiliated when called to perform the duties normally given to their 'younger siblings' (*nong*), and demand recognition of their evolving role as *phi*. Not all *dek salam* chose to run away as Wat did. However, others reacted to the imposed equality in a similar way. Biu, a 15-year-old boy who had been at Saint Jacob's for seven years, complained, for example: 'Now I get bored here. There are too many rules, and I am not a child any more'.

Many *dek salam* maintain a strong emotional bond with Father Nicola. However, those children who eventually decide to return to the slum – which is, significantly, identified as 'home' – tend to associate their experience as guests of a Western NGO with a childhood self that has now evaporated. Flight from the aid agency is conceived of as a 'rite of passage' (van Gennep 2002) by Wat and the other children, as a move that marks the transition from childhood to adulthood. In fact, in the eyes of many of the children social adulthood can only be achieved in the slum.

On the other hand, child-focused spaces such as Saint Jacob's can offer *dek salam* possibilities of agency that are limited in other environments, thereby providing poor children with powerful tools (both symbolic and economic) that allow the fugitives, on their way to adulthood, to return to the slum as apprentice leaders (*phu nam*). As Wat put it:

> Before coming to Saint Jacob's, I was just another child of the slum [*dek salam*]. Now I am a big boy. Saint Jacob's helped me to become an authoritative guide [*phu nam*] for the younger children [*nong*]. A *phu nam* is someone able to guide those who are younger, both within the family and in society, enabling them to grow up and become *phu yai*. I am a *nak leng* now, a good 'mafia person'. I have a lot of people counting on me – but don't tell Father Nicola! (Wat, March 2013)

By remaining with an organisation that is, in the eyes of the community, a rich Western NGO, Wat was able to 'appoint himself' as a leader in the slum and to go so far as to challenge inter-generational power relationships. One day, as Wat and I were going back to his house, we met his maternal uncle, who was having a whisky with friends. Evidently drunk, he shook my hand, while Wat, who kept on walking, boldly scoffed: 'You see? He's always drunk! He does nothing but drink whisky from morning till night!'

His circular movement from the slum to the NGO and back to the slum has equipped Wat with the symbolic capital to negotiate his own position within the local power structure. While a Western NGO like Saint Jacob's attempts to promote 'horizontal' relationships and values, Wat has managed to use the prestige associated with Saint Jacob's to 'vertically' ascend the local social hierarchy in the slum, which continues to be based on seniority.

Today, Wat is a recognised member of *mae* Pan's network. He has also been selected by CODI operators in the slum to work as an educator in a drug prevention programme for young people. He often calls Father Nicola to keep him updated on the latest developments in his life. Like other *dek salam*, he considers the missionary 'his real dad'. When they meet, Wat behaves like a devoted son. He proudly tells the missionary about the ways in which he is helping poor children, and he talks about religious topics, drawing parallels between Christian teachings and the direction that he wants to take in his life. Father Nicola's approval, his compliments and his pleased smiles thrill Wat. Yet, in the missionary's presence he carefully avoids wearing his showy golden pins, emblems of the Thai army and the monarchy.[1] He knows that Father Nicola might not appreciate his idealisation

---

1   The emblem of the Royal Army of Thailand is a chakra (*jak*) placed under the Thai version of *ohm* (a sacred sound and the spiritual icon of dharmic religions) and the Great Victory Crown

of military heroism. I last spoke to Wat on Skype in January 2015. His status read: 'I was born to have others in my power [*koet ma pheua hai khon yu tai amnat*]'.

Catholic teacher and prostitute

Naen arrived at Saint Jacob's in 2003 when she was six years old. She had previously lived with her mother and two half-brothers in Mit Phra Cha, one of the slums in Bangkok where Father Nicola was active. Naen never knew her real father and her stepfather had died of a heart attack. Her mother, a 40-year-old ex-peasant from Lampang, northern Thailand, ran a small restaurant out of her house.

In 2002, her mother decided to entrust Naen, her eldest daughter, to the Catholic NGO. She didn't want to send her sons to Saint Jacob's as they were often given small jobs by other people living in Mit Phra Cha. She also felt that Naen was not safe in the slum, as she was a very pretty child. Her mother feared that in a few years' time, when Naen became sexually mature, she would not be able to shield her from the (unwanted) attentions of men.

I met Naen at Saint Jacob's when she was 11 years old. She was a quiet, polite, graceful girl, the picture of Thai femininity. The staff at Saint Jacob's described her as a 'little angel' because she was particularly caring and motherly towards *nong*. Enrolled at a Catholic private school in Bangkok, she had only average marks, not outstanding enough for any special recognition. Nevertheless, she was very well liked by the headmistress of the school, a Thai nun, who appreciated the girl's well-mannered (i.e. Thai) behaviour – 'fairly uncommon among *dek salam*', as the nun pointed out.

Naen returned to Mit Phra Cha only during school holidays. While she was there, she took care of her younger siblings, helped her mother with household work, and regularly attended the Buddhist temple – all of which she did with great passion. After a few weeks in the slum, I saw that Naen was having a hard time making the transition back to Saint Jacob's; she looked mournful and lonely. She explained: 'I miss my mum and my brothers. I'd like to go back home. But mum doesn't want me to. She asked me to stay here, to study, to become *phu di* [a good, 'decent' person] to help the family. It is my duty to do this'. Morally bound to fulfil her mother's expectations, Naen had unwillingly accepted Saint Jacob's as her new home.

(the royal emblem of the Chakri dynasty, introduced by Rama IV). The official symbol of the Thai monarchy is the *garuda*: the mythological animal resembling a bird that in Hindu tradition serves as the vehicle of the god Vishnu. The *garuda* also appears in the Indonesian national emblem.

While at the Catholic NGO and at school Naen came across as a good Thai girl, in the absence of *phu yai* she showed sides of herself that the missionaries and her teachers would never have imagined existed. Behind the scenes, Naen was a powerful member of the *dohd diao* gang. As I would later find out, she was also quite forward. When, thanks to Ton's authorisation, I gained access to the gang's Facebook page, I was startled by Naen's posts on the forums of the group. There were several photos showing her smoking in flirtatious poses in the school toilets. In her posts, in 'non-Thai' slang, she mocked boys and teachers with disdainful comments, and advised other gang members on how to trick authority figures. It was clear that she was speaking as a leader. She was said by friends to be a very moral person, with her morality expressed mainly in the form of financial assistance to *nong* in distress.

In 2012, something happened that collapsed the boundaries between Naen's contradictory foreground and background identities, which the girl had hitherto been able to keep hermetically separated, dramatically revealing her 'self-bifurcation' (Rieber 2006). The teachers at her school called Saint Jacob's staff to say that Naen had been caught in a compromising position, to put it mildly: she had led a raid against a rival girl, accused of smiling at her boyfriend, and had assaulted her with a knife at the back of the school. In response to this shocking event, Naen came under a much higher level of supervision, both at school and at Saint Jacob's.

A few months later Naen began to behave strangely. One night she woke the Thai staff at Saint Jacob's, yelling and sobbing uncontrollably. She was convinced that she was haunted by her maternal grandfather's ghost, who kept commanding her to kill herself. While the *farang* at Saint Jacob's felt that the girl's increasingly inexplicable behaviour might require psychiatric treatment, Naen just wanted to go back home, where she was sure that her grandfather's spirit would not torment her any more. Father Nicola eventually acceded to Naen's desperate request.

In Mit Phra Cha, her family and acquaintances interpreted the girl's illness as a form of demonic possession. There is a widespread belief in this in (non) Thai popular culture, despite Buddhist authorities' historical attempts to eliminate ethnic minorities' allegedly 'superstitious beliefs' from 'authentic' (state) Buddhism (e.g. see Siani 2016; Pattana Kitiarsa 2005). Without the knowledge of those running Saint Jacob's, Naen's mother turned to the spirit medium (*mho phi*)[2] in her community. The medium held a healing session at which all the members of Naen's family were present, and which I also attended. It closed

---

2   In stark contrast to what happens in hospitals, which have been moulded by the globalisation of the Western 'bio-medical' paradigm (Good 1994), what may be described as the 'ethno-psychiatric systems' approach of many ethnic minority groups treats what are seen as demonic manifestations in individuals as social or ritual disorders (rather than as organic or

with a series of (surprisingly) Buddhist normative prescriptions: the whole family had to visit the temple on every *wan phra* (Buddhist celebration), and they had to perform a variety of merit-making rituals there. The treatment plan prescribed by the spirit medium proved effective. In Mit Phra Cha, the ghost of Naen's grandfather never showed up again. Naen begged her mother to let her stay home, but without success. The support they were getting from Saint Jacob's was too precious for her mother, who did not have a husband. Naen was persuaded to return.

One night not too long after this Naen ran away from the Catholic NGO, vanishing without trace. While the missionaries had no idea where she was, every so often from then on Naen would appear in Mit Phra Cha and would deliver large amounts of money to her mum, who did not inquire about her whereabouts in return. Some of her classmates told me that Naen, who was by then 16, had recently fallen in with a very strange crowd, a group of *mai di* ('not good') friends. It was rumoured that she was making money as a highly paid prostitute. Father Nicola continued to search for her.

In 2014, Naen suddenly reappeared at the Catholic charity, as if nothing had happened. She said she missed her *nong* and the staff at Saint Jacob's, who had been so kind and patient over the years. Relieved to see the girl in good shape and touched by her apparent 'redemption', Saint Jacob's missionaries proposed that Naen work at the NGO as a teaching assistant. Since then Naen has been part of the staff at Saint Jacob's, and is a favourite among *dek salam*.

In January 2015, during a flying visit to Mit Phra Cha, I witnessed yet another twist in the story: Naen arrived at the slum with a 55-year-old partner – he was the Sino-Thai headmaster of a prestigious high school in Bangkok. Naen's mother pleaded with me to maintain the utmost discretion in relation to this: 'Please don't say anything to the people at Saint Jacob's. They wouldn't understand. I know he's much older than Naen, but he's a good man. He has enrolled all of my children in his school. He's taking charge of our lives'. Deeply troubled by the situation, in the end I agreed and reassured Naen's mother, planning to talk to Naen alone at the earliest opportunity. An occasion to do this presented itself soon after, when her partner left the slum. With a mischievous smile on her face, Naen quietly told me all about her relationship: 'I'm fine now. I live in a huge house. I have money; I can help mum and my siblings. I can also get my diploma without studying. It's his school! He's a good man and anyway now I have a house of my own, one that I'm in charge of. Please don't say anything to the missionaries'. Naen casually

---

bodily alterations). There is a widespread belief in spirits in Thailand and across Asia, including in Thai pop culture (see e.g. Pattana Kitiarsa 2012).

wore designer clothes and accessories, brought expensive gifts to her brothers and proudly showed off her brand-new iPhone to all and sundry.

As far as I know, Naen is still working at Saint Jacob's as a teacher. The missionaries see her faithfully participating in all Catholic ceremonies and religious events and demonstrating continuous spiritual growth. Her ongoing sugar-daddy relationship appears to be unknown to the *farang* at the NGO. Naen seems able to keep her contradictory roles separate, as indeed she must. Struggling to keep the different parts of herself together, she is striving to combine her filial moral obligations with her 'burning desires' (Sopranzetti 2012) for consumption, status and recognition.

'They exchanged me at birth'

Two is a 21-year-old young Karen man born in Mae Hong Son, near the Thai–Myanmar border – a crossroads for ethnic minorities and refuges from Burma. Until the age of six, he lived with his extended family in a Christianised *chao khao* ('hill tribe') village in the Thai highlands. In the 1990s, as part of the Thai army's counterinsurgency strategies, Two's village was heavily militarised when the Thai state intensified its campaign of national Thaification in the ethnic north and northeast. His family was forcibly relocated to a lowland area, and Two's care and his primary education were entrusted to a hostel for ethnic minority children run by the Catholic Diocese of Chiang Mai.

In 2003, a wealthy, refined 43-year-old widow from Bangkok, who is now called *mae* Toi ('mum Toi'), visited the Catholic hostel where Two was living, representing the pastoral council at her parish, transforming his life forever. During her visit, the woman decided to adopt the child as her *luk bun tham* ('foster child') so as to make him a Thai *phu di* ('a decent Thai man'). Having been married to a high-ranking Thai military official, *mae* Toi had inherited her husband's sizeable capital, and was in Chiang Mai to demonstrate – not very discreetly – her Catholic benevolence. Two remembers how painful it was for his biological mother to bear the separation from her son. However, *mae* Toi's offer was impossible to turn down. Moving to Bangkok as *mae* Toi's son, Two was able, first of all, to gain a high school diploma from one of the best secondary schools in the capital. He was then enrolled as an international business student at Assumption University, the biggest (and very expensive) private Catholic university in Thailand. His new mother's influential connections also granted him access to Thai citizenship. But not all that glitters is gold.

In 2012, at the age of 18, Two broke free from *mae* Toi's suffocating embrace. He ran away from her big house, where he felt like a prisoner, and found shelter at Father Nicola's NGO. The boy stood out from the other guests at Saint Jacob's: he came to church for Sunday mass on his own motorcycle, wearing fashionable, stylish clothes and Rayban sunglasses. We quickly became close, and he soon felt the need to share his story, including his tormented relationship with *mae* Toi:

> At first I was grateful to her because she put me through school. But she always spoke ill of my real parents. She said they were 'forest people' [*khon pa*], 'primitives' [*bohran*] and dirty. She didn't want me to talk to them on the phone, nor that I should tell anyone where I come from. She was ashamed of my origins. I suffered, hearing her talking about my family in that way, but I never said anything because she had helped me. Last month [June 2012] she asked me to disown them, never to visit them again and to consider only her as my mother. She claims that I became Thai thanks to her, and that I should be grateful. I couldn't accept this, and I left. But now I have to pay the university fees on my own. Fortunately, Father Nicola is helping me. (Two, July 2012)

Two spoke perfect Thai. His rich friends – all students at Assumption University – would never have imagined that he was a Karen from Mae Hong Son. After years of cultural training in *mae* Toi's company, Two had built an impenetrable 'Thai armour', which allowed him to disguise himself as a member of Bangkok's high society. His true role models, however, were *farang*: 'I like espresso coffee. In the morning I enjoy it with a croissant for breakfast. Thai food is disgusting! I listen to *farang* music and watch *farang* movies. Also, when I talk to *farang* we just get each other. I feel so much more at ease with you than with Thai people. I am sure that they have exchanged me at birth. It's possible that I really am *farang*. I dream about this often, too.'

The *farang* self with which Two identified did not entirely fit the transnational Euro-American model that Thai youngsters encountered in the shopping malls, 'mediascapes' and 'technoscapes' of the 'global capital' (Appadurai 1996). Nor was he fascinated by the East Asian pop culture (especially Korean) that is becoming increasingly influential among urban Thai youths. Rather than Hollywood celebrities, K-pop stars, YouTube and Instagram influencers, Two's access to *farang* culture was mediated by Catholic missionaries such as Father Nicola, white people whom he saw as rich but generous, devoted to fighting for the rights of Thailand's ethnic minority groups. Over several conversations, Two openly expressed his contempt for Thai people:

> Since I was a child I've been discriminated against because I'm not Thai. They think they are superior. At school my way of speaking and my accent made everybody laugh. Teachers always used to tell me off in

public: 'Speak properly! We're not in the mountains here!' Thai people
here in Bangkok only think about themselves; being rich has made them
extremely selfish. They think they are intelligent but they let the army
rule without saying a single word.   (Two, July 2012)

While Two regarded Thais as representing a sort of anti-self, he developed an
image of *farang* as representing an idealised, almost mythologised, true self that
he wanted to emulate. He explained that his perfect Thai appearance was just a
mask that enabled him to gain status in a hostile world, a necessary step to access
education and citizenship – which he thought of as essential tools for achieving
his true target: Europe.

When he talked about his childhood in Mae Hong Son, Two became a totally
different person, becoming brooding and nostalgic. His stories were filled with
animals, sacred towering trees, the beauty of simplicity and the profound reality
of poverty. He described his parents as warm-hearted, simple people, scared of
city life. He treasured vivid, romantic and essentialised memories of (non-Thai)
'forest people's' social solidarity, which he viewed as being in sharp contrast with
urban Thai people's selfish individualism and wasteful consumerism. This was a
perspective that I often came across in the slums.

When he visited Mae Hong Son, which was about once every six months,
he deliberately rid himself of all traces of 'modernity': he took off his designer
suit, his exclusive watch and his sunglasses, to put on Karen traditional clothes
and his maternal grandmother's magic amulet: a tooth pendant made with her
yellowed molar, symbol of genealogical roots and ancestry. I was struck by the
radical opposition between the boy I knew in Bangkok and the Karen returning
to his village. I asked him whether he had spoken to anyone else about his origins, and how he was able to cope with these identity shifts.

Sometimes I feel guilty. When I'm at university or among Thai friends
I feel like I'm rejecting my origins. They don't know I'm Karen. When I
go to Mae Hong Son, I am afraid that my Thai friends might find out. I'm
ashamed, thinking that they might see where my parents live. There is no
electricity in the village; everything is really dirty. One thing I can't forgive
myself for yet is the fact that I disowned my mother. One summer she came
to see me in Bangkok at *mae* Toi's. That afternoon one of my classmates was
at the house. I pretended she was the housekeeper. He still thinks my real
mum is Toi.   (Two, December 2014)

Two seems to deal with his inner conflict by relating to the Christian *farang*
model, as a buffer between his two contradictory concepts of self (Thai and
Karen). His self-identity project, moreover, envisions a firm repudiation of

'Thainess' when the time is right: 'Now I'm among Thais. No one knows I'm Karen. I study at a reputable university and no one discriminates against me. When I have my degree and become a famous businessman, then that fiction comes to an end. I'll be rich and no Thai will be able to say anything. With the help of *farang*, I'll go back to my village and build houses and roads for everybody'.

He has two dreams, motivated by a barely-concealed aspiration for social redemption: to modernise his parents' village and to guide the development of his people. Perhaps he does not fully realise that his quest for the liberation and prosperity of the Karen overlaps, rhetorically, with the long-standing development strategy of the Thai state, which has the aim of achieving political control of the country's ethno-linguistic peripheries.

Searching for a sense of self

Yut, 17 years old, lived at Saint Jacob's for eight years. When he was four, Father Nicola saw him wandering around the slum. His mum had recently started a relationship with a new partner who did not, Father Nicola told me, tolerate her children from her previous relationship. For Yut, the atmosphere at home felt hostile, and he therefore preferred to spend his time walking around the slum. When Father Nicola suggested that his mother bring Yut along to the Catholic NGO, she did not hesitate, lured by the promise of financial help from the *farang*.

In July 2012, while I was conducting research at Saint Jacob's, Yut was a concern for the people in charge: his progress at school was slow, his teachers reported frequent unexplained absences and they suspected that he had started to take *ya ba* (amphetamine).

In an effort to establish a loving relationship with Yut, still unwittingly affected by a Eurocentric idea of childhood, I decided that I would behave with him as a peer – in contrast to how local adults related to him – so as to favour the emergence of a horizontal relationship between us. I wanted Yut to regard me as a special *farang*, who did not want to influence his choices. I was very surprised when, irritated by my manoeuvres aimed at achieving this, he angrily refused to play along, protesting: 'You're not one of my friends [*pheuan*]. You're my elder brother [*phi*]'.

Thai society's socio-political hierarchies tend to be internalised, and are embodied by individuals through concepts of self that define who they are. These selves are multiple; thus children, like adults, have more than one self, and this means that they switch from being *nong* to being *phi*, depending on the context and on the other person with whom they are interacting at any one time. The *phi–nong* relationship has both a cognitive and an emotional quality. For Yut, the standard dyad *phi–nong* was the only vehicle for affection in the context of a caring relationship that he recognized. He therefore, paradoxically, regarded my horizontal approach to a relationship with him as creating interpersonal distance, rather than the closeness I was aiming for.

One evening in July 2012, away from the prying eyes of the Thai staff at Saint Jacob's, Yut told me: 'Younger children [*nong*] here don't obey me. I don't want to do the same things they do any more. I'm big now [*phu yai*]. I can't stay here any more. I have found an apartment and a job. You are my *phi* now; I can talk to you about these things! I'm going to leave the NGO soon!'

At the end of July, Yut took action: he ran away from Saint Jacob's, seeking adventure in a spiral of improvised excursions, with the aim of working out for himself a means of living as an autonomous adult. Thanks to information from some of his ex-schoolmates, the staff at Saint Jacob's found him in a drug dealer's house. This man had promised the child an apartment, a moped and a salary if he agreed to deal *ya ba* for him. Taken back to Saint Jacob's, Yut ran off again. He had publicly announced to his peers that he was leaving. Had he stayed, his reputation would have been compromised. He had to prove he was *phu yai*.

He returned to Akhan Daeng, where his mother insisted that he go back to the Catholic NGO. She was vexed by the fact that her son had deprived her of her precious financial link with the *farang* at Saint Jacob's, and consequently she would not take him back. The last I heard from Father Nicola, Yut now seems to be working for a travelling circus. Unlike Wat, it seems that Yut, unfortunately, does not have what it takes to be a *nak leng*.

In his analysis of the 'rhetoric of walking in the city', Michel de Certeau (1984: 100–103) claims that 'to walk is to lack a place'. Continuous displacement implies an inability to find a place where one can feel represented. Yut's movements seem to express an undefined process of transience, an anomie of the self. His endless wandering can be regarded as an apt spatial metaphor to express the 'predatory nature of contemporary cities' (Kleinmann 2011), which condemns some individuals to be forever excluded.

Yut, like many other *dek salam*, had come to Saint Jacob's seeking social mobility. After years at the NGO, he could no longer bear the status equality imposed on all minors at Saint Jacob's, which was interpreted by some of the children as a culturally incongruous form of infantilisation. He regarded the Saint Jacob's Centre as a place of childhood, unsuited to his new status and from which he needed to escape. Yut, like Wat, felt stuck between the NGO's horizontal interpretation of childhood and the role that hierarchy plays in Thailand – as well as within his own group – as a cognitive, emotional, moral and political tool to be drawn on in one's understanding of one's own self and that of others.

This type of discomfort, triggered by the experience of internal and external contradictions within oneself and within others, is also felt by adults in the slums – who are considered *phu yai*, so long as they don't leave the slum. In fact, it is even more strongly felt, because it has been strengthened over time. This is true even for those, like *mae* Pan, who come across as strong leaders.

MAE PAN IN THE KINGDOM OF THE THAI

In Akhan Daeng, *mae* Pan was very popular. She was a sort of social whirlwind: she would walk confidently through the tentacle-like alleyways of the slum, joking with everybody, sometimes indulging in long-winded sermons. She was quite able to silence her male interlocutors, using sarcasm in a funny, yet authoritative, way to communicate. Her language could be rough. It was rich in idiomatic expressions in Isan (the Thai-Lao region in the northeast of Thailand). Like the members of the *dohd diao* gang, *mae* Pan rarely employed standard Thai subject pronouns, or the particles used as politeness tags at the ends of sentences in Thai to mark agreement, comprehension or acknowledgement, and which also mark and codify the speaker's gender (*kha* for females; *khrap* for males). By doing this, she was boldly neutralising the gendered hierarchies of Thai language. When there was no-one from the humanitarian or missionary world to hear her, Pan's 'non-Thai' exuberance was manifest. Outside of her own social universe, however, things were quite different.

In August 2012, I presented my research at Chulalongkorn University, the most important institution of higher learning in Thailand, known as 'Chula' and 'Pillar of the Kingdom'. The majority of Chula students were members of the Bangkok upper class, quintessential *phu di*. A few of them, fascinated by my analysis of the centrality of women in the slums, invited me for lunch, requesting that I bring my foster mother along. With a certain reluctance, *mae* Pan eventually accepted the invitation.

Together with her sons Dao and Nut (aged 13 and 19 respectively), we worked out how to reach the students' house, which was a large 12th floor apartment in Thong Lo district, one of the wealthiest parts of the capital. We decided to travel on the BTS Skytrain, the elevated rapid transit system of Bangkok – the fastest way to get around the congested city, ideal for cooling off from the midday heat. *Mae* Pan had never used it before. The internal stratification within Bangkok, which runs along class and ethnic lines, is reflected in huge inequalities in urban transport and mobility (Sopranzetti 2017b). *Mae* Pan, like most Akhan Daeng residents, only used motorcycle taxis or *rot me*, inexpensive public buses, which take hours to cover short distances. The Skytrain, she explained to me, was reserved for white-collar workers, tourists and 'those rich Thais who work in the city centre'. It shocked me to see a woman whose grit and determination I had always admired looking lost as soon as she crossed the metaphorical threshold between her world and that of Bangkok's middle classes.

When we arrived at the students' house, *mae* Pan became unusually quiet and awkward: she barely opened her mouth, and when she did, it was with feeble one-word answers. Although the students tried their best to make her feel safe and comfortable, Pan was like a fish out of water. It was one of the few occasions when I heard her using the politeness tag *kha*. Even more surprising was her self-deprecating use of *nu* (literally 'mouse') for 'I' – a first-person subject pronoun that children may use when they are speaking to *phu yai*. *Mae* Pan was talking to much younger students, but considered their higher social class as the principal criterion for determining her own position in the social hierarchy. As a poor slum woman, she felt *nu* compared to these full-blown representatives of the central Thai world.

What appeared to be an inferiority complex on *Mae* Pan's part, faced by students from Chula, was in open contradiction with her usual statements on slum dwellers' and 'village people's' (*khon ban nok*) moral superiority over 'city people'. But in what was essentially the kingdom of the latter, the social stigma that she had experienced when she first moved to Bangkok resurfaced as feelings of self-inadequacy and mediocrity, feelings that were usually silent or neglected. By contrast, Pan's sons, Dao and Nut, were initially at ease, both on the Skytrain and in the students' apartment. Long-term guests at Saint Jacob's, they were more used to middle/upper class material wealth. Gradually, though, I saw their enthusiasm fade. They seemed disoriented by the transformation in their mother. Soon after, they turned into 'good Thai children': silent, obliging, sitting properly beside their mother; emptied of their usual vitality.

Dek salam are trained to despise their own origins. Their ethnic, linguistic and cultural characteristics are variously labelled backward, inferior, immoral and abnormal, generating processes of what could be described as 'self-clandestinisation', especially in public contexts. *Mae* Pan's and her sons' behaviour during their visit to the students' house illustrates the way in which the stigmatising discourse of the state vis-à-vis slum dwellers can be internalised as a hostile concept of self that lies just below the surface of their consciousness – one that demands of the urban poor a resigned acceptance of their (externally imposed) position as Thai society's *phu noi*.

THE THAI (ANTI)SELF

Over the last few decades, the notion of 'Thai self' has been the subject of intense scholarly debate. Discussing the 'desire to be Thai in the context of the "non-Thai" demands imposed by globalisation', Thai political scientist Kasian Tejapira (1996b) has argued that Thai young people display symptoms of 'cultural schizophrenia': a fragmented subjectivity, split between the 'introjected Thai self, perceived as authentic, and a "non-Thai" self, projected externally in the shape of fashion trends, consumer behaviour, and Western-like activities' (ibid.: 394–395). This generational pathology is, Kasian suggests, linked to the 'post-modernisation of Thainess' (Kasian Tejapira 2002), and to a dysfunctional adjustment on the part of Thai young people to alien cultural forces. On the other hand, Thai anthropologist Pattana Kitiarsa (2002) has analysed Thai young people's consumption of foreign popular culture (social media, music bands, fashion trends, movies and TV shows, etc.) as a form of generational rebellion against the official paradigm of 'Thainess'. As Pattana has put it, Thai children and young people feel free to express hybridised forms of creative self-expression that are in contrast with the 'authoritative looks of old-fashioned parents, teachers, and officials', which are aligned with Bangkok's political traditionalism (ibid.).

The political and socio-psychological diagnosis of the situation made by Kasian Tejapira may partly explain slum children's self-identity contradictions, but there are some fundamental ways in which this does not fully explain the experiences of *dek salam*. Firstly, none of the children I have written about thus far perceive the 'Thai self' as an authentic, original or constitutive dimension of themselves. On the contrary, in these children's and young people's subjective experience the 'Thai self' most often operates as an introjected ethno-psychological artefact of self-alienation. It is also worth pointing out that the notion of 'Thai self' cannot be understood as an essentialised construct that exists outside of its historical context. It is clearly embedded in political contexts and can only be explained as a product of Thai ethno-nationalism. Thongchai Winichakul's critical conceptualisation (2000b) of ethnic minorities as Thailand's 'other within' is particularly insightful in this regard. If ethnic minority groups are historically constructed as the 'non-Thai' Other in the context of the Thai nation-state's geopolitical structure, they themselves are surely likely, in their turn, to experience the national norm of 'Thainess' as an adverse Alter (an alternate or dissociative identity) that contributes to shaping their selfhood while at the same time undermining its worth.

Psychoanalyst William Fairbairn (Fairbairn 1981) has argued that children are likely to introject experiences of neglect, discrimination or/and violence

169

in the form of dissociated states of being that produce self-stigma: the psychic equivalent of an autoimmune disease, what Fairbairn calls the 'internal persecutor or saboteur' (Fairbairn 1981). As a defence against an attack from the external world, this 'internal persecutor' may launch a pre-emptive strike against his/ her host, so as to forestall a repetition of the external violence. In a similar vein, political philosopher and psychiatrist Frantz Fanon (Fanon 2008) has explained the feeling of self-hatred experienced by black people as internalised colonial oppression: an 'epidermalisation of inferiority' that has shaped black people's self-image, in line with the racist discourse of white colonisers.

I would argue that the 'Thai self' acts as an 'internal persecutor' for *dek salam*: the identity they are expected to embody in public contexts (the 'Thai self') effectively establishes their deviant, abnormal and sub-human nature as 'non-Thai-enough' subjects. *Mae* Pan's feelings of inadequacy, Two's guilt, Naen's and Wat's fragmented subjectivities – all of these may be understood as rooted in an internalisation of what could be described as the Thai state's 'stigmatising parenthood'. However, as a way of being human that ensures status, wealth, and power, the 'Thai self' may nevertheless be ardently desired as an unattainable goal, generating self-ambivalence and the multiplication of contradictory trajectories, lacking coherence and direction. This is what has happened with Yut.

In this context, there is the potential for alternative parenting styles and different affective environments, as well as the various conceptual approaches to childhood, poverty, ethnicity, and citizenship that *dek salam* may encounter in their interactions with NGOs, missionaries, monks or peers, to acquire significance, as the story of Kla demonstrates. *Khon jon pen phiset nai phra jao* ('the poor are special for God') is Father Nicola's favourite spiritual statement. Children like Kla have drawn on this kind of discourses to rehabilitate concepts of self that they had previously repressed. This is a cultural and psycho-political operation that has the capacity to mitigate effectively against the fury of the 'internal Thai persecutor', thereby revalorising the 'non-Thai' self as worthy of respect.

RELIGIOUS SELVES

As a number of scholars have shown, religions set up powerful ideological and emotional frameworks for the cultural socialisation of children (see e.g. Campigotto et al 2012; Cusack 2011; Hemming and Madge 2012; Ridgely 2012). On the other hand, encounters with religion may also provide a space for self-definition and the exercise of choice (Hefner 1993 [ed.]; Bauman and Young 2012). The story of Kla highlights the way in which religion and the alternative models of care that poor children encounter at religious NGOs such as Saint

Jacob's and the Suan Kaeo Foundation can become an important reference point in these children's efforts to make sense of their lives, and even to reframe their concepts of self in ways that entail a powerful political critique of their ethnic and socio-economic subordination.

Kla took on Father Nicola's Catholicism to resist social stigma, to reject his position as *phu noi* within Thai society, and to boost his (ethnic) self-esteem. Through affective interactions with the missionary, the young boy learnt to re-conceptualise himself as God's beloved son – rather than as *dek salam* (in other words, as someone who is both inferior and morally abnormal). He also linked this self-formulation to his multiple attachments with younger peers in the slum, construed as political victims for whom he was morally responsible. Not all children, however, internalised Father Nicola's political-theological approach to *dek salam* as Kla did.

Consider, for example, the case of Miu, a 14-year-old guest at Saint Jacob's who, unlike Kla, had both parents; wanted to integrate into school and mainstream Thai society; and chose to move to the NGO purely to benefit from the Catholic organisation's financial support. During an interview that I conducted with her, she explained her relationship with Buddhism and Catholicism: 'Both Jesus and Lord Buddha teach people how to be good. Father Nicola comes to Akhan Daeng to help us. He is generous [*jai di*]. He brings us to his Centre and supports our education. But I'm Thai, so I must be Buddhist!' While she saw Father Nicola's Catholicism as being primarily a form of charity given to slum children, she experienced Buddhism as an essential dimension of her identity as a Thai citizen. Significantly, she added: 'I really like Jesus because he sacrificed himself for the salvation of humankind. I'd like to be a soldier, so as to give my life for the country and for the Thai people. That would bestow great merit [*bun*]!' She understood the sacrifice made by Christ, like that made by a soldier, in the framework of 'Thainess': as a patriotic sacrifice ensuring the accumulation of karmic merit (*bun*). Rather than using Catholicism to counter the 'Thai self', as Kla did, Miu identified in Jesus yet another symbol of Thai normative morality. His crucifixion epitomised, for her, the inspiring example of the selfless solder serving the nation.

The two ways in which Kla and Miu responded to Father Nicola's religious construction of childhood are strikingly at odds. Their stories demonstrate the wide and varied interpretations of this that are inherently possible for these children as they attempt to construct a sense of self. Although Father Nicola's political theology of childhood clearly undermined Thai dominant hierarchies, and his parenting style deviated fundamentally from that of Thai *phu yai*, some children nonetheless saw him in that light – as a *phu yai* himself, though a different kind of *phu yai.* This is demonstrated in a parallel that Wat drew between the missionary and King Bhumibol (the 'father' of the Buddhist nation), who had recently died:

> In Thailand, the king is the best and most generous kind of man because he is patient and is an example to us all. He helps everyone and takes care of us children [Thai citizens]. But here at Saint Jacob's the greatest man is my dad [Father Nicola] because he is able to see deep into people's hearts, he cares about everyone, and he considers all of us to be his children.
>
> (Wat, July 2011)

In the context of patriarchal regimes like Thailand, where the dominant political ethos revolves around belief in a father who is omnipotent and benevolent, and whose actions are intended to benefit his children, subjects are likely to develop affective bonds with charismatic authority figures who are deemed able to provide protection and caring (Sennett 2006). While this relationship provides subordinate subjects with a sense of security, it implies their dependency, passivity, and a substantial lack of agency. Moreover, the bond of affection, kinship, and filial devotion that links marginalised children to those cast as their 'saviours' is not without risk. 'Holy fathers' can turn into predators, as is demonstrated by cases of clerical child sex abuse (see e.g. Scheper-Hughes 1998).

In slum children's self-formation, a key role is simultaneously played by a number of caregivers – these may include a biological parent, a friend, a Catholic priest, or a symbolic 'parent' with whom there is no physical proximity, but an emotional bond, such as King Bhumibol, who plays this symbolic role for most Thai people. The fact that children have different models to emulate and embody, through different relationships, may well result in multi-layered, and ambivalent, psycho-political and cultural configurations of selfhood.

Multiple emotional, religious, and political dimensions are entangled in these children's experiences of self. Among *dek salam* who prioritised Father Nicola as a role model with whom to identify, many did not convert to Catholicism or, if they did, they still considered themselves to be Buddhists, and maintained multiple attachments to (foster) mothers, grandmothers, relatives or friends in the slum. The relationship they established with their caregiver's religion was not, moreover, necessarily easy to understand from a logical point of view.[3] Some took on Father Nicola's religious beliefs simply out of their willingness to please their 'dad'. These words of Fa, a 12-year-old orphan at Saint Jacob's, demonstrate this: 'When

---

3   Opposing an 'intellectualistic' understanding of conversion, Robert Hefner described it as a social process 'emerging both from the ideas and intentions of individuals and from the institutions and circumstances that constrain and routinise the world in which people act, often outside their full awareness' (Hefner 1993, p. 27).

I talk to dad [Father Nicola] I often get emotional. He touches my heart because he always asks me about my feelings. Dad hugs me and always tells me that we [i.e. *dek salam*] are God's most beloved children. That is why Catholicism is good'.

In fact, the reason why some *dek salam* became Catholic for a while was not just for political reasons, or as a contextual identity strategy to fight against discrimination, but because of their desire to benefit from Father Nicola's caring and affectionate attention. It is certainly the case that Saint Jacob's, as an alternative context for their socialisation, provided *dek salam* with possibilities for self-formation that were distinct from Thai school teachers' and public officials' stigmatising view of the poor. Their emotional bond with Father Nicola, in particular, offered some of the children a religious space where their ethnic, class, and generational identities could be revalorised and potentially transformed into subversive political selves.

IDEAL SELVES

What do *dek salam* want to be when they imagine themselves in the future? What are their ideal selves? How do they plan to accomplish the goals they wish to achieve? Throughout Asia, many disadvantaged children, when asked 'What would you like to do when you grow up?', reply that they would like to have a government job, because this ensures both status and social security benefits (see e.g. Chea and Huijsmans 2017; Naafs and Skelton 2017). This is also what I found in Bangkok. Approximately 60% of the *dek salam* whom I interviewed[4] stated that they dreamt of becoming government officials (*kharachakan*, literally 'servants of the king'): soldiers, teachers, policemen, and nurses. The remaining 40%, however, pictured themselves as aid workers, or as socially engaged religious: NGO workers, Buddhist monks, even Christian missionaries.

When I analysed the children's answers, I found that there were significant differences based on gender. While most boys wanted to become soldiers, girls mainly yearned for social status as teachers. Predictably, this gender polarisation reflects dominant cultural representations of masculinity and femininity in Thai society. Since the establishment of the Wild Tigers unit by King Vajiravudh, and the institutionalisation of Thai scouting (*luk seua*, Tiger Cubs) as a core subject in the school curriculum, soldiers have been publicly regarded as the moral and physical prototype of Thai manhood – a gender stereotype further invigorated by

---

4   I have interviewed 65 slum children on this subject (35 male, 30 female), 40 of whom were living at Saint Jacob's, 10 at the Suan Kaeo Foundation, and the rest at another child-focused NGO.

Thailand's current Prime Minister and his junta government. Particularly since the coup in 2014, military heroism is obsessively propagandised as the ultimate bastion of 'Thainess'. The state-controlled media constantly portray soldiers both in warlike postures and in contexts where they are portayed as compassionate. His Majesty's army is projected as involved not only in (grossly exaggerated) military drills, but also as serving the nation through providing social services for the poor and for Thailand's vulnerable rural communities (helping monks to clean temples, volunteering as teachers in remote village schools, leading drug prevention programmes in the slums of Bangkok, or carrying out natural disaster relief operations). Prayut, head of the military government and now Thai prime minister, would appear on TV each Friday while I was carrying out my fieldwork, to give a one-hour monologue in which the military's efforts to 'return happiness' (*kheun khwamsuk*) to the population were constantly being pointed out (McCargo 2009). The army's paternalistic role as the primary guarantor of royal *dharma* was being emphasised here, presented in opposition to the previous government's political corruption.

As Thai people's *phi*, in the service of the nation's 'father' (the king), soldiers feature prominently as role models for many young Thai men. Teaching, on the other hand, is regarded as a mainly female profession in Thailand. As living tropes of motherhood and nationhood, schoolteachers (*khru*) are publicly charged with educating the (military and manly) nation's children in 'Thainess'.

While soldiers and teachers are common role models, in the context of their structural assocation with the 'Thai self', Christian missionaries, socially engaged monks, NGO workers, and children's rights activists are less obvious ideal selves. A significant proportion of institutionalised *dek salam* – both boys and girls – identified with members of these groups, inspired by their humanitarian, political and religious commitment to Thailand's minority groups. As previously observed, most of these children have developed deep emotional connections with alternative caregivers such as Father Nicola, who are regarded as 'non-Thai', understanding and generous parent-like figures. Some may well indignantly (if conflictingly) reject the 'Thai self', proudly claim their identity as *dek salam* or 'non-Thai' citizens, and openly question 'Thainess' and the associated discriminatory practices of Thai *phu yai*. Some may convert to Catholicism, while others re-interpret the missionary's political theology strategically, in order to create a certain impression, or as a means of self-acceptance and/or of achieving leadership.

For a few, however, this all comes with a price: expulsion from school, further marginalisation, and social exclusion. As Phillips (2006: 316) put it: 'Performing within the bounds of one's subject position provides for certain levels of social rewards, at the very least the lack of censure or disciplining, while the violation of the bounds of decorum which surround one's position can lead to various forms of social punishment [...], exclusion and, therefore, a kind of social death'.

Thai or 'non-Thai'? Am's conflicted sense of self

The dreams that some slum children have of becoming soldiers or teachers reveal their desire to achieve a secure (and higher status) position as full citizens, with an identity that is recognized as purely Thai. These children think of private schools and NGOs as instrumental transit stations towards 'Thainess'. However, their desire for social inclusion, status and consumption often entails strategies of self-concealment, for they must disguise or remove their ethnic and class profiles from their public presentation of self, generating tensions in the process. Am's story exemplifies this internal conflict well.

Am, a 23-year-old woman born at Akhan Daeng, managed to complete her education on scholarships from Saint Jacob's and, in 2012, she finally graduated as a Thai language teacher. Today she is employed at the same Catholic private school that she attended as a child, which has significantly increased her social standing: she has moved to the city centre with her boyfriend, who is a Royal Thai Navy officer; she socialises with well-educated Thai professionals, and displays her devotion to 'Thainess' on every available occasion. On the other hand, Am's grandmother and mother, originally from Chiang Rai (in northern Thailand), complained that she had not been back to visit them in months: 'She sends us money, but rarely comes to the slum. She has never brought her partner or her friends home. She's ashamed of us! We had a fight because she accused us of being stupid. She says that we're still here in Akhan Daeng because we like to live surrounded by garbage and among criminals! Now she plays the *phu di* ['sophisticated city person'].'

Previously a *dek salam* from a 'non-Thai' family, Am has replaced her childhood self with an identity model created by those who have sought to subdue her group. She has identified with the normative 'Thai self', introjected as an 'internal persecutor' that has required her to erase her origins and move away from her family, as a 'bargaining chip' to access the privileged status of Thai *phu di*. Am's disgust at her mother's and her grandmother's lifestyle displays her attempt to differentiate herself from her former, neglected self, whom she has apparently abandoned.

Bourdieu and Wacquant have claimed that 'symbolic violence [...] is that form of violence that is exercised on social agents with their own complicity'

(Bourdieu and Wacquant 1992: 129). The ethno-ideology of 'Thainess' is a pervasive discourse in the country. Through militarised education at school, in particular, children internalise the 'Thai self' as the 'natural order of things' and 'common sense knowledge', which produces consonances between Thai society's hierarchical social order and children's cognitive structures. This leads to an unconscious collaboration on the part of those who are dominated in their own domination (Bourdieu and Passeron 1977). Unsurprisingly, Am's depiction of her family members as 'stupid, dirty and criminal' echoes schoolteachers' dominant narratives about dek salam.

I have known Am since she was a child and I could not believe she could be so cynical. I remember her being very attached to her mother. I thus sought to dig deeper into her emotions. One afternoon in 2013, I decided to meet her in a café, a neutral location between the slum and her apartment. We had a long, heart-to-heart conversation, during which Am burst into tears. Confused, and visibly in pain, she talked about her new life and her past life in contradictory terms. Her new friends did not know her true origins; her family and old friends did not recognise the person whom she had become. Her cognitive and emotional complicity with the Thai model, previously embodied brilliantly, seemed to waver. Am struggled to reconcile her filial obligations to her elderly parents (as prescribed by the Buddhist state discourse) with their public personae as 'non-Thai' slum dwellers, experiencing an excruciating fragmentation of her sense of self in the process. Her suffering may be regarded as an outcome of Thai society's symbolic violence on 'non-Thai' minority groups, inasmuch as the latter are forced to barter their childhood in exchange for social mobility. During our conversation, Am's sense of self had lost coherence, continuously redefining itself in multiple and precarious forms. What she was, what she became, and what she will be was not clear to Am, while the introjected 'Thai self' blatantly endangered her existential stability.

CONCLUDING REMARKS: SELF-POLYSEMY AS CHILDREN'S AGENCY

The last time I met Am, in April 2015, she looked remarkably serene. Her family noticed incredible changes in her bearing and attitude: 'She was lost, and now she has found herself'. She was back in Akhan Daeng every weekend, teaching English to slum youngsters as a volunteer for a Buddhist NGO. She had broken up with her boyfriend and, more significantly, she had become an advisor for the Four Regions Slum Network – an astonishing metamorphosis, which Am explained like this:

> I understood that poor people need help. If they stay at the slum it is because wealth isn't fairly distributed in this country. It is not their fault. The *khon meuang* ['city people'] of Bangkok cannot keep sponging off the rural provinces of Thailand. This is not democracy. I do not need to hide any more. Although I was born in a slum, I have managed to become a teacher. I was a *dek salam*, today I'm part of Thai society. I'm in an ideal position to help my people. I've got some new friends I can be myself with. While we appreciate the help that *farang* and NGOs provide, slum dwellers are our brothers and sisters. It is primarily our own responsibility to defend their rights.   (Am, December 2015)

Am appears to have managed to bend the 'Thai self' to her will, turning 'Thainess' from an unattainable, self-mutilating ideal into a useful socio-political mask, essential for negotiating rights for her own people with the authority of a full, respected citizen. Through collaboration with slum activists, 'red shirt' supporters and progressive intellectuals, Am's multiple and previously conflicting concepts of self have now integrated into a relatively harmonious whole – a hybrid identity that is Thai in a different way, enabling her to call for recognition of the rights of Thailand's minorities.

Am's breakthrough was warmly received not only by her family but also by the missionaries at Saint Jacob's and by the Buddhist inhabitants of the slums, who considered her motherly commitment to their children's education to be highly meritorious and praiseworthy.

Am's sense of self, like those of Kla, Wat, Naen, Two and Yut, is multiform and polysemic. They are, in fact, inhabited by multiple selves, and this means that they may experience subjective fragmentation. However, this self-polysemy does not necessarily foreshadow a cultural schizophrenia, for it can also enhance these children's capacity to address (and competently embody) an increasingly diverse range of societal pressures and cultural influences. As Phillips (2006: 316–317) has pointed out: 'The multiplicity of subject positions [...] also affords a multiplicity of potential social existences and, as such, a multiplicity of interests and desires. The memories of these past positions, then, may create a potential space in which to formulate challenges to one's present position. [...] The same power relations that dictate the position and form from which one speaks also, simultaneously, provide a form of agency that is a potential tool for resistance and reformulation.'

The nature of childhood for *dek salam* is disputed by ideologically heterogenous institutions, which pluralise these children's experiences of socialisation, their cultural repertoires, subject positions and their political dispositions. Competing cultural politics around the notions of 'childhood', 'poverty', 'ethnicity' and 'nationhood' structure children's interactions with caregivers in different positions, while they navigate endlessly through the complex maze of their potential futures. As alternative role models, Catholic missionaries, children's right activists, Buddhist monks, *farang* or senior gang members all have the potential to destabilise the authority of standard *phu yai* (parents, schoolteachers, state officials, soldiers, and royal persons), and even to promote children's critical awareness of 'Thainess' as Thai society's '*doxa*' (Bourdieu and Eagleton 1992): the taken-for-granted, unquestioned, arbitrary truth that naturalises the primacy of the Central Thai perspective – socio-morally, economically and politically – as constituting common sense for the country's entire population.

While Am's cultural subjectivity is still discontinuous, dynamic and multi-vocal, she is no longer a passive spectator of her life as something constructed by others. She shows political awareness of her multiple selves, which are now well-orchestrated and flexibly organised, as she strategically enacts her many roles for the greater good: social justice. Her commitment to slum dwellers' and children's rights invokes a multi-cultural reformulation of the 'Thai social body' (Aulino 2014), which she aims to make as inclusive and plural as her own new sense of self.

Conclusion: Thai
Childhoods Revisited

Children is a relational term; it is rendered meaningful by its opposition to the unmarked category *adults*. If we take the former seriously as an object of study, the latter is made productively stranger, too.

(Malkki 2010: 80).

Most studies of the social history and political anthropology of Thailand have focused attention on the shifting roles of kingship, Buddhism and the militarised nation-state in a rapidly changing society. While transnational processes of globalisation, neoliberal developmentalism, and political authoritarianism have profoundly reconfigured Thai society's prime cultural institutions, these latter remain at the core of scholarly analyses, as structural dimensions of Thailand's 'patriarchal social order' (Lindberg-Falk 2007).

In this book, on the other hand, I have prioritised 'childhood' over (royal, military, and state) 'parenthood' as the main analytical lens through which to investigate contemporary 'cultural politics' in Thailand (Jordon and Weedon 1995; Schiller 1997): the use of cultural representations (ideas, discourses, values, symbols, and daily practices) related to 'childhood' to maintain, assert, contest or subvert social relations of inequality during a complex period of Thai history (2010–2016). Through a 'childhood-centric' (Thomas and O'Kane 1998) approach to Thai cultural politics, this study has thus sought to reverse more conventional patterns of scholarship in this field, devoting greater epistemological attention to 'politically unnoticed' and 'ontologically uncommon' subjects (Brekhus 1998), notably poor children.

This book has been about 'slum children' (*dek salam*), their disputed childhoods and the multiple channels through which their anti-normative condition is being addressed in the increasingly globalised context of Bangkok's urban poverty. Throughout, I have demonstrated that 'childhood' is best understood in Thailand as a political category, and that attempts by the militarised state to 'repair' slum children's childhood – which is supposedly 'not-Thai-enough', and thus considered damaged – reflects a progressive infantilisation of the Thai polity. In an era of authoritarian rule and resurgent monarchical paternalism, I would

179

argue that any analysis of Thailand's ethno-political structure, social hierarchy and wealth inequality, must include serious consideration of the symbolic value of childhood in this context.

This book has been about slum children's multiple childhoods in Bangkok, including the modern construction of childhood, crafted in the West and circulated globally through humanitarian intervention, transnational moral economies, and legislation relating to children's rights. It was through an endeavour grounded in this globalised concept of childhood that I first met the protagonists of this book more than 10 years ago, when I arrived in Bangkok as a first-time volunteer at the Saint Jacob's Centre. Together with other child-focused organisations – local and international, secular and religious – this NGO challenges state sovereignty in the Thai capital's poorest districts, infusing new ethics and alternative discourses on 'childhood', 'poverty', 'ethnicity', and the 'nation' into the everyday lives of *dek salam*.

I have argued that the slums of Bangkok are no longer closed communities of rural migrants, but humanitarian landscapes of cosmopolitan interactions and child-centred power fields that are redefining the urban poor's positionality in the context of Bangkok's political structures. I have argued, furthermore, that the humanitarian circulation of *dek salam* (in and out the slums) makes them focal points of intersection between conflicting moral systems and political discourses that need to be 'translated' in multiple directions (Latour 1986). This is reflected in the fact that, unlike upper-middle class children in Bangkok, *dek salam* are hardly ever at home.

In the first part of this book, I explored the different ways in which slum children's 'childhood' is interpreted and addressed by local, national and supranational, both secular and religious actors (schoolteachers, development monks, Catholic missionaries, slum dwellers, NGO workers and the Thai state) in a variety of social locations. I began the book by analysing the Thai model of 'childhood' as it is formulated by the state and enforced in schools, the environment where *dek salam* spend most of their time (Chapter 1). Here children are exposed to the 'good Thai child' standard, an ethno-nationalist ideal that seeks to shape the nation's future citizens as obedient and grateful *phu noi* – sons and daughters devoted to the King (the nation's 'father'), Buddhism and the Army. I then turned to an analysis of Buddhist aid organisations addressing child poverty in Bangkok (Chapter 2). Unlike the state Buddhism associated with 'Thainess' (as it is displayed in schools), the approach of some development monks to *dek salam* reveals contrasting (yet ambivalent) visions of morality and the social order, shedding light on the doctrinal and political fragmentation of Theravada (*therawat*) Buddhism in the context of contemporary Thai society. In Chapter 3, I focused on Saint Jacob's Centre, and demonstrated the increasingly relevant political and economic roles of missionary aid organisations in Thailand's peripheral ethnic regions, in city slums, and in peri-urban areas where the ('non-Thai') poor live. I concluded Part One of this book with a detailed analysis of *dek salam*'s birth-place (the slums) as an ethno-linguistic and political 'other within' in the city of Bangkok (Thongchai Winichakul 2000a). I explored the ways in which city slums have been re-cast as spaces of child-focused humanitarian intervention; and I highlighted the political value of slum children's (socially constructed) 'victim-hood' as part of women's emerging leadership as the new, maternal spokespersons of the urban poor.

As 'victims', 'social dangers', 'spiritually immature individuals' and 'God's favourites', as *phu noi* and as not-Thai (enough) citizens, Bangkok's slum children embody a range of diverse futures, projecting competing images of the social body onto the screen of the national imagination. These (politically conflicting) notions of childhood shape and are being shaped by Thai young people, creating a broad constellation of experiences, constraints, opportunities and expectations. I have shown how children are actively appropriating, redefining and/or contesting local and global discourses on childhood, constructing in the process child (counter)cultures and their own senses of self.

Part Two of this book focused on *dek salam* as competent social agents rather than only as targets of policies and representations. The young protagonists of this study are exposed to conflicting cultural politics of childhood, different parenting styles and contrasting pedagogies. This ideological heterogeneity produces fragmented subjectivities, hybrid concepts of self, and a plurality of social identities, which children can actively manipulate to achieve economic, affective and social goals (Chapter 5). As I have shown, children's embodiments of different concepts of self are culturally mediated by processes of cognitive and emotional identification with (and political subordination to) multiple caregivers, including Catholic missionaries, parents, soldiers and/or the king. While the individual outcomes of this process are highly variable, I have argued that it is possible to trace some common features that define the psycho–political constitution of (non)Thai poor children's selves, in (and beyond) the slums of Bangkok (Chapter 6).

As Stoler (2004: 9) wrote: 'The role of the state is not only as Antonio Gramsci defines it, in the business of educating "consent". [...] Such consent is made possible [...] by shaping appropriate and reasoned affect, by directing affective judgments, by severing some affective bonds and establishing others'. All *dek salam* are confronted with the 'good Thai child' ethno-nationalist norm, while at the same time they are structurally precluded from accessing the class privileges associated with this norm. The Thai state prescribes a filial obligation to the nation's Buddhist parents (the king, soldiers and schoolteachers) on the part of aspiring citizens. However, it denigrates these children's real parents in the slums, as primitive, dangerous and 'insufficiently Thai' citizens, seeking to violently replace children's biological families with its corrective parenthood. This brutal shakedown, institutionalised through an increasingly militarised school system, has the potential to generate severe self-bifurcations, creating a split between children's inner experiences of self and an internalised, malignant 'Thai self'.

However, like other categories of children deemed to be 'at risk', *dek salam* are no longer taken care of only by state institutions and Buddhist temples. Over the last few decades, the globalisation of children's rights and the transnational expansion of the humanitarian enterprise have caused a number of international NGOs and child-focused aid agencies to take on roles as new political and economic players in Thailand's ethnic margins, both urban and rural, with religious aid organisations at the forefront of this. Such global (and often universalising) 'forces of compassion' (Redfield and Bornstein [eds] 2011) have not escaped the national logic of 'Thainess'. They have introduced a wide range of new assumptions about marginal childhoods, children's agency, state and parental authority, education, religion, and citizenship in the context of Thailand's 'non-Thai' political landscapes. In the process, Catholic NGOs, socially engaged Buddhist monks and advocates of children's rights have not only reconfigured existing geographies of inclusion/exclusion; they have also favoured the emergence of new moral economies, and further (de)politicised childhood. They have, in addition, provided *dek salam* with alternative discourses, social venues, role models, caregivers, religious ethics, financial tools and possibilities of 'subjection' (Butler 1997; Schofer 2012). Finally, and no less importantly, the fact that children and young people have privileged access to new media and technological tools, foreign pop-culture, and the global connectivity of social networks (e.g. see Singer and Singer 2012) means that they have yet another (digital) space in which selves (both individual and collective) can be developed – a virtual framework for subversive expression, which has the potential to be a channel for fierce generational dissent, and a place where Thai social norms are constantly questioned, reconfigured or reinforced.

Rather than being a symptom of 'cultural schizophrenia' (Kasian Tejapira 1996b), slum children's hybrid, multi-vocal and polysemic selves may therefore be regarded as a valuable resource against state violence. The slums of Bangkok are now transnational arenas of child development and religious charity. Compared with upper-middle class urban young people, *dek salam* are less embedded in the ritualised world of 'Thainess', and more used to playing with cultural diversity.

Their socio-political and economic exclusion from the city's bourgeois opportunities paradoxically opens up a space for connections with new local and international actors, such as missionaries, *farang*, NGOs, activist monks, grassroots social movements, and academic researchers. I would argue that these children's 'bottom-up cosmopolitanism' (Appadurai 2013) makes them ideal mediators of cultural languages and generational brokers of national and post-national (local and global) imaginaries, which has the capacity to turn the militarised monolith of 'Thainess' into a future that could be Thai in a different way.

On the other hand, this book has also shown how slum children's agency is often enacted 'ambiguously' (Durham 2000, 2008), and not always in ways that match Western projections of children as innocent and vulnerable victims (Bordonaro and Payne 2012). Mahony (2018) has made the important point that the exercise of agency in one field of action may produce unintended consequences in other, related social realms, so that attempts by *dek salam* either to participate in or stand against dominant cultures can result in counter-productive outcomes. Although they may be performed as resistance strategies, drug abuse, prostitution, street life, and gang violence threaten global conceptualisations of 'natural childhood' and what is deemed to be morally appropriate in the 'best interest of the child' (Thomas 2005). Children and young people living in the slums of Bangkok – like those living in other marginal urban spaces around the world – may violently assert their worth through mutual aid groups or gangs, posing moral and political conundrums for policy makers, practitioners and humanitarian workers.

More research is urgently needed in these areas. In the post-Bhumibol era, indeed, Thailand's many 'marginal childhoods' (stateless children along the Thai–Myanmar border, Muslim children in the deep south, migrant child workers in the coastal provinces, etc.) appear to be particularly in danger, as the pedagogists in charge of their education may well be soldiers holding war weapons.

Coda – Small People's
Generational Dissent

After the conclusion of this study, the death of King Bhumibol in 2017 led to a cosmological crisis that is affecting Thailand's cultural and political order. In the midst of current attempts by the Army both to preserve and invigorate the national ethos of royal fatherhood, several grown-up citizens are daring to criticise the militarisation of Thai society (and, linked to this, the new King's apparent inability to uphold the moral standards expected of a Buddhist ruler and benevolent father).

The following are just a few of the biting lyrics from 'What Has My Country Got?' (*prathet ku mi*), an anti-establishment song uploaded on YouTube on 22 October 2018 by a group of Thai young musicians who call themselves 'Rap Against Dictatorship'. The video reached up to 20 million views online in the first week after release, suggesting it may become the most watched YouTube video ever in Thailand (New York Times 2019). All of the *dek salam* with whom I am still in contact are mad about the song.

> The country whose parliament is the playground of its soldiers
> The country in which rebels are made to obey like ants
> The country in which whatever you do will be intruded upon by the leader
> The country in which the big fish eat the small fish
> The country in which high-ranking officials succeed all the time, no matter
> how immorally they act,
> This is my country, this is my country.

Ten male young rappers take turns singing, using harsh rhythms, denouncing what is wrong in their country and demolishing the fiction of the supposed good deeds and doctrines of the Army. The black and white video sinisterly evokes the dramatic scene of 6 October 1976, captured famously by Neal Ulevich in a Pulitzer Prize winning photo: this shows a hysterical crowd cheering a man who is beating the corpse of a student hanging from a tree with a chair. As ethnomusicologist James Mitchell (2018) has observed: 'What makes this song so unique is the number of barbs directed at the military. [...] Thus, the music video accomplishes what the Thai education system cannot, since school history

www.youtube.com/watch?v=qBu88GaHBHs.

Figure 9. Use of the three-finger salute is a common feature of student demonstrations across Thailand since 2014. Screenshot of an image from YouTube. Colour version, p. 232.

textbooks do not include the events of 6 October'. The junta's reaction to the song – the most daring act of political dissent expressed against the military government since the 2014 coup – was to threaten the singers, their families and anyone sharing the video with jail under Thailand's highly illiberal Computer Crimes Act, 2017.

In December 2014, during a visit by General Prayut Chan-o-cha, then leader of the NCPO, to Khon Kaen (the stronghold of the 'red-shirt' movement), five Isan student activists belonging to the Dao Din group protested against the Prime Minister, flashing the three-finger salute of *The Hunger Games* (Prachathai 2014d). As some of my *dek salam* friends in Bangkok explained to me later, the 2012 American film is set in the fictional state of Panam, an authoritarian regime governed by an opulent capital city that maintains its hyper-individualistic and consumerist lifestyle through exploitation of the external districts. In both fiction and reality, the three-finger salute is thus a symbol of resistance against the tyranny of the capital (Figure 9).

This was one of the few moves made against the military junta in a country that has otherwise been subdued, and whose historical political parties have almost disappeared from the public scene. It was followed by the sentencing of 23-year-old Jatupat 'Pai' Boonpattararaksa, a former student of Law at Khon Kaen University and the leader of Dao Din, to five years in prison, under Thailand's *lèse-majesté* law, for sharing a BBC portrait of King Maha Vajiralongkorn on his Facebook account.

The Project Director of the Isan Culture Maintenance and Revitalisation Programme, John Draper (2018), is of the view that Dao Din young activists are involved in a centre-vs-periphery separatist struggle that is based on both class and ethnicity and that is aiming to establish village-based direct democracy, a decentralisation of power and the pluralisation of 'Thainess'. Members of Dao Din share their ideals with affiliated groups of young people, such as the Federation of Pattani Students and Young People in the far south, Community Activists North in the north, and the New Democracy Movement. Am, who is a former *dek salam* and is now an activist with the Four Regions Slum Network, is very sympathetic to Dao Din's political endeavours.

These courageous actions against the Thai nation's *phu yai* (Bangkok-based military and royalist elites) do not originate in political parties but from the country's class, ethnic and generational *phu noi*: (non)Thai children and young people from all Thailand's regions, *dek salam* included. Since the 2014 military coup, bold acts of civil disobedience have most often been carried out by those who are commonly referred to as *dek* ('children'), even when they are no longer that young. It is these whom I am describing as the 'belittled citizens' of Thailand.

Compared to more organised political activities, these 'children's' generational rebellion has some distinctive traits: it does not formally side with either political party (although it is tinged with 'red'); it often constitutes a spontaneous challenge to Thai conservative politics and etiquette; it is organised and coordinated through social media; and it draws creatively – as Pattana Kitiarsa (2002) has correctly pointed out – on alien cultural ideas and concepts, including American rap, human rights, engaged Buddhism, Latin-American liberation theology, and digital democracy.

Like Bangkok's *dek salam*, these young rebels, who are Thai in a different way from that laid down by 'Thainess', simultaneously access and draw on multiple discourses, which go well beyond the geo-political, ethnic, class, and gendered boundaries imposed by the Thai state. Unlike Thai *dek di* ('good children'), and unlike children and young people belonging to previous generations, they are actively expanding their hybrid selves, challenging generational hierarchies while redefining 'childhood' – and thus the nation's possible futures – in a country that has, until now, been focused on and defined by *phu yai*. Before he was arrested, Jatupat 'Pai' sat down for an interview with Thai online newspaper *Prachathai* (2014e):

We went [to protest against the coup] because today there are more and more human rights violations. We can't stand this any more [...] Dictatorship fears people. It may be difficult to do something, but please just do it. It's something a human must do. This is the era of young people [...] We want you to fight.   (Jatupat, November 2014).

Although the outcomes of recent elections have frustrated Pai's expectations, Thailand's 'bad children' continue to be convinced that the generational wheel will eventually turn in their favour.

References

Adler, P. and P. Adler

1998. *Peer Power: Preadolescent Culture and Identity*. New Brunswick: Rutgers University Press.

Akin Rabibhadana

1963. 'The Organization of Thai Society, and the Process of Change in the Early Bangkok Period (1782–1873)'. PhD. thesis, Cornell University.

1976. *Rise and Fall of a Bangkok Slum*. Bangkok: Thai Khadi Research Institute, Thammasat University.

2010. *Mong sangkhom phan chiwit nai chumchon* ('Observing society through everyday life in slum communities'). Bangkok: Sirindhorn Anthropology Centre.

Allen, D.L., J.W. Carey, C. Manopaiboon, R.A. Jenkins, W. Uthaivoravit, P.H. Kilmarx and F. van Griensven

2003. 'Sexual health risks among young Thai women: Implications for HIV/STD prevention and contraception.' *AIDS and Behavior* 7 (1): 9–21.

Althusser, L.

1970. 'Ideologia e apparati ideologici di stato' [Ideology and state ideological apparatuses]. *Critica marxista* 5: 23–65.

Amaladoss, M.

2000. *Oltre l'inculturazione: Unità e pluralità delle chiese* ('Beyond inculturation: Unity and plurality in churches'). Bologna: Editrice Missionaria Italiana.

Anand Panyarachun

1996. *His Majesty's role in the making of Thai history*. Paper presented at the 14th International Association of Historians of Asia, May 20, 1996, Chulalongkorn University, Bangkok.

Anderson, B.

1978. 'Studies of the Thai state: The state of Thai studies.' In E.B. Ayal (ed.), *The Study of Thailand: Analysis of Knowledge, Approaches, and Prospects in Anthropology, Art History, Economics, History, and Political Science*, pp. 193–247. Athens, Ohio: Ohio University Center for International Studies.

1983. *Imagined Communities: Reflections on the Origin and Spread of Nationalism*. London: Verso Editions and New Left Books.

Appadurai, A.

1996. *Modernity at Large: Cultural Dimensions of Globalization*. Minneapolis and London: University of Minnesota Press.

2013. *The Future as Cultural Fact: Essays on the Global Condition*. New York: Verso Books.

Appayut Jantarapaa

2009. *Khreua khai salam si phak: tuaton lae prasobkan kankleuaiwai* [The Four Region Slum Network: Identity and experience of a movement]. Bangkok: Four Region Slum Network.

Arendt, H.

1963. *Eichmann in Jerusalem: A Report on the Banality of Evil*. London: Penguin.

Ariès, P.

1962. *Centuries of Childhood: A Social History of Family Life*. New York: Alfred A. Knopf.

Asia

1981. 'A fairy godmother for Bangkok's slum children.' (By W. Warren). *Asia* March–April, 1981.

Asian Correspondent

2011. 'Inter-school violence and the value of life in Thailand.' (By Saksith Saiyasombut & Siam voices). *Asian Correspondent* Feb 22. Retrieved from: asiancorrespondent. com//48889/inter-school-violence-and-the-value-of-life-in-thailand/.

2014a. 'Thai students required to recite Prayuth's 12 core values daily.' (By Bangkok Pundit). *Asian Correspondent* Sep 22. Retrieved from: asiancorrespondent.com/ 126873/all-thai-students-required-to-recite-daily-prayuths-12-core-values/.

2014b. 'Education reform comes to Thailand… Criticism of the junta banned in schools.' (By Bangkok Pundit). *Asian Correspondent* Jun 10. Retrieved from: asiancorrespondent. com/123618/education-reform-comes-to-thailand-criticism-of-the-junta-banned-at-shcools/.

Askew, M.

1994. 'Bangkok: Transformation of the Thai city.' In M. Askew & W. S. Logan (eds), *Cultural Identity and Urban Change in Southeast Asia: Interpretive Essays*, pp. 85–116. Victoria, Australia: Deakin University Press.

2002. *Bangkok. Place, Practice and Representation*. London: Routledge.

Aulino, F.

2014. 'Perceiving the social body: A phenomenological perspective on ethical practice in Buddhist Thailand.' *Journal of Religious Ethics* 42: 415–441.

Avila, C.

1976. *Peasant Theology: Reflections by the Filipino Peasants on Their Process of Social Revolution*. Bangkok: WSCF Asia.

Baker, C.

1999. 'Assembly of the poor: The new drama of village, city and state.' *Thai Development Newsletter* 37: 15–21.

Baker, C. and Pasuk Phongpaichit

2005. *A History of Thailand* (2nd ed.). Cambridge: Cambridge University Press.

Bangkok Post

2003. 'MP's to check parents' claims of schools' new surcharges.' *Bangkok Post* May 13. Home Section, p. 4.

2009. 'Turning slums into communities. A lion-hearted woman fights for housing rights.' (By Janchitfah Suparah). *Bangkok Post,* June 4.

2014a. 'Thai education system needs fundamental reform.' *Bangkok Post* April 9. Retrieved from: www.bangkokpost.com/opinion/opinion/404095/thai-education-system-needs-fundamental-reform.

2014b. '"Good deeds" passports for students. Education project to foster ethical living.' *Bangkok Post* July 22. Retrieved from: www.bangkokpost.com/news/local/421749/education-project-to-foster-ethical-living.

Bao, J.

2008. 'Denaturalizing polygyny in Bangkok, Thailand.' *Ethnology* 47(2–3): 145–161.

Barmé, S.

1993. *Luang Wichit Wathakan and the Creation of Thai Identity.* Singapore: Institute of Southeast Asian Studies.

Barnett, M.N.

2011. *Empire of Humanity: A History of Humanitarianism.* Ithaca: Cornell University Press.

Baron–Gutty, A. and Supat Chupradit (eds)

2009. *Education, Economy and Identity. Ten Years of Educational Reform in Thailand.* Bangkok: IRASEC.

Bauman, C.M. and R.F. Young

2012. 'Minorities and the politics of conversion with special attention to Indian Christianity.' In R. Robinson (ed.), *Minority Studies,* pp. 185–203. New Delhi: Oxford University Press.

Bauman, Z.

1989. *Modernity and the Holocaust.* Cambridge: Polity Press and Blackwell Publishing Ltd.

Beatty, A.

2013. 'Current emotion research in anthropology: Reporting the field.' *Emotion Review* 5: 414–422.

Beazley, H.

2003. 'Voices from the margins: Street children's subcultures in Indonesia.' *Children's Geographies* 1(2): 181–200.

Bechstedt, H.D.

1991. 'Identity and authority in Thailand.' In C. J. Reynolds (ed.), *National Identity and its Defenders. Thailand Today,* pp. 238–261. Chiang Mai: Silkworm Books.

Benthall, J.

1992. 'A late developer? The ethnography of children.' *Anthropology Today* 8(2): 1.

Berner, E. and R. Korff

1994. *Globalization and Local resistance: The Creation of Localities in Manila and Bangkok.* Bielefeld: Working paper No 205, University of Bielefeld.

Bhumibol Adulyadej (His Majesty the King)

1980. 'A statement on good teaching.' *Friends of Teachers Magazine,* p. 23.

Biehl, J., B. Good and A. Kleinman (eds)

2007. *Subjectivity: Ethnographic Investigations.* Berkeley: University of California Press.

Bloch, M. (ed.)

2003. *Governing Children, Families and Education: Restructuring the Welfare State.* New York: Palgrave Macmillan.

BMA (Bangkok Metropolitan Administration)

2007. *Statistical profile of Bangkok Metropolitan Administration 2007.* Bangkok: Strategy and Evaluation Department, BMA.

Bobilin, R.

1988. 'Buddhist and Christian movements for social justice in Southeast Asia.' *Buddhist–Christian Studies* 8: 5–12.

Boff, L.

1977. *Teologia della Cattività e della Liberazione* ('The Theology of Captivity and Liberation'). Brescia: Queriniana.

Bolotta, G.

2016. 'The good child's duties: Childhood in militarized Thailand.' In Pavin Chachavalpongpun (ed.), *The Blooming Years: Kyoto Review of Southeast Asia,* pp. 551–556. Kyoto: Center for Southeast Asian Studies.

2017a. "God's beloved sons': Religion, attachment, and children's self-formation in the slums of Bangkok.' *Antropologia* 4(2): 95–120.

2017b. 'Playing the NGO system: How mothers and children design political change in the slums of Bangkok.' In S. Vignato (ed.), *Dreams of Prosperity: Inequality and Integration in Southeast Asia,* pp. 203–234. Chiang Mai: Silkworm.

2018a. 'Religious and secular NGOs in the slums of Bangkok: Why a sharp dividing line is unhelpful and mistaken.' In M.R. Feener and P. Fountain (eds), *Religion and NGOs.* Part of the Oxford Department of International Development (ODID) blog. Retrieved from: www.qeh.ox.ac.uk/blog/religious-and-secular-ngos-slums-bangkok-why-sharp-dividing-line-unhelpful-and-mistaken.

2018b. 'Development missionaries in the slums of Bangkok: From the Thaification to the de-Thaification of Catholicism.' In C. Scheer, P. Fountain, and M.R. Feener (eds), *The Mission of Development: Techno-Politics of Religion in Asia*, pp. 135–164. Leiden: Brill.

2019. 'Making sense of (humanitarian) emotions in ethnography with vulnerable childhood: The case of Bangkok slum children.' In T. Stodulka, S. Dinkelaker and F. Thajib (eds), *Affective Dimensions of Fieldwork*, pp. 29–48. New York: Springer.

Bolotta, G., D. Boone, G. Chicarro, N. Collomb, D. Dussy and A.S. Sarcinelli (eds)

2017. À *quelle Discipline appartiennent les enfants? Croisements, échanges et reconfigurations de la recherche autour de l'enfance*. Marseilles: La Discussion.

Bolotta, G., P. Fountain and R.M. Feener (eds)

2020. *Political Theologies and Development in Asia: Transcendence, Sacrifice and Aspiration*. Manchester: Manchester University Press.

Bolotta, G. and S. Vignato

2017. 'Introduction: Independent children and their fields of relatedness.' *Antropologia* 4(2): 7–23.

Boltansky, L.

1993. *La Souffrance à distance*. Paris: Éditions Métailié.

Boonlert Visetpricha

2008. *Slum Development as a Technique of Governmental Control*. Paper presented at the 10th International Conference on Thai Studies, January 9–11 2008, Thammasat University, Bangkok.

Bordonaro, L.I. and R. Payne

2012. 'Ambiguous agency: Critical perspectives on social interventions with children and youth in Africa.' *Children's Geographies* 10(4): 365–372.

Bornstein, E.

2001. 'Child sponsorship, evangelism, and belonging in the work of World Vision Zimbabwe.' *American Anthropologist* 28(3): 595–622.

2011. 'The value of orphans.' In P. Redfield and E. Bornstein (eds), *Forces of Compassion: Humanitarianism between Ethics and Politics*, pp. 123–148. New Mexico: School for Advanced Research Press.

Bourdieu, P.

1987. *Choses Dites*. Paris: Les Éditions de Minuit.

2005. *Il Senso Pratico* ('The Logic of Practice). Roma: Armando Editore.

Bourdieu, P. and T. Eagleton

1992. 'Doxa and common life.' *New Left Review* 199: 111–121.

Bourdieu, P. and J. C. Passeron

1977. *Reproduction in Education, Society and Culture*. London: Sage Publications.

Bourdieu, P. and L. Wacquant

1992. *Réponses. Pour une Anthropologie Réflexive*. Paris: Seuil. Translation into Italian: Torino, Bollati Boringhieri, 1992.

Bowie, K.

1992. 'Unravelling the myth of the subsistence economy: The case of textile production in nineteenth century Northern Thailand.' *Journal of Asian Studies* 51(4): 797–823.

1997. *Rituals of National Loyalty. An Anthropology of the State and the Village Scout Movement in Thailand*. New York: Columbia University Press.

2008. 'Standing in the shadows of matrilocality and the role of women in a village election in northern Thailand.' *American Ethnologist* 35(1): 136–153.

Boyden J.

1997. 'Childhood and the policy makers: A comparative perspective on the globalization of childhood.' In A. James and A. Prout (eds), *Constructing and Reconstructing Childhood: Contemporary Issues in the Sociological Study of Childhood*, pp. 190–229. Oxford: Routledge.

Brekhus, W.

1998. 'A sociology of the unmarked: Redirecting our focus.' *Sociological Theory* 16(1): 34–51.

Bressan, L.

2005. *A Meeting of Worlds: The Interaction of Christian Missionaries and Thai Culture*. Bangkok: Assumption University Press.

Bressan, L. and M. Smithies

2006. *Thai–Vatican Relations in the Twentieth Century*. Bangkok: Amarin.

Brown, B. and R.M. Feener

2018. 'Configuring Catholicism in the anthropology of Christianity.' *The Australian Journal of Anthropology* 28(2): 139–151.

Buddhadasa Bhikkhu

1986. *Dhammic Socialism* (edited and translated by Donald K. Swearer). Bangkok: Munnithi Komonkhimthong.

Bunge, M.J. (ed.)

2001. *The Child in Christian Thought*. Cambridge: Wm. B. Eerdmans Publishing Co.

Bunge, M.J. and J. Wall

2011. 'Christianity.' In D.S. Browning and M.J. Bunge (eds), *Children and Childhood in World Religions: Primary Sources and Texts*, pp. 83–150. New Brunswick: Rutgers University Press.

Buono, G.

2000. *Missiologia: Teologia e Prassi* ('Missiology: Theology and Praxis'). Milano: Paoline Editoriale Libri.

Burkhart, L.M.

1989. *The Slippery Earth. Nahwa–Christian Moral Dialogue in Sixteenth-Century Mexico.* Tucson: The University of Arizona Press.

Burman, E.

2017. *Deconstructing Developmental Psychology* (3rd ed.). Oxford: Routledge.

Burr, R.

2006. *Vietnam's Children in a Changing World.* New Brunswick: Rutgers University Press.

Butler, J.

1990. *Gender Trouble. Feminism and the Subversion of Identity.* New York and London: Routledge.

1993. *Bodies that Matter.* New York: Routledge.

1997. *The Psychic Life of Power: Theories in Subjection.* Stanford: Stanford University Press.

Callahan, W.A.

2005. 'The discourse of vote buying and political reform in Thailand.' *Pacific Affairs* 78(1): 95–113.

Campigotto M., E. Razy, C.E. de Suremain and V. Pache Huber (eds)

2012. 'Children and religion. Children's religions.' *AnthropoChildren* No 2, October 2012.

Canella, G.S. and R. Viruru

2004. *Childhood and Post-Colonization: Power, Education, and Contemporary Practice.* New York: Routledge.

Carreon, J.R. and C. Svetanant

2017. 'What lies underneath a political speech? Critical discourse analysis of Thai PM's political speeches aired on the TV programme "Returning Happiness to the People".' *Open Linguistics* 3: 638–655.

Carsten, J.

1991. 'Children in-between: Fostering and the process in kinship on Pulau Langkawi, Malaysia.' *Man* 26(3): 425–443.

Cash, K.

1999. 'Understanding the psychosocial aspects of HIV/AIDS prevention for Northern Thai adolescent migratory women workers.' *Applied Psychology: An International Review* 48(2): 125–137.

Cassaniti, J.

2012. 'Agency and the Other: The role of agency for the importance of belief in Buddhist and Christian traditions.' *Ethos* 40(3): 297–316.

CDO (Community Development Office)

2002. *10 pi samnakngan phatthana chumchon* ('10 years of the community development office'). Bangkok: Community Development Office, Bangkok Metropolitan Administration.

Chaiyan Rajchagool

1994. *The Rise and Fall of the Thai Absolute Monarchy: Foundations of the Modern Thai State from Feudalism to Peripheral Capitalism*. Bangkok: White Lotus.

Chapin, B.L.

2013. 'Attachment in rural Sri Lanka: The shape of caregiver sensitivity, communication, and autonomy.' In N. Quinn and J. Mageo (eds), *Attachment Reconsidered: Cultural Perspectives on a Western Theory*, pp. 143–164. New York: Palgrave Macmillan.

Chayan Vaddhanaphuti

1991. 'Social and ideological reproduction in rural Northern Thai schools.' In C.F Keyes (ed.), *Reshaping Local Worlds: Formal Education and Cultural Change in Rural Southeast Asia*, pp. 153–173. New Haven: Yale University Southeast Asia Studies, Monograph no. 36.

Chea, L. and R. Huijsmans

2017. 'Rural youth and urban-based vocational training: Gender, space, and aspiring to "become someone".' *Children's Geographies* 16(1): 39–52.

Cheney, K.E.

2004. *Pillars of the Nation: Child Citizens and Ugandan National Development*. Chicago and London: University of Chicago Press.

2013. 'Malik and his three mothers: AIDS orphans' survival strategies and how children's rights hinder them.' In K. Hanson & O. Nieuwenhuys (eds), *Reconceptualizing Children's Rights in International Development: Living Translations*, pp. 152–172. Cambridge: Cambridge University Press.

Christensen, P. and A. Prout

2002. 'Working with ethical symmetry in social research with children.' *Childhood* 9(4): 477–497.

Clarke M. (ed.)

2012. *Mission and Development: God's Work or Good Works?* London: Continuum International Publishing Group.

Clewley, J.

2000. 'Thailand: songs for living.' In M. Ellingham, O. Duane, and J. McConnachie (eds), *World Music. The Rough Guide. Latin and North America, Caribbean, India, Asia and Pacific Vol. 2*, pp. 241–253. London: Rough Guides Ltd, Penguin Group.

Cohen, A.P.

1994. *Self-Consciousness. An Alternative Anthropology of Identity*. London: Routledge.

Cole, A.

2011. 'Buddhism.' In D.S. Browning and M.J. Bunge (eds), *Children and Childhood in World Religions. Primary Sources and Texts*, pp. 277–336. New Brunswick: Rutgers University Press.

Cole, J. and D. Durham (eds)

2008. *Figuring the Future: Globalization and the Temporalities of Children and Youth*. Santa Fe: School for Advanced Research Press.

Coles, R.

1986. *The Political Life of Children*. New York: Grove Press.

Collins, S. and J. McDaniel

2010. 'Buddhist "nuns" (*mae chi*) and the teaching of Pali in contemporary Thailand.' *Modern Asian Studies* 44(6): 1373–1408.

Comaroff, J. and J. Comaroff

1986. 'Christianity and colonialism.' *American Ethnologist* 13(1): 1–22.

2005. 'Children and youth in a global era.' In A. Honwana and F. de Boeck (eds), *Makers and Breakers: Children and Youth in Postcolonial Africa*, pp. 19–30. Oxford: James Currey.

Condominas, G.

1980. *L'Espace social: A propos de l'Asie du Sud-Est*. Paris: Flammarion.

Connors, M.K.

2003. *Democracy and National Identity in Thailand*. London and New York: Routledge Curzon.

2005. 'Ministering culture: Hegemony and the politics of culture and identity in Thailand.' *Critical Asian Studies* 37(4): 523–551.

Cook N.

1998. '"Dutiful daughters", estranged sisters. Women in Thailand.' In K. Sen and N. Stevens (eds), *Gender and Power in Affluent Asia*, pp. 250–290. London: Routledge.

Corsaro, W.A.

2011. *The Sociology of Childhood* (third ed.). Los Angeles: Sage.

Cunningham, H.

2014. *Children and Childhood in Western Society since 1500*. London: Routledge.

Cusack, M.

2011. 'Some recent trends in the study of religion and youth.' *Journal of Religious History* 35(3): 409–418.

Cuturi, F. (ed.)

2004. *In nome di Dio: L'impresa missionaria di fronte all'alterità* ('In the name of God: Mission and cultural alterity'). Roma: Meltemi.

Daily News

2013. 'Sun khunatham prakad rangwan haengchat pii 2556' ('The Centre for the Promotion of National Morality announces Thailand Morality Awards 2013'). June 25, 2013. Retrieved from: m.dailynews.co.th/News.do??contentId==19972.

Darlington, S.M.

2000. 'Rethinking Buddhism and development. The emergence of the environmentalist monks.' *Journal of Buddhist Ethics* 7: 1–14.

2012. *Ordination of a Tree: The Thai Buddhist Environmental Movement.* Albany: State University of New York Press.

Darunee Tantiwiramanond and S. R. Pandey

1991. *By Women, for Women: A Study of Women's Organizations in Thailand.* Singapore: Institute of Southeast Asian Studies, Paper no. 72.

Davies, B. and R. Harre

1990. 'Positioning: The discursive production of selves.' *Journal for the Theory of Social Behaviour* 20(1): 43–63.

Davies, J. and D. Spencer (eds)

2010. *Emotions in the Field. The Psychology and Anthropology of Fieldwork Experience.* Stanford: Stanford University Press.

Davies, M.

2008. 'A childish culture? Shared understandings, agency and intervention: An anthropological study of street children in Northwest Kenya.' *Childhood* 15(3): 309–330.

Davis, M.

2006. *Planet of Slums.* London: Verso.

de Boeck, F.

2005. 'The divine seed: Children, gift and witchcraft in the Democratic Republic of Congo.' In A. Honwana and F. de Boeck (eds), *Makers and Breakers: Children and Youth in Postcolonial Africa*, pp. 188–214. Oxford: James Currey.

de Certeau M.

1984. *The Practice of Everyday Life.* Berkeley: University of California Press.

de Rooij, L.

2015. 'The King and his cult: Thailand's monarch and the religious culture.' In D.W. Kim, *Religious Transformation in Modern Asia*, pp. 274–296. Leiden and Boston: Brill.

de Sardan, J.-P.O.

2005. *Anthropology and Development. Understanding Contemporary Social Change*. London: Zed Books.

de Vries, H.

2006. 'Introduction: Before, around, and beyond the theological–political.' In H. de Vries and L.E. Sullivan (eds), *Political Theologies: Public Religions in a Post-Secular World*, pp. 1–90. New York: Fordham University Press.

Delalande, J. (ed.)

2009. *Des enfants entre eux. Des jeux, des règles, des secrets*. Paris: Autrement.

Di Fiore, G.

2001. 'Strategie di evangelizzazione nell'Oriente asiatico tra cinquecento e settecento' ('Evangelisation strategies in the Asian Orient between the 15th and the 17th centuries'). In G. Martina and U. Dovere (eds), *Il cammino dell'evangelizzazione: Problemi storiografici* ('The progress of evangelisation: Historiographical problems'), pp. 97–162. Bologna: Il Mulino.

Doneys, P.

2002. 'Political reform through the public sphere: Women's groups and the fabric of governance.' In D. McCargo (ed.), *Reforming Thai Politics*, pp. 163–182. Copenhagen: NIAS Press.

Draper, J.

2018. 'Isaan update: Focus on the Dao Din (Part 1).' *Prachathai* January 4, 2018. Retrieved from: prachatai.com/english/node/7537 (Accessed March 1, 2018).

DPF (Duang Prateep Foundation)

2013. 'The origin of Duang Prateep Foundation.' Video file. *Youtube* September 27, 2013. Retrieved from: www.youtube.com/watch?feature=player_embedded&v=93PBkkeY4_g.

Dumont, L.

1980. *Homo Hierarchicus: The Caste System and its Implications*. Chicago and London: University of Chicago Press.

Durham, D.

2000. 'Youth and the social imagination in Africa.' *Anthropological Quarterly* 73(3): 113–120.

2008. 'Apathy and agency. The romance of agency and youth in Botswana.' In J. Cole and D. Durham (eds), *Figuring the Future: Globalization and the Temporalities of Children and Youth*, pp. 151–178. Santa Fe: School for Advanced Research Press.

Elinoff, E.

2012. 'Smouldering aspirations: Burning buildings and the politics of belonging in contemporary Isan.' *South East Asia Research* 20(3): 381–398.

2014. 'Sufficient citizens: Moderation and the politics of sustainable development in Thailand.' *Political and Legal Anthropology Review* 37(1): 89–108.

Ennew, J. and J. Swart-Kruger

2003. 'Introduction: Homes, places and spaces in the construction of street children and street youth.' *Children, Youth and Environments* 13(1): 81–104.

Essen, J.

2005. *Right Development: The Santi Asoke Buddhist Reform Movement of Thailand.* Oxford: Lexington Books.

Fairbairn, W.R.D.

1981. *Psychoanalytic Studies of the Personality.* London: Routledge and Kegan Paul.

Fanon, F.

2008. *Black Skin, White Masks.* Sidmouth: Pluto Press.

Fassin, D.

2005. 'A l'écoute de l'exclusion.' *Sciences Humaines* 159: 20–25.

2012. *Humanitarian Reason. A Moral History of the Present.* Berkeley and Los Angeles, California: University of California Press.

2013. 'Children as victims. The moral economy of childhood in the time of AIDS.' In J. Biehl and A. Petryna (eds), *When People Come First. Critical Studies in Global Health,* pp. 109–129. Princeton: Princeton University Press.

Feener, R.M. and P. Fountain

2018. 'Religion in the age of development.' *Religions* 9: 382.

Feener, R.M. and C. Scheer

2018. 'Development's missions.' In C. Scheer, P. Fountain, and M.R. Feener (eds), *The Mission of Development: Religion and Techno-Politics in Asia,* pp. 1–27. Leiden and Boston: Brill.

Ferguson, J.

1994. *The Anti-Politics Machine: 'Development', Depoliticization, and Bureaucratic Power in Lesotho.* Minneapolis: University of Minnesota Press.

Fine, G.A., and K. L. Sandstrom

1988. *Knowing Children. Participant Observation with Minors.* San Francisco: SAGE Publications.

Firestone, S.

1970. *The Dialectic of Sex: The Case for Feminist Revolution*. London: Jonathan Cape.

Forest, A.

1998. *Missionnaires français au Tonkin et au Siam, XVII–XVIII siècles: Analyse comparée d'un relative succès et d'un total èchec*. Paris: L'Harmattan.

Foucault, M.

1982. 'The subject and the power.' In H.L. Dreyfus & P. Rabinow (eds), *Michel Foucault: Beyond Structuralism and Hermeneutics*, pp. 208–226. London: Harvester Wheatsheaf.

1994. 'The ethics of care for the self as a practice of freedom: An interview.' In J. Bernauer and D. Rasmussen (eds), *The Final Foucault*, pp. 112–131. Cambridge: MIT Press.

Fountain, P., R. Bush and R. M. Feener (eds)

2015. *Religion and the Politics of Development*. Basingstoke: Palgrave–Macmillan.

Freire, P.

2011. *La pedagogia degli oppressi* ('The pedagogy of the oppressed'). Torino: Gruppo Abele.

Gabaude, L.

1988. *Une herméneutique buddhique contemporaine de Thailande: Buddhadasa Bhikkhu*. Paris: EFEO.

Geertz, C.

1973. *The Interpretation of Cultures*. New York: Basic Books.

1980. *Negara: The Theatre State in Nineteenth Century Bali*. Princeton: Princeton University Press.

Gellner, E.

1983. *Nations and Nationalism*. Oxford: Basil Blackwell.

German, D., S. G. Sherman, B. Sirirojn, N. Thomson, A. Aramrattana and D. D. Celentano

2006. 'Motivations for methamphetamine cessation among young people in northern Thailand.' *Addiction* 101: 1143–1152.

Gibellini, R. (ed.)

1978. *Teologia nera* ('Black theology'). Brescia: Queriniana.

Giles Ungpakorn

2009. 'Why have most Thai NGOs chosen to side with the conservative royalists, against democracy and the poor?' *Interface* 1(2): 233–237.

Gillogly, K.

2005. 'Developing the "hill tribes" of Northern Thailand.' In C.R. Duncan (ed.), *Civilizing the Margins. Southeast Asian Government Policies for the Development of Minorities*, pp. 116–149. Ithaca and London: Cornell University Press.

Glauser, B.

1997. 'Street children: Deconstructing a construct.' In A. James and A. Prout (eds), *Constructing and Reconstructing Childhood: Contemporary Issues in the Sociological Study of Childhood*, pp.145–164. Oxford: Routledge.

Goddard, J., S. McNamee, J. Goddard and A. James (eds)

2005. *The Politics of Childhood: International Perspectives, Contemporary Developments.* New York: Palgrave MacMillan.

Goffman, E.

1997 [1956]. *La vita quotidiana come rappresentazione.* (Original title in English: *The Presentation of Self in Everyday Life*). Bologna: Il Mulino.

2003a [1961], *Espressione e Identità. Gioco, ruoli e teatralità.* (Original title in English: *Encounters. Two Studies in the Sociology of Interaction*). Bologna: Il Mulino.

2003b [1963]. *Stigma: L'identità negate.* (Original title in English: *Stigma: Notes on the Management of Spoiled Identity*). Verona: Ombre Corte.

Goldman, L.R.

1998. *Child's Play: Myth, Mimesis, and Make-Believe.* New York, Oxford: Routledge.

Gombrich, R.

1988. *Theravada Buddhism. A Social History from Ancient Benares to Modern Colombo.* London & New York: Routledge.

Good, B. J.

1994. *Medicine, Rationality and Experience. An Anthropological Perspective.* Cambridge: Cambridge University Press.

Goodman, J.

2013. 'The meritocracy myth: National exams and the depoliticization of Thai education.' *Journal of Social Issues in Southeast Asia* 23(1): 101–131.

Goody, J. E. and S. J. Tambiah

1973. *Bride, Wealth and Dowry.* Cambridge: Cambridge Papers in Social Anthropology No 7.

Gross, R.

2006. 'Scarce discourse: Exploring gender, sexuality, and spirituality in Buddhism.' In K.M. Yust, A.N. Johnson, S.E. Sasso and E.C. Roehlkepartain (eds), *Nurturing Child and Adolescent Spirituality: Perspectives from the World's Religious Traditions*, pp. 411–422. Lanham: Rowman & Littlefield.

Gutiérrez, G.

1981. *La forza storica dei poveri* ('The historical force of the poor'). Brescia: Queriniana.

Haberkorn, T.

2011. *Revolution Interrupted: Farmers, Students, Law and Violence in Northern Thailand.* Madison: University of Wisconsin Press.

Hall, S.

1996. 'Who needs identity?' In S. Hall and P. Du Gay (eds), *Questions of Cultural Identity*, pp. 1–17. New York: Routledge.

Halliday, M.A.K.

1976. 'Anti-languages.' *American Anthropologist* 78: 570–584.

Handley, P.

2006. *The King Never Smiles: A Biography of Thailand's Bhumibol Adulyadej*. New Haven and London: Yale University Press.

Handwerker, W.P.

1990. 'Politics and reproduction: A window on social change.' In W.P. Handwerker (ed.), *Births and Power: Social Change and the Politics of Reproduction*, pp. 1–38. Boulder: Westview Press.

Hanks, L.M.

1962. 'Merit and Power in the Thai Social Order.' *American Anthropologist* 64: 1247–1261.

Hanson, K. and O. Nieuwenhuys (eds)

2013. *Reconceptualizing Children's Rights in International Development. Living Rights, Social Justice, Translations*. Cambridge: Cambridge University Press.

Harkness, S. and C. M. Super

1992. 'Parental ethnotheories in action.' In I.E. Sigel, McGillicuddy–DeLisi, and J.J Goodnow (eds), *Parental Belief Systems: The Psychological Consequences for Children* (2nd ed.), pp. 373–392. Erlbaum: Hillsdale.

Harkness, S. and C.M. Super (eds)

1996. *Parents' Cultural Belief Systems*. New York and London: The Guilford Press.

Harrison, R. and P. Jackson

2009. 'Introduction: Siam's/Thailand's constructions of modernity under the influence of the colonial West.' *South East Asia Research* 17(3): 325–360.

Hefner, B. (ed.)

1993. *Conversion to Christianity: Historical and Anthropological Perspectives on a Great Transformation*. Berkeley: University of California Press.

Hemming, P.J. and N. Madge

2012. 'Researching children, youth and religion: Identity, complexity, and agency.' *Childhood* 19(1): 38–51.

Herzfeld M.

1997. *Cultural Intimacy: Social Poetics in the Nation-State*. New York: Routledge.

2002. 'The absent presence: discourses of crypto-colonialism.' *The South Atlantic Quarterly* 101(4): 899–926.

2003. 'Pom Mahakan: Humanity and order in the historic centre of Bangkok.' *Thailand Human Rights Journal* 1: 101–119.

2016. *Siege of the Spirits: Community and Polity in Bangkok*. Chicago: University of Chicago Press.

Hewison, K.

1997. 'The monarchy and democratization.' In K. Hewison (ed.), *Political Change in Thailand. Democracy and Participation*, pp. 58–74. London: Routledge.

Heywood, C.

2001. *A History of Childhood: Children and Childhood in the West from Medieval to Modern Times*. Cambridge: Polity Press.

Hirshfeld, L.A.

2002. 'Why don't anthropologists like children?' *American Anthropologist* 104(2): 611–627.

Hoffman, D.M. and G. Zhao

2008. 'Global convergence and divergence in childhood ideologies and the marginalization of children.' In J. Zajda, K. Biraimah and W. Gaudelli (eds), *Education and Social Inequality in the Global culture*, pp. 1–16. Dordrecht: Springer.

Holland, D. and M. Eisenhart

1990. *Educated in Romance: Women, Achievement, and College Culture*. Chicago: University of Chicago Press.

Holland, D., D. Skinner, W. Lachicotte Jnr. and C. Cain

1998. *Identity and Agency in Cultural Worlds*. Cambridge: Harvard University Press.

Honwana, A. and F. de Boeck (eds)

2005. *Makers and Breakers: Children and Youth in Postcolonial Africa*. Oxford: James Currey.

Igunma, J.

2006. *Vajiravudh and the words: alphabetisation, book production and the ethos of modernisation in Thailand, 1910–1925*. Paper presented at the International Conference on Thai Language and Literature, November 10–12, 2006, Bangkok.

Il Messaggero

2014. 'Papa Francesco: "Il comunismo ci ha rubato la bandiera"' ('Pope Francis: "Communism stole our flag"'). *Il Messaggero*, July 29, 2014. Retrieved from: m. ilmessaggero.it/m/messaggero/articolo/primopiano/770510.

Isager, L. and S. Ivarsson

2010a. 'Strengthening the moral fibre of the nation. The King's sufficiency economy as etho-politics.' In S. Ivarsson and L Isager (eds), *Saying the Unsayable. Monarchy and Democracy in Thailand*, pp. 223–240. Copenhagen: NIAS Press.

2010b. 'Challenging the standard total view of the Thai monarchy.' In S. Ivarsson, S. and L. Isager (eds), *Saying the Unsayable: Monarchy and Democracy in Thailand*, pp. 1–28. Copenhagen: NIAS Press.

Ivarsson, S. and L. Isager (eds)

2010. *Saying the Unsayable. Monarchy and Democracy in Thailand*. Copenhagen: NIAS Press.

Iwanaga, K.

2008. *Women and Politics in Thailand*. Copenhagen: NIAS Press.

Jackson, M.

1998. *Minima Ethnographica: Intersubjectivity and the Anthropological Project*. Chicago: University of Chicago Press.

Jackson, P.A.

1987. *Buddhadāsa. Theravada Buddhism and Modernist Reform in Thailand*. Chiang Mai: Silkworm.

1989. *Buddhism, Legitimation, and Conflict: The Political Functions of Urban Thai Buddhism*. Singapore: Institute of Southeast Asian Studies.

1999. 'The enchanting spirit of Thai capitalism: The cult of Luang Phor Khoon and the post-modernization of Thai Buddhism.' *South East Asia Research* 7(1) 5–60.

2002. 'Thai Buddhist identity: Debates on the *Traiphum Phra Ruang*.' In C.J. Reynolds (ed.), *National Identity and Its Defenders*, pp. 155–188. Bangkok: Silkworm Books.

2010. 'Virtual divinity. A 21st century discourse of Thai royal influence.' In S. Ivarsson, and L. Isager (eds), *Saying the Unsayable. Monarchy and Democracy in Thailand*, pp. 29–60. Copenhagen: NIAS Press.

James, A.

1993. *Childhood Identities: Self and Social Relationships in the Experience of the Child*. Edinburgh: Edinburgh University Press.

1995. 'Talking of children and youth: Language socialization and culture.' In V. Amit–Talai and H. Wulff (eds), *Youth Cultures: A Cross-Cultural Perspective*, pp. 43–62. London: Routledge.

James, A. and A. James

2005. 'Introduction: The politics of childhood – An overview.' In J. Goddard, S. McNamee, Adrian James and Allison James (eds), *The Politics of Childhood: International Perspectives, Contemporary Developments*, pp. 3–12. New York: Palgrave Macmillan.

James, A. and A. Prout (eds)

1997. *Constructing and Reconstructing Childhood: Contemporary Issues in the Sociological Study of Childhood*. Oxford: Routledge.

Jenks, C.

1996. *Childhood*. London: Routledge.

Johnson, A.R.

2006. 'Leadership in a Bangkok slum: An ethnography of Thai urban poor in the Lang Wat Pathum Wanaram community'. PhD Thesis, University of Wales.

Jordon, G. and C. Weedon

1995. *Cultural Politics: Class, Gender, and Race and the Postmodern World*. Oxford: Blackwell.

Kammerer, C.A.

1990. 'Customs and Christian conversion among Akha highlanders of Burma and Thailand.' *American Ethnologist* 17(2): 277–291.

Kanokrat Lertchoosakul

2012. 'The Rise of the Octobrists: Power and Conflict among Former Left Wing Student Activists in Contemporary Thai Politics'. PhD thesis, London School of Economics and Political Science, London.

Kasian Tejapira

1996a. 'Cultural forces and counter-forces in contemporary Thailand.' In E. Thumboo (ed.), *Cultures in ASEAN and the 21st Century*, pp. 239–250. Singapore: Unipress.

1996b. 'The postmodernization of Thainess.' *Proceedings of the 6th International Conference on Thai Studies*, pp. 385–404. Chiang Mai: Chiang Mai University.

2002. 'The post-modernization of Thainess.' In Yao Souchou (ed.), *House of Glass. Culture, Modernity and the State in Southeast Asia*, pp. 150–172. Singapore: Institute of Southeast Asian Studies.

Kemp J.

1982. 'A tail wagging the dog: The patron–client model in Thai studies.' In C. Clapham (ed.), *Private Patronage and Public Power: Political Clientelism in the Modern State*, pp. 142–161. London: Frances Pinter.

Keyes C.F.

1971. 'Buddhism and national integration in Thailand.' *The Journal of Asian Studies* 30(3): 551–567.

1977. 'Millennialism, Theravada Buddhism and Thai society.' *The Journal of Asian Studies* 36(2): 283–302.

1978. 'Political crisis and militant Buddhism in contemporary Thailand.' In B.L. Smith (ed.), *Religion and Legitimation of Power in Thailand, Laos and Burma*, pp. 159–160. Chambersburg, Pennsylvania: Anima Books.

1984. 'Mother or mistress but never a monk: Buddhist notions of female gender in rural Thailand.' *American Ethnologist* 11(2): 223–241.

1989. 'Buddhist politics and their revolutionary origins in Thailand.' *International Political Science Review* 10(2): 121–142.

1991a. 'The proposed world of the school: Thai villagers' entry into a bureaucratic state system.' In C.F. Keyes (ed.), *Reshaping Local Worlds: Formal Education and Cultural Change in Rural Southeast Asia*, pp. 89–130. New Haven: Yale University Southeast Asia Studies. Monograph no. 36.

1991b. 'State schools in rural communities: Reflections on rural education and cultural change in Southeast Asia.' In C.F. Keyes (ed.), *Reshaping Local Worlds: Formal Education and Cultural Change in Rural Southeast Asia*, pp. 1–18. New Haven: Yale University Southeast Asia Studies. Monograph no. 36.

1993. 'Why the Thai are not Christian: Buddhist and Christian conversion in Thailand.' In R.W. Hefner (ed), *Conversion to Christianity. Historical and Anthropological Perspectives on a Great Transformation*, pp. 259–283. Berkeley: University of California Press.

Kirsch, A.T.

1977. 'Complexity in the Thai religious system: An interpretation.' *Journal of Asian Studies* 36(2): 241–266.

1978. 'Modernizing implications of nineteenth century reforms of the Thai Sangha.' In B.L. Smith (ed.), *Religion and Legitimation of Power in Thailand, Laos and Burma*, pp. 52–65. Chambersburg, Pennsylvania: Anima Books.

Kleinman A.

2011. *Social Suffering in Urban Space*. Public Lecture, December 13, 2011, SOUQ (Centro Studi sulla Sofferenza Urbana), Università degli Studi di Milano, Milan.

Komulainen, S.

2007. 'The ambiguity of the child's "voice" in social research.' *Childhood* 14(1): 11–28.

Korakod Narkvichetr

2009. *Juvenile Crime and Treatment of Serious and Violent Juvenile Delinquents in Thailand*. United Nations Asia and Far East Institute for the Prevention of Crime and the Treatment of Offenders Resource Material Series No 78. Retrieved from: www.unafei.or.jp/english/pdf/RS_No78/No78_16PA_Narkvichetr.pdf.

Korff, R.

1986. *Bangkok: Urban System and Everyday Life*. Saabrucken: Verlag Breitenbach.

Laclau, E., and C. Mouffe

1985. *Hegemony and Socialist Strategy: Towards a Radical Democratic Politics*. New York: Verso.

Lancy, D.F.

2008. *The Anthropology of Childhood. Cherubs, Chattel, Changelings*. Cambridge: Cambridge University Press.

2009. *Perspectives on Children in Cultural Preservation and Change*. Paper presented at the American Anthropological Association 105th Annual Meeting: 'Cultural Transmission and the Paradox of Children's Agency', December 2–6, 2009, Philadelphia.

Lanternari, V.

2003. *Movimenti religiosi di libertà e di salvezza dei popoli oppressi* ('Religious movements promoting oppressed populations' freedom and salvation'). Milano: Feltrinelli.

Lapthananon Pinit

2012. *Development Monks in Northeast Thailand.* Kyoto: Kyoto University Press.

Latour, B.

1986. 'The powers of association.' In J. Law and M. Callon (eds), *Power, Action and Belief: A New Sociology of Knowledge,* pp. 264–280. London: Routledge.

Lees, S.

1993. *Sugar and Spice: Sexuality and Adolescent Girls.* London: Penguin Books.

Levine, R.

2003. *Childhood Socialization: Comparative Studies of Parenting, Learning and Educational Change.* Hong Kong: Comparative Education Research Centre.

Levine, R. and K. Norman

2001. 'The infant's acquisition of culture: Early attachment re-examined in anthropological perspective.' In C. Moore and H. Mathews (eds), *The Psychology of Cultural Experience,* pp. 83–104. Cambridge: Cambridge University Press.

Lewis, A.

2011. 'Silence in the context of "child voice".' *Children and Society* 24: 14–23.

Lewis, D. and D. Mosse (eds)

2006. *Development Brokers and Translators: The Ethnography of Aid and Agencies* Bloomfield: Kumarian Press.

Li, T.

2007. *The Will to Improve: Governmentality, Development, and the Practice of Politics.* Durham: Duke University Press.

Lindberg–Falk, M.

2007. *Making Fields of Merit: Buddhist Female Ascetics and Gendered Orders in Thailand.* Copenhagen: NIAS Press.

2008. 'Gender and religious legitimacy in Thailand.' In Q. Wang, K. Iwanaga, C. Milwertz and W. Burghoorn (eds), *Gender Politics in Asia: Women Manoeuvring within Dominant Gender Orders,* pp. 95–119. Copenhagen: NIAS Press.

2010. 'Recovery and Buddhist practices in the aftermath of the tsunami in Southern Thailand.' *Religion* 40: 96–103.

Liow, J.C.

2009. *Islam, Education and Reform in Southern Thailand: Tradition and Transformation.* Singapore: Institute of Southeast Asian Studies.

Loos, T.

2006. *Subject Siam: Family, Law, and Colonial Modernity in Thailand*. Ithaca and London: Cornell University Press.

Lutz, C. and M.G. White

1986. 'The anthropology of emotions.' *Annual Review of Anthropology* 15: 405–436.

Mackenzie, R.

2007. *New Buddhist Movements in Thailand: Towards an Understanding of Wat Phra Dhammakaya and Santi Asoke*. London and New York: Routledge.

Mahony, S.

2018. *Searching for a Better Life: Growing Up in the Slums of Bangkok*. New York: Berghahn Books.

Malinowski, B.

1929. *The Sexual Life of Savages in North-Western Melanesia: An Ethnographic Account of Courtship, Marriage and Family Life among the Natives of the Tobriand Islands, British New Guinea*. London: Routledge and Sons.

Malkki, L.

2010. 'Children, humanity, and the infantilization of peace.' In I. Feldman and M. Ticktin (eds), *In the Name of Humanity: The Government of Threat and Care*, pp. 58–85. Durham: Duke University Press.

2015. *The Need to Help: The Domestic Arts of International Humanitarianism*. Durham: Duke University Press.

Manderson, L. and Liamputtong Pranee (eds)

2002. *Coming of Age in Southeast Asia: Youth, Courtship and Sexuality*. Surrey: Curzon Press.

Martin, J., C. Ungruhe and T. Häberlein

2016. 'Young future Africa – images, imagination, and its making: An introduction.' In J. Martin, C. Ungruhe, and T. Häberlein (eds), 'Images, imagination, and the making of future: Children, youth and the role of education.' Special issue of *AnthropoChildren* 6: 1–18.

Matichon

2008. *Seua daeng thayoi ruam kwham jing wat suan kaeo*' ('Red shirts' rally; "the truth" is starting at Suan Kaeo Temple'). *Matichon*, November 23, 2008. Retrieved from: tnews.teenee.com/politic/29484.html.

Mauss, M.

1936. 'Les techniques du corps.' *Journal de Psychologie* XXXII, 3–4, 15 Mars–15 Avril 1936.

McCargo, D.

2005. 'Network monarchy and legitimacy crises in Thailand.' *The Pacific Review* 18(4): 499–519.

2009. 'Thai politics as reality TV.' *The Journal of Asian Studies* 68(1): 7–19.

McCargo, D. and Ukrist Pathamanand

2005. *The Thaksinization of Thailand*. Copenhagen: NIAS Press.

McDaniel, J.

2011. *The Lovelorn Ghost and the Magic Monk: Practicing Buddhism in Modern Thailand*. New York: Columbia University Press.

Mead, G.H.

1934. *Mind, Self and Society*. Chicago: University of Chicago Press.

Mead, M.

1928. *Coming of Age in Samoa*. New York: Wm. Morrow and Co.

Mesnard, P.

2004. *Attualità della vittima: La rappresentazione umanitaria della sofferenza* (Original title in French: *La victime écran: La représentation humanitaire en question*). Verona: Ombre Corte.

Mickelson, R. (ed.)

1999. *Children on the Streets in the Americas: Globalization, Homelessness, and Education in the United States, Brazil and Cuba*. London: Routledge.

Miller–McLemore, B.J.

2001. '"Let the children come" revisited: Contemporary feminist theologians on children.' In M.J. Bunge (ed.), *The Child in Christian Thought*, pp. 446–473. Grand Rapids: Wm. B. Eerdmans Publishing.

Mills, M.B.

1999. *Thai Women in the Global Labor Force: Consuming Desires, Contested Selves*. New Brunswick: Rutgers University Press.

Ministry of Labour and Social Welfare of Thailand

1998. *Rule of the Ministry of Labour and Social Welfare on the Entry of Foreign Private Organizations to Operate in Thailand*. Foreign Working Administration Office, Department of Employment. Accessed January 11, 2015 at: wp.doe.go.th/ngo/documents/rule_2541_eng.pdf.

Mitchell, J.

2018. 'Thailand's rap against dictatorship.' *New Mandala* November 2, 2018. Retrieved from: www.newmandala.org/thailands-rap-against-dictatorship/ (Accessed December 01, 2018).

Mitchell, S.A.

1988. *Relational Concepts in Psychoanalysis: An Integration.* Cambridge: Harvard University Press.

Monod, P.K.

1999. *The Power of Kings: Monarchy and Religion in Europe, 1589–1715.* New Haven: Yale University Press.

Montesano, M.J., Pavin Chachavalpongpun and Aekapol Chongvilaivan (eds)

2012. *Bangkok May 2010: Perspectives on a Divided Thailand.* Chiang Mai: Silkworm Books.

Montgomery, H.

2001. *Modern Babylon? Prostituting Children in Thailand.* New York: Berghahn Books.

2009. *An Introduction to Childhood. Anthropological Perspectives on Children's Lives.* Hoboken: Wiley-Blackwell.

Morrison, L.

2004. 'Traditions in transition: Young people's risk for HIV in Chiang Mai.' *Qualitative Health Research* 14(3): 328–344.

Morrow, V.

1995. 'Invisible children? Toward a re-conceptualization of childhood dependency and responsibility.' *Sociological Studies of Children* 7: 207–230.

Mosse, D.

2012. *The Saint in the Banyan Tree: Christianity and Caste Society in India.* Berkeley: University of California Press.

Mounier, A. and Phasina Tangchuang (eds)

2010. *Education & Knowledge in Thailand.* Chiang Mai: Silkworm Books.

Mulder, N.

1992. *Inside Thai Society.* Bangkok: Duang Kamol.

1997. *Thai Images. The Culture of the Public World.* Chiang Mai: Silkworm.

Naafs, S. and T. Skelton

2017. 'Youthful futures? Aspiration, education, and employment in Asia.' *Children's Geographies* 16(1): 1–14.

New York Times

2019. 'The Saturday profile: A rap challenger to the Thai military junta.' February, 15, 2019. Retrieved from: www.newsstandhub.com/the-new-york-times/the-saturday-profile-a-rap-challenger-to-the-thai-military-junta (Accessed February 30, 2019).

Niphot Thienvihan

2016. *Rice Rituals and Building Community.* Paper presented at Sombath Symposium on 'Traditional, Cultural and Alternative Perspective on Humanity's Relationship with Nature', February 15–16, 2016, Chulalongkorn University, Bangkok.

Nitirat Sapsuntorn

2007. *Suwit Watnoo: nak rob pracha khiangkhang khon jon* ('Suwit Watnoo: Fighter for the people on the side of the poor'). Bangkok: Friends of the People Group.

Nusartlert, A.

2015. 'First person pronouns in Thai political language.' *Manusya: Journal of Humanities* 21: 1–13.

2017. 'Political language in Thai and English: Findings and implications for society.' *Journal of Mekong Societies* 13(3): 57–75.

Obeyesekere, G.

1968. 'Theodicy, sin and salvation in a sociology of Buddhism.' In E.R. Leach (ed.), *Dialectic in Practical Religion*, pp. 7–40. Cambridge: Cambridge University Press.

1972. 'Religious symbolism and political change in Ceylon.' In B.L. Smith (ed), *The Two Wheels of Dhamma: Essays on the Theravada Tradition in India and Ceylon*, pp. 58–78. Chambersburg, Pennsylvania: American Academy of Religion.

Ochs, E.

1982. 'Talking to children in Western Samoa.' *Language in Society* 11: 77–104.

1988. *Culture and Language Development: Language Acquisition and Language Socialization in a Samoan Village.* Cambridge: Cambridge University Press.

Ockey, J.

1996. 'Eviction and changing patterns of leadership in Bangkok slum communities.' *Bulletin of Concerned Asian Scholars* 20(2): 46–61.

1999. 'God mothers, good mothers, good lovers, godmothers: Gender images in Thailand.' *The Journal of Asian Studies* 58(4): 1033–1058.

2004. *Making Democracy. Leadership, Class, Gender, and Political Participation in Thailand.* Honolulu: University of Hawaii Press.

Office for the Registrar General of India

2001. *Census of India 2001: Slum Population in Million Plus Cities, 2001.* Office for the Registrar General of India. Retrieved from: censusindia.gov.in/Tables_Published/ Admin_Units/Admin_links/slum1_m_plus.html (accessed August 23, 2010).

Ortner, S.

1974. 'Is female to male as nature is to culture?' In M. Rosaldo and L. Lamphere (eds), *Woman, Culture, and Society*, pp. 67–87. Stanford: Stanford University Press.

Pache Huber, V. and L. Ossipow (eds)

2012. 'Les enfants comme enjeux et comme acteurs. Appartenances, relations interindividuelles et logiques institutionnelles.' *Tsantsa* 17 (Special issue): 19–35.

Pairin Jotisakulratana

2012. 'Mothers of all Peoples: Goddesses of Thailand from Prehistory until the Present'. PhD Dissertation, California Institute of Integral Studies, San Francisco.

Panter–Brick, C.

2002. 'Street children, human rights and public health: A critique and future directions.' *Annual Review of Anthropology* 31: 147–171.

Pasuk Phongpaichit and C. Baker

1996. *Thailand's Boom!* Chiang Mai: Silkworm.

2004. *Thaksin: The Business of Politics in Thailand.* Chiang Mai: Silkworm.

2008. *The Spirits, the Stars, and Thai Politics.* Public lecture, December 2, 2008, Siam Society, Bangkok.

Pattana Kitiarsa

2002. *The Politics of Thai Pop and Thai Anthropology.* Paper presented on May 21, 2002 at conference at Center of South-East Asian Studies, University of Washington, Seattle.

2005. 'Beyond syncretism: Hybridization of popular religion in contemporary Thailand.' *Journal of Southeast Asian Studies* 36(3): 461–487.

2012. *Mediums, Monks, and Amulets: Thai Popular Buddhism Today.* Washington: University of Washington Press.

Pavin Chachavalpongpun

2011. 'The necessity of enemies in Thailand's troubled politics.' *Asian Survey* 51(6): 1019–1041.

Payom Kanlayano

1992. *Phra kho khon duai* ('Phra Payom's excuse in May incident'). Nonthabury: Wat Suan Kaeo Pubblication.

Peacock, M.

2014. *Innocent Weapons: The Soviet and American Politics of Childhood in the Cold War.* Chapel Hill: The University of North Carolina Press.

Persaud, W.H.

2005. 'Gender, race and global modernity: A perspective from Thailand.' *Globalizations* 2(2): 210–227.

Phillips, E.

2006. 'Rhetorical maneuvers: Subjectivity, power, and resistance.' *Philosophy and Rhetoric* 39(4): 310–332.

Phya Anuman Rajhadon

1955. 'Me Posop, the rice mother.' *Journal of the Siam Society* 43: 55–61.

1963. *Thai Traditional Salutation.* Bangkok: The Fine Arts Department (Thai Culture Series no. 2).

Pitch Pongsawat

1993. *The Roles of the Sangha in Urban Thai Society: A Case Study of Phra Payom Kalayano.* Paper presented at 5th International Conference on Thai Studies, SOAS, London.

Pochetti, I.

2017. 'Care under constraint: Street children in a rehabilitation centre in Tijuana (Mexico).' In G. Bolotta and S. Vignato (eds), 'Independent Children' (Special Focus), *Antropologia* 4(2): 121–144.

Porphant Ouyyanont

2008. 'The Crown Property Bureau from crisis to opportunities.' In Pasuk Phongpaichit and C. Baker (eds), *Thai Capital After the 1997 Crisis*, pp. 155–186. Singapore: Institute of Southeast Asian Studies.

Prachathai

2013. 'Salam si phak nun sopopo. sanoe thuk phak long sathayaban kon leuak tang ruam kae rotono. Kae panha khrohngsang sangkhom' ('4 regions slum network supports AFDD'). *Prachathai*, December 12. Retrieved from: prachatai.com/journal/2013/12/50389.

2014a. 'Kanchaichai kanseuksa khong thai sung thisud nai lok' ('Thai educational budget is the highest in the world'). *Prachathai* February 2014. Retrieved from: prachatai.com/journal/2014/02/51674?utm_source=feedburner&utm_medium=feed&utm_campaign=Feed%3A+prachatai+%28ประชาไท+Prachatai.com.

2014b. 'When truth is missing from the land of (pretended) smiles.' *Prachathai* July 02, 2014. Retrieved from: prachatai.org/english/node/4182.

2014c. 'Kristachon katholik kab kwham rap phid chop to ban meuang nai thana phonlameuang khong chat' ('Catholic Christians, as citizens, are responsible to the country'). *Prachathai* 01/03/2014. Retrieved from: www.prachatai.com/journal/2014/01/50932.

2014d. '5 anti-coup activists arrested for 3-fingered salute during junta leader's visit to Khon Kaen.' *Prachathai* November 11, 2014. Retrieved from: www.prachatai.org/english/node/4501 (Accessed November 15, 2015).

2014e. 'Exclusive interview with Khon Kaen student activist detained for 3-fingered salute.' *Prachathai* November 20, 2014. Retrieved from: www.prachatai.org/english/node/4505 (Accessed November 22, 2014).

Punch, S.

2002. 'Research with children. The same or different from research with adults?' *Childhood* 9(3): 321–341.

Quaritch Wales, H.G.

1965. *Ancient Siamese Government and Administration*. New York: Paragon Book Reprint Corp.

Queen, C.S.

1996. 'Introduction.' In C.S. Queen and S.B. King (eds), *Engaged Buddhism. Buddhist Liberation Movements in Asia*, pp. 1–44. Albany: State University of New York Press.

Queen, C.S. and S.B. King (eds)

1996. *Engaged Buddhism. Buddhist Liberation Movements in Asia.* Albany: State University of New York Press.

Redfield, P. and E. Bornstein (eds)

2011. *Forces of Compassion: Humanitarianism between Ethics and Politics.* New Mexico: School for Advanced Research Press.

Reid, A.

2010. *Imperial Alchemy: Nationalism and Political Identity in Southeast Asia.* Cambridge: Cambridge University Press.

2015. *A History of Southeast Asia: Critical Crossroads.* Oxford: Wiley Blackwell

Reynolds, C.J. (ed.)

2002. *National Identity and its Defenders. Thailand Today.* Chiang Mai: Silkworm Books.

Ridgely, S.

2012. 'Children and religion.' *Religion Compass* 6(4): 236–248.

Rieber, R.

2006. *The Bifurcation of the Self: The History and Theory of Dissociation and Its Disorders.* New York: Springer.

Rigg, J.

1995. *Counting the Costs: Economic Growth and Environmental Change in Thailand.* Singapore: Institute of Southeast Asian Studies.

Rimmer, P.J. and H. Dick

2009. *The City in Southeast Asia. Patterns, Processes and Policy.* Singapore: NUS Press.

Roest–Crollius, A.

1984. 'What is so new about inculturation?' In A. Roest–Crollius and T. Nkerahimigo (eds), *Inculturation: Working Papers 1*, pp. 1–18. Rome: Gregorian University.

Rosaldo, M.

1984. 'Toward an anthropology of self and feeling.' In A.R. Levine and A.R. Shweder (eds), *Culture Theory. Essays on Mind, Self, and Emotion*, pp. 135–157. Cambridge: Cambridge University Press.

Rosen, D.

2007. 'Child soldiers, international humanitarian law, and the globalization of childhood.' *American Anthropologist* 109: 296–306.

Rossi, A.

2012. 'Turning red rural landscapes yellow? Sufficiency economy and royal projects in the hills of Nan province, Northern Thailand.' *Austrian Journal of South-East Asian Studies* 5(2): 275–291.

Rudnyckyj, D. and F. Osella (eds)

2017. *Religion and the Morality of the Market.* Cambridge: Cambridge University Press.

Russell, L.

1974. *Human Liberation in a Feminist Perspective – A Theology.* Philadelphia: Westminster Press.

Sanit Samakkarn

1994. '*Phi nong*' ('Elder and younger siblings'). In Suwanna Satha–Anand & Nuangnoi Boonyanate (eds), *Kham: rongroi khwam khit khwam cheua thai* ('Words: trace thinking, Thai belief;), pp. 164–171. Bangkok: Chulalongkorn Univeristy Press.

Santikaro Bhikkhu

1996. 'Buddhadasa Bhikkhu: Life and society through the natural eyes of voidness.' In C.S. Queen and S.B. King (eds), *Engaged Buddhism. Buddhist Liberation Movements in Asia*, pp. 147–194. Albany: State University of New York Press.

Sasson, V.R. (ed.)

2013. *Little Buddhas. Children and Childhood in Buddhist Texts and Traditions.* New York: Oxford University Press.

Satha–Anand, S.

1990. 'Religious movements in contemporary Thailand: Buddhist struggles for modern relevance.' *Asian Survey* 30(4): 395–408.

Scheer, C., P. Fountain and M.R. Feener (eds),

2018. *The Mission of Development: Religion and Techno-Politics in Asia.* Leiden and Boston: Brill.

Scheper–Hughes, N.

1987. 'The cultural politics of child survival.' In N. Scheper–Hughes (ed.), *Child Survival: Anthropological Perspectives on the Treatment and Maltreatment of Children*, pp. 1–29. Dordrecht: Reidel.

1992. *Death without Weeping: The Violence of Everyday Life in Brazil.* Berkeley: University of California Press.

1998. 'Institutionalized sex abuse and the Catholic Church.' In N. Scheper–Hughes and C. Sargent (eds), *Small Wars: The Cultural Politics of Childhood*, pp. 295–317. Berkeley and Los Angeles: University of California Press.

Scheper–Hughes, N. and P. Bourgois (eds)

2004. *Violence in War and Peace: An Anthology.* Oxford: Wiley–Blackwell.

Scheper–Hughes, N. and C. Sargent

1998. *Small Wars. The Cultural Politics of Childhood.* Berkeley and Los Angeles: University of California Press.

Schepler, S.

2014. *Childhood Deployed: Remaking Child Soldiers in Sierra Leone*. New York: New York University Press.

Schiller, N.G.

1997. 'Cultural politics and the politics of culture.' *Identities* 4(1): 1–7.

Schofer, J.W.

2012. 'Ethical formation and subjection.' *Numen* 59(1): 1–31.

Scott, J.C.

1972. 'Patron–client politics and political change in Southeast Asia.' *The American Political Science Review* 66(1): 91–113.

1985. *Weapons of the Weak: Everyday Forms of Peasant Resistance*. New Haven: Yale University Press.

2009. *The Art of Not Being Governed. An Anarchist History of Upland Southeast Asia*. New Haven: Yale University Press.

Sennett, R.

2006. *Autorità. Subordinazione e insubordinazione: L'ambiguo vincolo tra il forte e il debole* (Original title: *Authority. Subordination and Insubordination: The Ambiguous Relationship between the powerful and the powerless*). Milano: Mondadori.

Seri Phongphit

1988. *Religion in a Changing Society: Buddhism, Reform and the Role of Monks in Community Development in Thailand*. Hong Kong: Arena Press.

Shigetomi, S., Kasian Tejapira, and Apichart Thongyou (eds)

2004. *The NGO way: Perspectives and Experiences from Thailand*. Bangkok: Institute of Developing Economies, Japan External Trade Organization.

Siani, E.

2016. 'The return of the divine king.' *New Mandala* October 24, 2016. Retrieved from: www.newmandala.org/return-divine-king/.

Singer, D.G. and J.L. Singer (eds)

2012. *Handbook of Children and the Media* (second edition). Los Angeles: Sage.

Siwach Sripokangkul and M.S. Cogan

2019. 'Political demonology, dehumanization, and contemporary Thai politics.' *Asia–Pacific Social Science Review* 19(2): 115–130.

Smith, K.

2015. 'Deconstructing Discourses to Rupture Fairytales of the "Ideal" Childhood.' In: J. Wyn and Cahill H. (eds.) *Handbook of Children and Youth Studies*, pp. 21–33. Singapore: Springer.

Smith, R.T.

1973. 'The matrifocal family.' In J. Goody (ed.), *The Character of Kinship*, pp. 121–144. Cambridge: Cambridge University Press.

Somphong Čhitradab

2007. *Krung thep mahanakhon meuang sithaw khong dek lae yewachon* ('Bangkok metropolis: The grey city of children and youth'). Bangkok: Chulalongkorn University.

Somsak Jeamteerasakul

2001. *Prawatsat thi pheung sang: ruam bot khwam kiao kap korani somsak jiamthirasakul* ('History that has just been made: Collected articles related to the October 14 and October 6 events'). Bangkok: 6 October Commemoration Publishing.

Somsook Boonyabancha

1983. 'Causes and effects of slum eviction in Bangkok.' In S. Angel, R. Archer, S. Tanphiphat and E. Wegelin (eds), *Land for Housing the Poor*, pp. 254–283. Singapore: Select Publications.

Sopon Pornchokchai

1992. *Bangkok Slums: Review and Recommendations*. Bangkok: Agency for Real Estate Affairs.

Sopranzetti, C.

2012. 'Burning red desires: Isan migrants and the politics of desire in contemporary Thailand.' *South East Asia Research* 20(3): 361–379.

2017a. 'The tightening authoritarian grip on Thailand.' *Current History* 116(791): 230–234.

2017b. *Owners of the Map: Motorcycle Taxi Drivers, Mobility, and Politics in Bangkok*. Berkeley: University of California Press.

Spiro, M.E.

1993. 'Is the Western conception of the self "peculiar" within the context of the world cultures?' *Ethos* 21(2): 107–153.

Spyrou, S.

2018. *Disclosing Childhoods: Research and Knowledge Production for a Critical Childhood Studies*. London: Palgrave Macmillan UK.

Stephens, S. (ed.)

1995. *Children and the Politics of Culture*. Princeton: Princeton University Press.

Stodulka, T.

2014. '"Playing it right": Empathy and emotional economies on the streets of Java.' In T. Stodulka & B. Röttger-Rössler (eds), *Feelings at the Margins: Dealing with Violence, Stigma and Isolation in Indonesia*, pp. 103–127. Frankfurt: Campus.

2015. 'Emotion work, ethnography and survival strategies on the streets of Yogyakarta.' *Medical Anthropology: Cross-Cultural Studies in Health and Illness* 34(1): 84–97.

2016. *Coming of Age on the Streets of Java – Coping with Marginality, Stigma and Illness.* Bielefeld. Transcript.

Stoler, A.

2004. 'Affective states.' In D. Nugent and J. Vincent (eds), *A Companion to Anthropology of Politics*, pp. 4–20. Oxford: Blackwell.

Strate, S.

2011. 'An uncivil state of affairs: Fascism and anti-Catholicism in Thailand, 1940–1944.' *Journal of Southeast Asian Studies* 42(1): 59–87.

Strathern, A.

2019. *Unearthly Powers: Religious and Political Change in World History*. Cambridge: Cambridge University Press.

Streckfuss, D.

2010. 'The intricacies of lese-majesty. A comparative study of imperial Germany and modern Thailand.' In S. Ivarsson and L. Isager (eds), *Saying the Unsayable. Monarchy and Democracy in Thailand*, pp 105–146. Copenhagen: NIAS Press.

Sulak Sivaraksa

1989. *Crisis of Siamese Identity*. Keynote address, Symposium on Thai identity, September 8–9, 1989, Centre of Southeast Asian Studies, Monash University, Austria.

Swearer, D.K.

1996. 'Sulak Sivaraksa's Buddhist vision for renewing society.' In C.S. Queen and S.B. King (eds), *Engaged Buddhism. Buddhist Liberation Movements in Asia*, pp. 195–235. Albany: State University of New York Press.

2010. *The Buddhist World of Southeast Asia*. Second edition. Albany: State University of New York Press.

Tajfel, H.

1981. *Human Groups and Social Categories in Social Psychology*. Cambridge: Cambridge University Press.

Tambiah, S.J.

1969. 'Animals are good to think and good to prohibit.' *Ethnology* 8(4), 423–459.

1976. *World Conqueror & World Renouncer. A Study of Buddhism and Polity in Thailand against a Historical Background*. London: Cambridge University Press.

1977. 'The galactic polity: The structures of traditional kingdoms in Southeast Asia.' In S. Freed (ed.), *Anthropology and the Climate of Opinion*, pp. 69–97. New York: New York Academy of Sciences.

1984. *The Buddhist Saints of the Forest and the Cult of Amulets: A Study in Charisma, Hagiography, Sectarianism and Millennial Buddhism*. Cambridge: Cambridge University Press.

Tanner, N.

1974. 'Matrifocality in Indonesia and Africa and among black Americans.' In M.Z. Rosaldo and L. Lamphere (eds), *Woman, Culture and Society*, pp. 129–156. Stanford: Stanford University Press.

Taylor, J.

2016. *Buddhism and Postmodern Imaginings in Thailand: The Religiosity of Urban Space.* Surrey: Ashgate.

Thak Chaloemtiarana

2007. *Thailand. The Politics of Despotic Paternalism.* Chiang Mai: Silkworm.

Thomas, N.

2005. 'Interpreting children's needs: Contested assumptions in the provision of welfare.' In J. Goddard, S. McNamee, Adrian James and Allison James (eds), *The Politics of Childhood: International Perspectives, Contemporary Developments*, pp.13–31. New York: Palgrave MacMillan.

Thomas, N. and C. O'Kane

1998. 'The ethics of participatory research with children.' *Children and Society* 12: 336–348.

Thongchai Winichakul

1994. *Siam Mapped: A History of the Geo-Body of a Nation.* Honolulu: University of Hawaii Press.

2000a. 'The other within: Travel and ethno-spatial differentiation of Siamese subjects.' In A. Turton (ed.), *Civility and Savagery: Social Identity in Tai States*, pp. 38–62. Surrey: Curzon Press.

2000b. 'The quest for 'siwalai': a geographical discourse of civilizational thinking in the late nineteenth and early twentieth century Siam.' *Journal of Asian Studies* 59(3): 528–549.

2008. 'Toppling democracy.' *Journal of Contemporary Asia* 38(1): 11–37.

Thorbek, S.

1987. *Voices from the City: Women of Bangkok.* London: Zed Books Ltd.

Ticktin, M.

2017. 'A world without innocence.' *American Ethnologist* 44(4): 577–590.

Unger, D.

1998. *Building Social Capital in Thailand: Fibers, Finance, and Infrastructure.* Cambridge: Cambridge University Press.

United Nations

2009. *World Urbanization Prospects: The 2009 revision population database.* United Nations. Retrieved from: <u>esa.un.org/UNPP/p2k0data.asp</u> (accessed August 16, 2010).

2010. *Slum Populations as Percentage of Urban*. United Nations. Retrieved from: data.un.org/Data.aspx?d=MDG&f=seriesRowID:710#f__9 (accessed August 22, 2010).

United Nations Habitat

2006. *State of the World's Cities 2006/7*. Retrieved from: ww2.unhabitat.org/mediacentre/documents/sowcr2006/SOWCR%205.pdf (accessed August 22, 2010).

Uthai Dulyakasem

1991. 'Education and ethnic nationalism: The case of the Muslim–Malays in southern Thailand.' In C.F Keyes (ed.), *Reshaping Local Worlds: Formal Education and Cultural Change in Rural Southeast Asia*, pp. 131–152. New Haven: Yale University Southeast Asia Studies, New Haven. Monograph no. 36.

Vajiravudh (King of Siam)

1917. *The Jews of the Orient*. Bangkok: Siam Observer Press.

van der Cruysse, D.

1991. *Siam & the West: 1500–1700*. Chiang Mai: Silkworm Books.

van Gennep, A.

2002. *I Riti di Passaggio* (Original title: *Rites of Passage*). Torino: Bollati Boringhieri.

Vella, W.F.

1978. *Chaiyo! King Vajiravudh and the Development of Thai Nationalism*. Honolulu: University of Hawaii Press.

Vignato, S.

2017. 'Orphans, victims and families: An ethnography of children in Aceh.' *Antropologia* 4(2): 65–93.

2020. 'Motherly landscapes: Matrifocality, marriage, Islam and the change of generation in post-conflict, post-tsunami Aceh.' *East and West* 1(60): 405–434.

Virada Somswasdi and Kobkun Rayanakorn

1994. *Women's Legal Position in Thailand*. Chiang Mai: Women's Studies Center, Faculty of Social Sciences, Chiang Mai University.

Walker, A.

2010. 'Royal sufficiency and elite misrepresentation of rural livelihoods.' In S. Ivarsson and L. Isager (eds), *Saying the Unsayable. Monarchy and Democracy in Thailand*, pp. 241–265. Copenhagen: NIAS Press.

Wallace, M.

2003. *Today's Cultural Dilemma for the Thai teachers: Moral Parent and Critical Thinker*. Sewanee, The University of the South. Retrieved from: www.sewanee.edu/education/mwhomejan03/MWThaiteach03%202.pdf.

Watson, D.K.

1980. *Educational Development in Thailand*. London: Heinemann Educational Books Limited.

Wells, K.

2009. *Childhood in a Global Perspective*. Cambridge: Polity Press.

Whiting, B.B. (ed.)

1963. *Six Cultures: Studies of Child Rearing*. New York: Wiley.

Withitan Foundation

2004. *Dek thai wai muasum tid ya ba kem. Reuang thi po mae tong rianru* ('Thai Children in Gig Generation'). Bangkok: Withitan Foundation.

World Bank

1993. *The East Asian Miracle: Economic Growth and Public Policy*. Oxford and New York: Oxford University Press.

Wyatt, D.K.

1969. *The Politics of Reform in Thailand: Education in the Reign of King Chulalongkorn*. New Haven: Yale University Press.

1975. 'Education and modernization of Thai society.' In G.W Skinner and T.A. Kirsh (eds), *Change and Persistence in Thai Society. Essays in Honor of Lauriston Sharp*, pp. 125–150. Ithaca and London: Cornell University Press.

1994. *Studies in Thai History*. Chiang Mai: Silkworm.

Young, L.

2003. 'The "place" of street children in Kampala, Uganda: Marginalisation, resistance and acceptance in the urban environment.' *Environment and Planning D: Society and Space* 21: 607–627.

Young, R.F. and J.A. Seitz

2013. 'Introduction.' In R.F. Young and J.A. Seitz (eds), *Asia in the Making of Christianity: Conversion, Agency, and Indigeneity, 1600s to the Present*, pp. 1–26. Leiden: Brill.

Zimbardo, P.

2007. *The Lucifer Effect. How Good People Turn Evil*. New York: Random House.

Zupanov, I.

1995. *Missionary Tropics: The Catholic Frontier in India (16th–17th Centuries)*. Ann Arbor: The University of Michigan Press.

Glossary of Key Thai
Words and Phrases

Thai is the most widely-spoken language in the Tai-Kadai family. It is a tonal language (5 tones: mid, low, falling, high and rising) with a number of (short and long) vowels and consonants that are not found in English.

This glossary lists key Thai words and phrases used in the text. Words and phrases are provided in Thai script and I also provide a phonetic transcription. Entries are ordered alphabetically by the transcribed Thai term (left-hand column). There is no agreed transcription of Thai and the only correct spelling is that in Thai script. Rather than following the Royal Thai General System of Transcription (RTGS) – which is often incoherent, difficult to understand for non-specialist readers, and is largely ignored by most Thais – my phonetic transcription seeks to provide the average English-speaking reader with a consistent and easy-to-read spelling. Tonal marks and vowel length are thus excluded for the sake of simplicity. The translations into English that are provided (right-hand column) are basic. Since the meaning of many Thai lexemes varies according to the context in which they occur, more accurate translations are given within the body of the text.

Transcription	Thai	English Translation
akhan daeng	อาคารแดง	Red Building (name of slum area)
anapanasati	อานาปานสติ	mindful breathing (meditation technique)
ban dek	บ้านเด็ก	children's houses
ban meta	บ้านเมตตา	House of Compassion (juvenile detention centre)
bap	บาป	demerit; sin
barami	บารมี	charismatic power; prestige
binthabat	บิณฑบาต	collection of alms; food offering
bohran	โบราณ	primitive; antiquated; ancient
bun	บุญ	merit

Transcription	Thai	English Translation
chan rak meuang thai	ฉันรักเมืองไทย	I love Thailand (TV show)
chao khao	ชาวเขา	hill tribes
chat	ชาติ	nation
chon thai	ชนไทย	Thai people
chumchon aeat	ชุมชนแออัด	crowded communities; slums
dam	ดำ	black
dichan	ดิฉัน	I (female speaker)
dek	เด็ก	child
dek deu	เด็กดื้อ	obstinate child
dek di	เด็กดี	good child
dek doi ohkat	เด็กด้อยโอกาส	disadvantaged child
dek jon	เด็กจน	poor child
dek lao	เด็กลาว	Lao child
dek salam	เด็กสลัม	slum child
dek tang dao	เด็กต่างด้าว	foreign child; migrant child
dek wat	เด็กวัด	temple child
dohi samathi	โดยสมาธิ	by meditation
dom kao	ดมกาว	glue sniffing
du thuk	ดูถูก	to despise; humiliate
fai phatthana chumchon	ฝ่ายพัฒนาชุมชน	community development team
farang	ฝรั่ง	Westerner; white person
hia	เหี้ย	monitor lizard; asshole; shit
huana hong	หัวหน้าห้อง	class representative/president
jai di	ใจดี	generous; kind; benign
jai yen	ใจเย็น	to cool the heart; calm; patient
jak	จักร	chakra
kaeng dohd diao	แก๊งโดดเดี่ยว	Gang of Loners (gang name)
kam	กรรม	karma
kere	เกเร	undisciplined; rowdy; disobedient
kha	ค่ะ	yes; please (female speaker)
khaniyom	ค่านิยม	value

Transcription	Thai	English Translation
kharachakan	ข้าราชการ	public servant
kheun khwamsuk	คืนความสุข	to return happiness
kheun sawan	ขึ้นสวรรค์	to go to heaven
khlong	คลอง	canal
khon ban nok	คนบ้านนอก	countrymen; rural people
khon di	คนดี	good people
khon isan	คนอีสาน	people from the northeast of Thailand
khon jon pen phiset nai phra jao	คนจนเป็นพิเศษในพระเจ้า	the poor are special in God
khon meuang	คนเมือง	city people
khon pa	คนป่า	forest people
khon thai	คนไทย	Thai people
khrap	ครับ	yes; please (male speaker)
khreua khai salam si phak	เครือข่ายสลัมสี่ภาค	Four Regions Slum Network (slum organisation)
khrohngkan luang	โครงการหลวง	royal project
khru	ครู	teacher
khru phaen din	ครูแผ่นดิน	Teacher of the Land (royal title)
khun	คุณ	you
khunatham	คุณธรรม	morality; moral goodness
khwai	ควาย	water buffalo; stupid
khwam jing	ความจริง	truth
khwam katanyu	ความกตัญญู	gratitude
khwam pen thai	ความเป็นไทย	Thainess
khwam riaproi	ความเรียบร้อย	order; discipline; decency; neatness
koet ma pheua hai khon yu tai amnat	เกิดมาเพื่อให้คนอยู่ใต้อำนาจ	I was born to have others in my power.
krap	กราบ	to prostrate
krong thip	กรองทิพย์	Krong Thip (Thai cigarette brand)
ku	กู	I (informal)
lek	เล็ก	small
luang	หลวง	royal; venerable

Transcription	Thai	English Translation
luk	ลูก	son/daughter
luk bun tham	ลูกบุญธรรม	adopted child; foster child
luk seua	ลูกเสือ	Tiger Cubs (Thai scouting)
mae	แม่	mother; mum
mae chi	แม่ชี	Buddhist laywomen; nuns
mafia	มาเฟีย	crook; mafia
mai di	ไม่ดี	not good; bad
mai mi kham wa phi, mai mi kham wa nong, mi khae kham wa pheuan	ไม่มีคำว่า พี่ ไม่มีคำว่า น้อง มีแค่คำว่า เพื่อน	The words younger and older sibling don't exist. There's only room for the word friends.
mai mi khwam riaproi	ไม่มีความเรียบร้อย	There is no order/discipline.
mai mosom	ไม่เหมาะสม	inappropriate
mai rap phit chop	ไม่รับผิดชอบ	irresponsible; unaccountable
mai riaproi	ไม่เรียบร้อย	undisciplined; untidy
marayat	มารยาท	good manners; decorum; courtesy
mathayom	มัธยม	high school
meung	มึง	you (informal)
mho phi	หมอผี	spirit medium; shaman
mia noi	เมียน้อย	minor wife
mu ban	หมู่บ้าน	village
munithi	มูลนิธิ	foundation; NGO
munithi dek	มูลนิธิเด็ก	Children's Foundation (name of NGO)
nai - munnai	นาย - มูลนาย	feudal official; supervisor; boss; master
nak leng	นักเลง	gangster; ruffian
nang samathi	นั่งสมาธิ	to meditate
nen	เณร	novice (informal)
nipphan	นิพพาน	*nirvana*
nong	น้อง	younger brother/sister
nu	หนู	I (child/low-rank speaker); mouse
ohm	โอม	ohm (sacred sound in Dharmic religions)
ongkon	องค์กร	organisation

225

Transcription	Thai	English Translation
ongkon salam pheua prachathipatai	องค์กรสลัมเพื่อประชาธิปไตย	Slum Organisation for Democracy (NGO)
phatthana	พัฒนา	development; to develop
phasa thai	ภาษาไทย	Thai language
pheuan	เพื่อน	friend
phi	พี่	elder brother/sister
phithi poet	พิธีเปิด	opening ceremony/ritual
phleng pheua chiwit	เพลงเพื่อชีวิต	songs for life (music genre); folk songs
pho	พ่อ	father; dad
pho mai	พ่อใหม่	new father
phom	ผม	I (male speaker)
phra	พระ	monk
phra yesu jao nai chiwit prajam wan khong phom	พระเยซูเจ้าในชีวิตประจำวันของผม	Jesus in my everyday life.
phra mahakasat	พระมหากษัตริย์	King
phra nak phatthana	พระนักพัฒนา	development monk
phrai	ไพร่	commoners; plebeian
phu di	ผู้ดี	good people; decent people; aristocratic
phu nam	ผู้นำ	leader; guide
phu noi	ผู้น้อย	small people
phu tam	ผู้ตาม	follower
phu yai	ผู้ใหญ่	big people
phu yai ban	ผู้ใหญ่บ้าน	village head
phuchai dang	ผู้ชายดัง	popular boy
pit toem	ปิดเทอม	semester break
prachathipatai	ประชาธิปไตย	democracy
prathet ku mi	ประเทศกูมี	What Has My Country Got? (song)
prathom	ประถม	primary school
prawatsat	ประวัติศาสตร์	history

Transcription	Thai	English Translation
rap mai dai	รับไม่ได้	I can't accept it
ramakian	รามเกียรติ์	Ramakien (poem)
ran kem	ร้านเกม	video-game shop
rathaniyom	รัฐนิยม	state convention
rawang dek kat	ระวังเด็กกัด	Warning: children bite!
rohngrian	โรงเรียน	school
rohngrian phra rachathan	โรงเรียน พระราชทาน	royal award school (education award)
rot me	รถเมล์	bus
sabai sabai	สบายๆ	unconcerned; devoid of worries; casual
sakdina	ศักดินา	fields of power (Thai feudal system)
samanen	สามเณร	novice
sangkhom	สังคม	society
sanit jai	สนิทใจ	intimate; emotionally close
sasana	ศาสนา	religion
sati	สติ	awareness; consciousness; concentration
sethakit pho phiang	เศรษฐกิจพอเพียง	sufficiency economy
sia na	เสียหน้า	to lose face
sia sala	เสียสละ	sacrifice
siwilai	ศิวิไลซ์	to civilise; civilisation; civilised
sokaprok	สกปรก	dirty
sop khao	สอบเข้า	entrance examination
su - hin lek fai	สู้-หิน เหล็ก ไฟ	Fight: Stone Metal Fire (song)
sun khunatham	ศูนย์คุณธรรม	Centre for the Promotion of National Morality (public organisation)
talat pho phiang	ตลาดพอเพียง	sufficiency market
thai	ไทย	Thai
tham bun	ทำบุญ	merit-making
thamhai na rohngrian du di	ทำให้หน้าโรงเรียน ดูดี	to ensure that the school's 'face' looks good
thamma	ธรรมะ	dharma
thammachat	ธรรมชาติ	nature
thammasat	ธรรมศาสตร์	Buddhist law

227

Transcription	Thai	English Translation
therawat	เถรวาท	Theravada (Buddhism)
theuan	เถื่อน	wild; rough
tid mae	ติดแม่	attached to mother
uparat	อุปราช	regent (political post)
wai	ไหว้	Thai salutation; pay respect
wan dek	วันเด็ก	Children's Day
wan mae	วันแม่	Mother's Day
wan phra	วันพระ	holy day (Buddhist)
wannakam pheua chiwit	วรรณกรรมเพื่อชีวิต	literature about life (literature genre)
wat	วัด	temple
wat pa	วัดป่า	forest temple
watthanatham	วัฒนธรรม	culture
watthanatham thai	วัฒนธรรมไทย	Thai culture
wicha	วิชา	subject
wicha lak	วิชาหลัก	basic subject
wicha phoem toem	วิชาเพิ่มเติม	optional additional subject
ya ba	ยาบ้า	amphetamine

Photo: Takeway, Wikimedia Commons.

Figure 1. Children's Day 2012. Chiang Mai Royal Thai Air Force base. See p. 7.

Figure 2. Thai traditional saluta-tion training for primary school students. Thairath Witthaia School, Bangkok, August 2013. See p. 38.

Photo: Giuseppe Bolotta.

Figure 3. Thai students practising Buddhist meditation, October 2014. See p. 55.

Photo: Kochphon Onshawee, Wikimedia Commons.

Photo: Giuseppe Bolotta.

Figure 4. Reproduction of the painting Hapag ng Pag-asa ('Table of Hope') by Filipino artist Joey Velasco (1967–2010), displayed at the Saint Jacob's Centre. Bangkok, August 2008. See p. 76.

Photo: Giuseppe Bolotta.

Figure 5. Life along the railway tracks. Bangkok slums, April 2013. See p. 95.

Photo: Giuseppe Bolotta.

Figure 6. Akhan Daeng, May 2013. See p. 99.

Photo: Giuseppe Bolotta.

Figure 7. Children sitting and chatting along the railway tracks. Bangkok slums, April 2013. See p. 125.

Figure 8. *Rawang dek kat* ('Warning! Children bite'). Akhan Daeng, May 2013. See p. 128.

Photo: Giuseppe Bolotta.

www.youtube.com/watch?v=qBu88GaHBHs.

Figure 9. Use of the three-finger salute is a common feature of student demonstrations across Thailand since 2014. Screenshot of an image from YouTube. See p. 185.

Index